משנה

ArtScroll® Series

Rabbi Nosson Scherman / Rabbi Meir Zlotowitz
General Editors

Living
Published by
ArtScroll®
Mesorah Publications, ltd

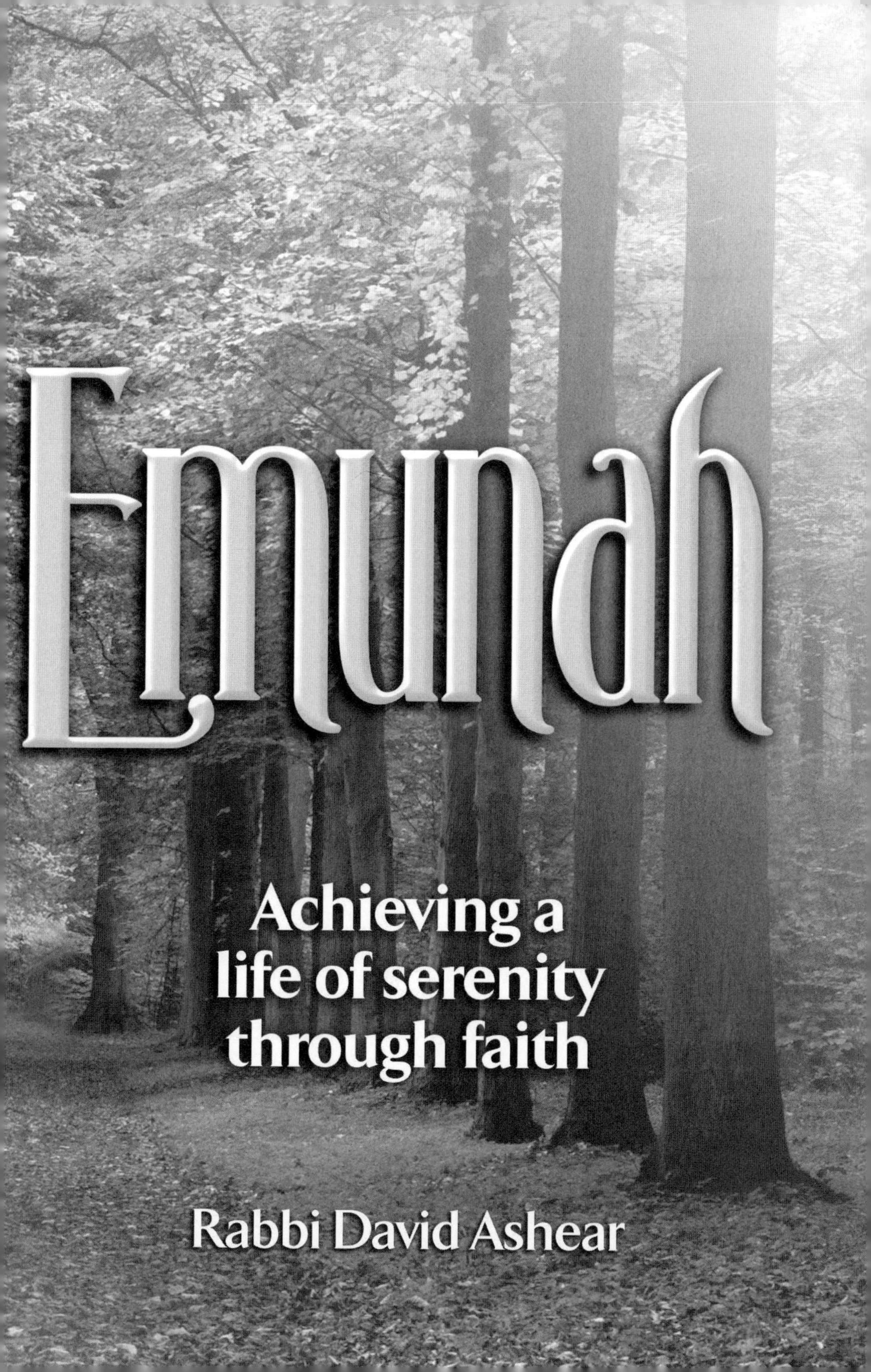

Emunah

Achieving a life of serenity through faith

Rabbi David Ashear

FIRST EDITION
First Impression ... July 2014

Published and Distributed by
MESORAH PUBLICATIONS, LTD.
4401 Second Avenue / Brooklyn, N.Y 11232

Distributed in Europe by
LEHMANNS
Unit E, Viking Business Park
Rolling Mill Road
Jarow, Tyne & Wear, NE32 3DP
England

Distributed in Israel by
SIFRIATI / A. GITLER — BOOKS
Moshav Magshimim
Israel

Distributed in Australia and New Zealand
by **GOLDS WORLDS OF JUDAICA**
3-13 William Street
Balaclava, Melbourne 3183
Victoria, Australia

Distributed in South Africa by
KOLLEL BOOKSHOP
Northfield Centre, 17 Northfield Avenue
Glenhazel 2192, Johannesburg, South Africa

ARTSCROLL® SERIES
LIVING EMUNAH

ISBN 10: 1-4226-1512-X / ISBN 13: 978-1-4226-1512-6

Typography by CompuScribe at ArtScroll Studios, Ltd.

Printed in the United States of America by Noble Book Press Corp.
Bound by Sefercraft, Quality Bookbinders, Ltd., Brooklyn N.Y. 11232

This volume is dedicated in memory of
our dear mother and grandmother

Diane Azrak ע"ה

דינה בת שרה ע"ה

23 Tevet 5774

שַׁמַּאי אוֹמֵר, עֲשֵׂה תוֹרָתְךָ קֶבַע.
אֱמוֹר מְעַט וַעֲשֵׂה הַרְבֵּה,
וֶהֱוֵי מְקַבֵּל אֶת כָּל הָאָדָם בְּסֵבֶר פָּנִים יָפוֹת

Shammai says, Make your Torah study a fixed practice;
say little and do much;
and receive everyone with a cheerful face
(Avot 1:15).

She was a lady who personified this Mishnah.

She never veered from the way of Torah, emunah and bitachon. Her trust in Hashem was absolute and uncompromising.

She was a woman of action. The needs of others were always foremost. Without a word she would do what had to be done.

She greeted everyone with a smile and a good word. She made everyone feel that he or she was unique and special.

It is fitting that this volume which will bring emunah into countless lives is dedicated to a woman who personified this ideal.

Victor & Cheryl Azrak & Family
Elliott & Annie Azrak & Family
Adam & Frieda Azrak & Family

RABBI YAAKOV HILLEL
Rosh Yeshivat
Hevrat Ahavat Shalom
45 Arzey Habira St. Jerusalem

יעקב משה הלל
ראש ישיבת
חברת אהבת שלום
רח' ארזי הבירה 45 ירושלים

בס"ד

Approbation

Our Sages teach that *emunah*, belief and faith in Hashem, is the cornerstone of our holy Torah. The Torah consists of six hundred and thirteen *mitzvot*, condensed into the Ten Commandments. The first of these fundamental Commandments is belief and faith in Hashem as the Ruler of the world: "I am Hashem your G-d Who took you out of the Land of Egypt" (*Shmot* 20:2). The Sages cite the prophet Havakuk, who taught that "everything depends on one principle, as it says, 'and a righteous man will live by his faith'" (*Havakuk* 2:4; *Makkot* 24a). Belief and faith are the basis of the entire Torah.

Our generation lives in the darkness of a world suffering from widespread evil and denial of the Al-mighty's unlimited control of man's affairs. Many today believe that "My might and the strength of my hand made me this wealth" (*Devarim* 8:17). In response to the needs of the times, Rabbi David Ashear has written a book entitled "Living *Emunah*." This book educates the reader about the *mitzvot* of true *emunah* and *bitahon*. Fortunate are those who invest the time to study about this vital topic and implement these teachings in their daily lives. They are sure to benefit greatly.

May the author and his readers be blessed with the fulfillment of King David's words, "One who trusts in G-d is surrounded by *hesed*" (*Tehillim* 32:10).

Rabbi Yaakov Hillel

בס"ד

עש"ק פרשת מסעי שנת תשע"ד לפ"ק

ראיתי חיבור על אמונה בהשם יתברך הנקרא "ליווינג אמונה" שחברו איש אשר רוח בו ובעל השקפה ברורה ואיתנה כ"ש **מורה"ר ר' דוד אשקר שליט"א** מפלטבוש ארה"ב. והנה הגם שלא נתנני הזמן לראות אלא חלק קטן מהספר מ"מ אומר שהספר מצא מאוד חן בעיני בין מצד התוכן ובין מצד סגנון הכתיבה. ותקותי חזקה שימצא חן בעיני אחינו בני ישראל הצריכים כל כך חיזוק ועידוד בזמן הזה בכל דבר הנוגע לאמונה ובטחון. וכידוע שלפני ביאת המשיח יתרבו הנסיונות וכמו שהנחש נושך בעקב שהוא בשר המת שבחי וממית בלב ובראש כן האינטרנט מתחילים עמו בדבר שנראה שלא יזיק וסופו להרעיל המוח והלב של האדם ר"ל. ולכן יש צורך גדול להמציא להציבור דברים המושכים את הלב עם דברי תורה קצרים אבל קולעים אל המטרה, וסיפורים אמתיים של גדולי ישראל והוא מצרכי השעה. ואשרי למחברינו שזכה לכתוב ספר שיעשה זאת בע"ה, ויהא לאחיעזר ואחיסמך לאחינו הצריכים משענת להעמידם בקרן אורה. ואחשוב שכל אחד ימצא חיזוק בהדברים היקרים שהביא בתוך דבריו. ואני תפלה שחפץ ה' בידו יצליח ויזכה להמשיך ולהעשיר בתי בני ישראל עם ספרים שיביא אורה של אמונה בתוך משכנותם.

החותם לכבוד התורה ולכבוד המחבר שדואג לחזק האמונה בה' ובתורתו הקדושה,

פסח אליהו פאלק

פסח אליהו פאלק

Table of Contents

Publisher's Preface

We are proud to publish *Living Emunah*, which deals with one of the most important issues of our time. The vast majority of serious people — leaders and laymen, men and women — agree that it is important for all of us to find ways to increase our *emunah*/faith in Hashem. Many of us remember grandparents or great-grandparents who exemplified "*emunah peshutah*," simple faith in Hashem. Modern life with its medical miracles, scientific discoveries, and powerful machines is in many ways the enemy of *emunah*, for we can easily think that nearly everything is in man's power. We can also forget that Hashem controls everything and that whatever He does is ultimately for the good whether we understand it or not — even when it is not what we wanted.

RABBI DAVID ASHEAR has the unique ability to transmit *emunah*. His 4-minute "Daily Emunah" presentations are read or heard by thousands of people every day, and they are shared with thousands more. These people are a broad cross-section, Sephardi and Ashkenazi, chassid and misnaged, young and old, men and women. They read and listen to Rabbi Ashear because his down-to-earth, content-filled presentations are both practical and inspirational. Few authors can accomplish that, and few authors have such a positive effect on so many grateful readers and listeners. This book, therefore, will be of enormous benefit to countless people.

We are grateful to Rabbi Ashear for assembling his presentations in book form, and to the others who have made it possible:

The AZRAK FAMILY has dedicated this volume in memory of their mother and grandmother. A book that will improve the lives of so many people is a wonderful tribute to a woman who exemplified faith and kindness.

RABBI DAVID SUTTON of the Yad Yosef Torah Center encouraged the author to create these presentations and shepherded the manuscript to publication. Rabbi Sutton is an imaginative and dynamic spiritual leader and teacher. His popular classes and personal interaction with countless people are transformational. We are privileged to enjoy his friendship.

RABBI MORDECHAI YEHUDAH GRONER of Yeshiva Ateres Shimon created and maintains the email site that brings "Daily Emunah" and many other Torah projects to the public.

ELI KROEN designed the cover with his customary skill and imagination. MENDY HERZBERG was involved in every step of the production, with unfailing efficiency and cheerfulness.

MRS. JUDI DICK edited and made valuable suggestions that Rabbi Ashear found to be very helpful. MRS. FAYGIE WEINBAUM proofread with her usual diligence. MRS. ESTIE DICKER paginated the book and RIVKY PLITTMAN designed the page layout.

We are confident that people will turn to this volume day after day as an invaluable source of strength and faith. It will enhance the lives of its readers and their communities, and it is our privilege to present it to the public.

Rabbi Meir Zlotowitz / Rabbi Nosson Scherman

Av 5774 / August 2014

Acknowledgments

כי ממך הכל ומידך נתנו לך

"For everything is from You, and what we give You is from Your hand" (*Divrei HaYamim I* 29:14).

The lessons and stories found in this volume are the direct result of Hashem's kindness. He has put me in the right places at the right times, enabling me to learn all this material, and I thank Him with all my heart for allowing me to be His messenger in disseminating *emunah*.

Hashem has also sent me numerous individuals along the way without whom this project would never have materialized, and to whom I feel eternally indebted.

RABBI DAVID J. SUTTON has, from day 1, been the driving force behind this book. It was his idea that I should deliver brief discourses on *emunah*, and it was his idea to compile them into a book. Rabbi Sutton took the initiative to care for everything that needed to be done to bring this idea to fruition, whether it was scheduling meetings, finding sources in the works quoted in these classes, or all the other behind-the-scenes work that he dealt with. Thank you so much, Rabbi Sutton, for getting it all done.

I am indebted as well to two of our generation's outstanding disseminators of Torah — RABBI EPHRAIM WACHSMAN and RABBI PESACH ELIYAHU FALK, whose dynamic *shiurim* shaped my thoughts to allow me to see the world and life from an entirely new vantage point. Those classes were the seeds that produced this undertaking.

I wish to thank all my Rabbis who have taught me Torah and guided me along the proper path.

Thank you, RABBI DAVID OZERI, for your ongoing guidance and support.

Thank you, RABBI MORDECHAI YEHUDA GRONER and RABBI SCHNEUR GRONER, for your unbelievable work spreading the *emunah* lessons worldwide. I am truly amazed at all of your selfless work on a daily basis at Yeshivah Ateres Shimon, bringing people closer to Hashem.

Thank you, DAVID SILVERBERG, for your terrific work transcribing all the lectures. I am consistently amazed by your ability to capture the essence of each and every class, and to find the perfect words to express the ideas in the most effective and meaningful way.

I express my heartfelt gratitude and appreciation to VICTOR, ELLIOTT, and ADAM AZRAK for graciously sponsoring this book in memory of their dear mother, MRS. DIANE AZRAK, *a"h*. Your generosity is bringing the lessons of faith to Jews across the world, and I am confident that this incalculable merit will bring great merit to the soul of your beloved mother. May her memory be a source of blessing and inspiration to you, your entire family, and all *Am Yisrael*, אמן.

I owe an enormous debt of gratitude to the entire ArtScroll family. Despite their demanding schedules, RABBI MEIR ZLOTOWITZ and RABBI NOSSON SCHERMAN always made themselves available to me to offer their advice. Thank you, MENDY HERZBERG, for coordinating this entire project, and to MRS. JUDI DICK for her tireless efforts editing the text and helping me decide which lessons should be included in this volume and which points required greater emphasis. Thank you as well to ELI KROEN for the beautiful cover design, MRS. FAYGIE WEINBAUM for her proofreading, MRS. ESTIE DICKER for her corrections and pagination, and RIVKY PLITTMAN for her layout design.

Many people contributed to this work by sending me their personal stories and accounts of how the *yad Hashem* was apparent in their lives. Thank you all for assisting me in spreading this message of *emunah*.

Last but certainly not least, words cannot express my heartfelt appreciation to my loving family for all their support. My parents, MORRIS and LOUISE ASHEAR, have always been a constant source of unlimited love, guidance, and encouragement. I could not have done this without you. I thank my wonderful in-laws, DR. ROBERT and MRS. BARBARA MATALON, for all their love and advice. Finally, and mostly, I thank my dear wife and our children for everything they do and for everything they are.

Introduction

Approximately twelve years ago, I began listening to a series of recorded lectures by Rabbi Ephraim Wachsman entitled "Faith at Work," an in-depth study of the *Shaar HaBitachon* section of the work *Chovos HaLevavos*. This experience proved to be life-altering, and to this day I remain inspired by the messages conveyed in these masterful discourses. I made a point of listening to them several times in order to fully internalize the fundamental concepts of faith and *emunah*. I then began sharing this new goldmine that I had discovered with others, by delivering lectures on these topics. Everybody who heard these talks had the same reaction: "This is unbelievable!" "You changed my life!"

Learning about *emunah* gives a person an entirely new perspective on life. It allows him to rise above all the pettiness that too many people waste their time and energy dwelling upon, so he can truly enjoy life the way Hashem intended. The centrality of *emunah* is underscored by the Gemara at the end of *Makkos*, which teaches that the prophet Chabakkuk summarized all the concepts of the Torah in three words: וצדיק באמונתו יחיה — "A righteous man lives with faith." If we want to experience real "life," then we need *emunah*.

Emunah is so vitally important because life does not always go according to our plans. We come upon many twists and turns along the journey of life, and many obstacles get in our way. Sometimes the challenges seem too great to bear. I recall one occasion when I was dealing with a very difficult situation. I felt I couldn't handle the pressure, and I walked around upset and agitated. Although my feelings were indiscernible on the outside, inside they crushed me. I had no appetite and I felt anxious throughout the day. Finally, I told myself, "I've been speaking about *emunah* for several years already. This situation is precisely the time when I need *emunah* more than any other." I then began reviewing in my mind the basic principles of *emunah*, over and over again, until I felt as though a mountain was lifted off my shoulders. I felt completely relaxed and at ease, and the pressure I was facing suddenly seemed trivial and insignificant. "Hashem is so kind," I told myself. "He gave me this problem because He knows that I can handle it and it's going to improve me."

This experience taught me something very important: *emunah* is ineffective if it remains confined to the mind. I knew all the principles of *emunah*, but this wasn't enough to keep me calm. It has to move from the mind to the heart. And this can only happen by regularly reviewing and reinforcing the concepts.

A person might think, *Of course I know that Hashem controls everything and always does what is best for me*. True, most of us would likely score 100 on a test about *emunah*. But many of us are nevertheless unable to properly deal with difficult challenges when they arise, and this is because we have not fully internalized these concepts. We might draw a comparison to the Rambam's remark in his commentary to the Mishnah that it is preferable to donate one dollar to charity each day for one hundred days than to donate one hundred dollars in a single lump sum. The act of giving, the Rambam explains, has an effect on a person's character, making him more sensitive and giving, and the more the act is repeated, the more significant is this impact. Small doses of good deeds repeated consistently over an extended period of time have the effect of molding us into better people, and it is thus preferable to give frequent small amounts, in order to train ourselves to become more selfless and generous. This applies to *emunah*, as well. Repeatedly learning and reviewing the concepts of faith and trust in Hashem train us to approach life with the proper mindset. By reading stories about how ordinary people like us saw Hashem's hand unmistakably guiding them, we strengthen our *emunah* and receive the hope and encouragement that we all need.

Readers of this volume will learn about how much Hashem loves them and wants to help them, how actively involved He is in every aspect of their lives, and how He yearns for them to build a relationship with Him. These concepts will be conveyed in different ways and from different angles in order to help the reader internalize them.

We all have times in life when our *emunah* is put to the test, when we have unanswered questions, requiring us to strengthen our faith and hang onto it very tightly. There are also times when as a nation, our collective *emunah* is put to the test. This volume is being published at such a time. Just over two months ago, on June 12, 2014, three Israeli yeshivah boys — Naftali Fraenkel, Gil-ad Shaar and Eyal Yifrach — were abducted at a bus stop in Gush Etzion. For eighteen days, during which their fate was unknown, Jews across the world united in prayer on their behalf. But then, on June 30, we heard the tragic news that they had been brutally murdered minutes after their abduction, and we are still reeling in pain. This was a loss felt by every Jew, as we all bear this burden of grief. This is the source of our nation's strength — we are united together as an extended family. One person's sorrow is everyone's sorrow. This is a tragedy that none of us will ever forget. We beseech Hashem to console the grieving families and fill the massive void in their hearts.

During this painful time, we are left with difficult questions. How could our loving Father, the One Who controls everything, the *Shomer Yisrael*, allow such a thing to happen? How could three pure, innocent boys be taken from us in such brutal fashion?

We are not alone in asking this question. This question has been asked throughout the ages, whenever tragedy befell good people. This question was posed by the prophets, and even by Moshe Rabbeinu. Hashem answered him, לא יראני האדם וחי — we cannot know the answer to this question. This is one of the greatest tests in life — to see one thing with our eyes and to still believe that Hashem is a merciful Father Who always does what is best for us, and Who loves each and every one of us more than a parent could ever love his or her child. *Emunah* means "belief," which means knowing something even when it is not obvious. If something is obvious, we don't have to "believe" it, because we can see it.

Hashem is always the *Shomer Yisrael*, Who guards and protects us in ways of which we are totally unaware. We don't hear about the hundreds of attempts made by terrorists to harm us but were unsuccessful. We don't know of the countless times Hashem has saved each and every one of us from harm. He is constantly performing kindness for us and taking care of us.

I overheard a child nervously talking about how he is scared of being kidnaped. What do we tell him? Our children need to know that no one has any power besides Hashem. As the *pasuk* says (*Eichah* 3:37), מי זה אמר ותהי ה' לא צוה — "Who can say they will do something if Hashem does not want it?" The *Chovos HaLevavos* writes that no person can cause another person harm or provide a benefit to another person unless this is willed by Hashem. If something is meant to happen, it will happen, no matter what. Hashem makes all the decisions, and we believe in complete faith that Gil-ad, Naftali and Eyal all lived the precise number of years allotted to them by G-d. They could have been taken from us in a car accident or in some other way, but Hashem decided they would die על קידוש ה', through which, as the Gemara (*Pesachim* 50a) teaches, one earns the highest place in *Gan Eden*. It says in the Torah (*Vayikra* 10:3), בקרובי אקדש — Hashem takes only the most precious among our people על קידוש ה'. These boys were the *korban* for our entire generation.

Hashem did not let us know the boys' fate for eighteen days, during which time their abduction inspired millions of heartfelt prayers recited numerous times each day by Jews across the globe — prayers recited in public and in private, *Tehillim* readings, and rivers of tears. These boys will receive the merit of each and every prayer. And Hashem will use those prayers — each and every one — to protect us in the future and to bring us salvation. The three boys will then receive the merit of having brought about that salvation.

These boys were the catalysts of extraordinary unity among *Klal Yisrael*, the likes of which have not been experienced in a very long time. Everyone came together with a single goal, and this, too, will be credited to these three קדושים.

They are now happy in a better place, while we are left here with questions. We don't know why this had to happen, and we are in pain. We are allowed to cry, but we also need to know that Hashem is and always will be our loving G-d. He is our Guardian, and we should always feel that we are in His loving embrace.

The *pasuk* says (*Tehillim* 126:2), "אז ימלא שחוק פינו" — In the future when Hashem reveals Himself and we will see why everything had to happen the way that it did, then our mouths will be filled with laughter because it will be so clear that it was all חסדי ה'. We pray that Hashem will bring us to that glorious day במהרה בימנו אמן.

To sign up for Rabbi David Ashear's daily emunah email, visit his website www.dailyemunah.com or subscribe@dailyemunah.com

1 Worry-Free Life

Learning about *emunah* is the most effective way for someone to improve the quality of his life. Many people have remarked that the study of this topic has changed their lives, and they are so much calmer and more relaxed because of *emunah*. One person mentioned that *emunah* is like oxygen without which he cannot survive. *Emunah* is a powerful tool that enables us to live our lives to the very fullest, which is precisely what we all desire.

> "*Emunah is a powerful tool that enables us to live our lives to the very fullest.*"

Rabbi Ephraim Wachsman observed that we live in a society where we are consistently bombarded by people trying to sell us something or to convince us to do something. Buy this, invest here, travel there, join us, vote for me, and so on. Everyone has more or less the same sales pitch: some variation of, "If you listen to me, you'll be happy." And, indeed, happiness is what we are all pursuing. Let us imagine asking an average American high-school student, who works very hard in school, why he invests so much effort into his studies. He'd probably say that he's studying hard so he could get into a good college. We might then continue the conversation by asking, "Why do you want to get into a good college?"

"So I can then get a good job and make a lot of money."

"And why do you want to make a lot of money?"

"So I can have a nice house, take care of my family, and invest."

"And what then?"

"When I'm ready to retire, I'll have so much money that I can buy a condominium on the eighth hole of a golf course in Florida and live the last fifteen years of my life in unbridled joy and tranquility, without having to worry about anything."

We are taught that material assets and financial success are what bring us happiness and serenity, and this is the goal that the vast majority of people in our society are pursuing. So much of the despair and depression that people experience result from the frustration and disappointment of being unable to attain this goal, which is supposedly the key to happiness.

But imagine mastering a skill that will take us right to that desired level of tranquility, immediately, without having to spend sixty-five years working hard to attain it. ברוך הגבר אשר יבטח בה'; if one trusts in Hashem, his life is a blessing. What a shame it would be to spend one's whole life without this skill, enduring anxiety and insecurity irrespective of what one has accomplished. This is the difference between life with *emunah* and life without *emunah*. The *Chovos HaLevavos* (introduction to *Shaar HaBitachon*) states that it is impossible for a person to be worry-free without trusting in Hashem. There is no other means to avoid anxiety. Without *emunah*, a person's mind is prone to becoming overrun by worry even when a minor problem arises. Too often, people miss out on the joys and delights of life because they're too preoccupied worrying about their problems. A man takes his family out on a nice Sunday afternoon, but throughout the trip he cannot stop thinking about his business. He lost a whole day of meaningful and enjoyable time with his family, all because of his stress. And the more stress one has, the more difficult it is to maintain a tranquil environment in the home. It often happens that the husband will come home after a tense day at the office and snap at his wife, who then responds in kind. The children feel intimidated and the entire evening is ruined — all because of stress and pressure.

When we work on our *emunah*, we avoid these problems because we understand that Hashem, Who loves us and cares for us, is in charge and running our lives, and we trust that He knows exactly what He's doing. The more these concepts become part of our way of looking at things, the happier we will be and the more serenity we will enjoy.

2

How Much Is Hashem Really Involved?

How involved is Hashem in our everyday lives?

The Gemara (*Chullin* 7a) cites the following remark of Rabbi Chanina:

אין אדם נוקף אצבעו מלמטה אלא אם כן מכרידין עליו מלמעלה

A person does not even stub his toe down below, on Earth, unless this was decreed upon him from Above, in the heavens. Even small, seemingly insignificant incidents such as stubbing one's toe are the result of *hashgachah pratis* (individual Divine providence). The stubbing itself is a manifestation of Hashem's love and affection, as the Gemara continues that when one bleeds, the blood rises to Hashem as an atonement like the blood of an offering. Everything that happens in a person's life, whether big or small, is caused directly by Hashem, Who always does what is best for us.

"Everything that happens in a person's life, whether big or small, is caused directly by Hashem, Who always does what is best for us."

This concept is further developed as the Gemara (*Arachin* 16b) raises the question, עד היכן תכלית יסורין — "How far does the definition of suffering extend?" Which minor inconveniences are considered יסורין, punishments brought upon a person by Hashem? The Gemara cites several Rabbis who give different examples indicating how even the smallest events are orchestrated by Hashem. Rabbi Elazar says that even if one had clothing tailored, and when he receives it from the tailor it does not quite fit, this is aggravation from Hashem. Another Rabbi gives the example of one who asks a bartender to add hot water to his wine, but he mistakenly adds cold water. A third Rabbi gave the example of one who accidentally puts his shirt on backward when he gets dressed in the morning, and thus has to take it off and put it on again. Rava says that even if one puts his hand in his pocket to remove three coins, but only removes two, and thus he has to put his hand back into his pocket to take out the third — this is anguish sent from Hashem. The Gemara notes that this information is important to know, because if a person goes through a period of forty days without any *yissurim* at all, then he must be concerned that he has been given his eternal reward already in this world.

One might ask, how does a person know that he is getting his share of the Next World in his lifetime just because he did not experience any of these kinds of inconveniences over the course of forty days? Perhaps he always had a careful bartender and skilled tailor, and was always attentive when he put on his shirt or took money out of his pocket? The answer is that neither the tailor nor the bartender has the final say on what happens to us. Hashem is directly involved in the tailoring of our clothing, the preparation of our drinks, and even when we get dressed and take cash out of our wallet. This is the extent to which *hashgachah pratis* extends.

When we realize that Hashem is with us twenty-four hours a day, in every aspect of our lives, down to the smallest and least significant details, and that He always deals with us kindly, it becomes much easier to respond to the day-to-day inconveniences that we face with a smile. We will not be disturbed when the shirt does not fit, and even when we are injured and bleed, we can feel gratified knowing that we have just brought a *korban* (sacrificial offering) that was lovingly accepted by Hashem.

3

Emunah Is the Root of Good Middos

E*munah*, faith in Hashem, is the root of all *middos tovos* (fine qualities).

One who truly believes that Hashem governs the world, and wishes only for his well-being, will never be envious of other people. *Kinah*, jealousy, is one of the most destructive qualities, and, in fact, Shlomo HaMelech stated that jealousy is what causes one's bones to decay. Rabbeinu Yonah writes that a person's health depends upon the heart, and nothing is more harmful to the heart than jealousy. Indeed, modern medicine has determined that stress is one of the most harmful conditions for one's health. And so much of the stress that we experience comes from jealousy. We look around us and see what other people have, and we begin to ask ourselves, *Why am I not as accomplished and successful as he?* These thoughts cause overbearing pressure that can directly lead to both physical and emotional ailments.

One who has *emunah*, however, when he sees other people's success he thinks, *What does this have to do with me? Hashem gives me exactly what I need to serve Him and fulfill my role in the world. Why does it matter that other people have more?*

A person berates himself when he invests effort but doesn't see the desired results and doesn't earn a comfortable living. He assumes it's his fault, that this is because he wasn't good enough, that he is a failure, and that others look at him as a "good-for-nothing." This is a totally incorrect approach. Our success depends not upon our efforts, but on Hashem. We invest our effort, but only Hashem determines the outcome.

A person with *emunah* also does not become angry. After all, anger occurs when things do not work out the way a person wants them to. But if one has *emunah*, he is not upset when events do not turn out to his liking. He says to himself, *It is Hashem's will that things should turn out this way, and if this is Hashem's will — then this is my will, as well!*

> *"It is Hashem's will that things should turn out this way, and if this is Hashem's will — then this is my will, as well!"*

Likewise, a person with *emunah* is humble. He realizes that everything is determined by Hashem, and that even his successes and achievements are the result not of his own skills and efforts, but rather Hashem's grace and compassion. Everything he has and everything he has achieved was graciously given to him by Hashem. If he had the wisdom to earn money, it is because Hashem enabled him to do so. With this perspective, a person can never become arrogant or look down on others.

> A parable is told of a poor man who was invited to the wedding of a fabulously wealthy cousin. The man could not afford a proper suit for the affair, and so he approached his well-to-do neighbor and asked if he could borrow a suit. The neighbor lent him an exquisite $1,000 suit to wear to the wedding. And so the guest arrived at the wedding in this $1,000 suit, and when he looked around, he noticed many guests wearing far less fancy attire. He felt very proud of the suit he was wearing, and looked at the other guests with scorn.

Quite obviously, this reaction is completely irrational. Does it make sense for a person to take pride in something he borrowed for one evening? Does he have anything of which to be proud?

This is how the person with *emunah* looks at all his possessions and achievements. Everything is borrowed, something given to him mercifully by Hashem, and there is thus no room for any sort of hubris or pride.

4

Living With Nobility

One who lives his life with *emunah* will automatically bring glory to Hashem. When others see the way he carries himself and lives his life with such serenity and nobility, they will see G-dliness. Avraham Avinu taught *emunah* to the world, and the people revered him, calling him a נשיא אלוקים — "a prince of Hashem." A person with *emunah* never loses himself or becomes upset regarding those things that normally upset others. He knows that everything is from Hashem, and that Hashem is always doing what is best for him, even when he doesn't understand how.

> *"A person with emunah never loses himself or becomes upset regarding those things that normally upset others."*

A man told me he came into work one morning to find that his business' computer system was malfunctioning. He called a team of technicians, and their initial assessment was that all the data was lost. The system contained everything: eight years' worth of information had been wiped out. All the orders that were to be shipped over the next six months, all the records of businesses that owed him money and to which he owed, all the charges and credit: all were gone. The business was a mess. The owners had *emunah* and accepted the will of Hashem with joy. They carried on to the best of their ability, but the employees were anxious and complaining, wondering how to proceed without that data.

After four days, the technicians were able to solve the problem, and not one piece of information was missing. The office celebrated, and during the celebration one of the employees came over to the man and said, "Boss, we are awestruck by the way you handled the situation. You never lost your cool. We all couldn't believe it. You are our role model for life." This is a *kiddush Hashem*.

❖ ❖ ❖

An acquaintance of mine had a doctor's appointment in Manhattan for a procedure that was to have taken up most of the day. He took the day off, canceling all his meetings, and went to the doctor's office. After one hour in the waiting room, he was finally taken in and he underwent a series of tests and preparatory procedures. He then had to wait for another hour, after which the doctor came out and said very apologetically, "I am so sorry, the machine I need for the procedure is broken. This has never happened to me in all my years as a doctor. I feel terrible, but we cannot do the procedure today. We'll have to reschedule."

The man understood that there are no accidents, that everything is caused by Hashem, and so he didn't lose his cool. He said, "O.K., we'll reschedule." The doctor could not believe how calmly the person responded. He was certain he would be furious, having wasted an entire day. This created a wonderful *kiddush Hashem*.

Emunah lends a person nobility. He knows Hashem is calling all the shots, there are no mistakes, everything happens precisely the way Hashem wants, and He only wants to do what is best for us. There are many people who have reasons to complain but they walk around with a smile, happy and content, and in so doing, they create a *kiddush Hashem*.

A student of the Chazon Ish owned a printing shop in Bnei Brak, and someone opened a similar shop nearby. Most people would be furious when this happens, but this man strengthened his *emunah* and repeatedly reminded himself that his livelihood comes only from Hashem. *Hashem gives me my parnassah*, he kept saying to himself, *and I am not going to start a fight over this*. He befriended his competitor, warmly welcoming him to the area and offering to help in any way he can.

The competitor couldn't believe it. But those with *emunah* never compromise their dignity, and always remain calm and composed.

We must work toward developing our *emunah* so we respond properly to adverse situations, which will then bring glory to Hashem.

5 There Is Only One Boss

Part of the "American dream" is to enjoy a life of tranquility, without trepidation. Yet, most people live each day with numerous fears and worries. People are afraid of the boss, the IRS, the wealthy individuals around them, or generally about the future. By contrast, the *Chovos HaLevavos* (*Shaar HaBitachon*) states, a person with *bitachon* has no fears. Moreover, he writes, בני אדם החשובים והנכבדים ביותר מפחדים ממנו; important and distinguished people are afraid of him, rather than the other way around. And even the stones upon which he treads seek to please him.

People often harbor negative feelings and resentment toward those who they feel have caused them harm or wronged them in some way. These feelings reflect a deficiency in one's *emunah*. After all, people have no power to cause someone else harm unless Hashem decided that it should happen. When you look at someone and realize that he has no control or say in your life you won't fear him. Of course, there is an obligation of *hishtadlus*, to make an effort, and we must therefore live normally and take reasonable precautions. But we must also recognize that ultimately Hashem has absolute control over everything that happens, and once we come to this realization we will cease to be fearful.

Unfortunately, people put great effort into flattering and complimenting others in order to find favor in their eyes, thinking that this will benefit them. But in truth, there is no guarantee at all that this approach is effective. I know of a business where the president decided to cut the salaries of all the low-wage employees, without exception. One employee affected by the cut was the best friend of the company's vice president, and all the high-ranking members of the company were very fond of him. They tried to intercede on his behalf, but to no avail. He had tried so hard over the years to build close relationships with the influential people in the company, but in the end, Hashem decided that his income should be reduced, and this is what happened.

Certainly, we should be respectful to our employers and every other individual, and, moreover, we should be in the habit of giving people compliments and praise. In fact, one of the questions we will be asked when we leave this world is, המלכת את חברך — "Did you make your fellow a king?" (*Reishis Chochmah, Shaar HaYirah,* Chapter 12). We are to make the people around us feel good about themselves by complimenting them and expressing admiration, but we are to do so because this is the Divine will, and not for ulterior motives. If we truly want to help ourselves, we should concentrate on pleasing the One, True Boss, Who is really the Only One Who can benefit us.

> *"If we truly want to help ourselves, we should concentrate on the One, True Boss, Who is really the Only One Who can benefit us."*

One of the advantages of *emunah*, then, is that it makes us more genuine people, people who do not need to give insincere praise and compliments, and who instead focus on doing the truly right thing.

6 Giving Emunah Is Giving Life

One of the greatest gifts we can give a person is to teach him *emunah*, the powerful tool that enables one to go through life with genuine happiness, knowing that everything that happens comes directly from Hashem, Who loves Him and always has his best interests in mind.

The Chafetz Chaim asked someone, "How are you today?"

"Well, it could be better," the man replied.

"This isn't true," the sage said. "If it could be better, then it would be better. Everything is precisely the way it is supposed to be."

"If it could be better, then it would be better."

By giving somebody *emunah*, one gives him life, as he is filled with contentment and serenity.

An oft-quoted *pasuk* (*Tehillim* 34:13) states, מי האיש החפץ חיים אוהב ימים לראות טוב — "Who is the man who desires life, who loves days in which to see goodness..." The *Shefa Chaim* (232) explains this to mean that the person who truly "desires life" and "loves days," who wants to enjoy life, will ensure לראות טוב, to always see goodness, to view everything in his life in a positive light. Even if he experiences hardship, such as in earning a living or raising his children, he will nevertheless see everything that happens as טוב, goodness.

Parents should train their children from a young age to live with *emunah*, to know how much Hashem loves them and controls everything that happens in their lives. They should be told that even when they are hurt, it is Hashem cleansing them of their misdeeds and purifying them so they will experience greater enjoyment in the Next World. Just as a mother lovingly changes her infant's diaper despite his protests, because she very much wishes him to be clean, similarly, Hashem at times makes us uncomfortable for our own long-range benefit.

> I taught a weekly class to boys ages 8 to 12 on these concepts of *emunah*, in which I discussed how everything is ultimately for the best, and how we must thank Hashem and avoid complaining. Every week, they would relate amazing incidents. One boy reported that he fell off his bicycle and scraped his knee, but instead of crying he thanked Hashem. Another boy said he was not picked for the basketball game in school, but instead of complaining about it, he said "thank you" to Hashem. Every week, we were treated to yet another remarkable story. I made a point of emphasizing to the boys that when a child rides his bicycle for hours without falling, of course that is because Hashem is protecting him; and when a kid is picked for the game, this happened because Hashem wanted it. Everything is from Hashem.

Someone I know asks his children at bedtime each night to thank Hashem for something that happened that day. Usually, the kids mention the special candy they received, or the delicious ice cream they ate. But sometimes, they'll even say "thank you" for the boo-boo they got, or for the snack they lost. They might not actually mean it, but they are being trained to recognize that everything is from Hashem and is for our benefit, even if we cannot possibly understand how. This is a fundamental life skill. And the more we set this standard for our children, the more we ourselves will follow it in order to be consistent, and when things go wrong at home we will not become upset, but we will instead say "thank you" to Hashem, knowing that they didn't go *wrong;* they went exactly as they were supposed to. We will then be people who truly "desire life," who "see goodness" in everything that happens.

7 No Regrets

A person with *emunah* never has regrets. Rather than dwell on the past and on what might have been, he accepts the outcome without frustration or distress. He recognizes that he made his *hishtadlus* (effort), and if it did not work out, this can only be because this was the best thing for him. And even if, in retrospect, he realizes that he could have put in more effort, he does not fret over the mistake he made. Instead, he accepts the fact that this, too, was ordained from Above.

A *pasuk* in *Koheles* (3:2) says, עת ללדת ועת למות — "There is a time to give birth, and a time to die." What is the wisdom underlying this statement? Is it not obvious that there is a time for birth? When a baby is born, we can simply look at the clock and determine the time of birth. What is the profound message in King Shlomo's teaching, "There is a time to give birth"?

> I heard a beautiful explanation of this verse from Rabbi Pesach Eliyahu Falk that he had told a young couple who were married for several years without children. They went to doctors and underwent numerous treatments, and they also prayed tearfully, but to no avail. As the years went by and their prayers went unanswered, they grew despondent.
>
> Ten years after they married, they heard that a certain renowned *tzaddik*, who was known for the power of his blessings, was visiting their neighborhood and would be staying very close to their home.
>
> The wife turned to the husband and said, "Look, the *tzaddik* is coming practically to our door. Why not go and receive a *berachah* from him?"
>
> The husband agreed, and he went to the *tzaddik* who assured the man that he would be blessed with a child

within the year, and, sure enough, his *berachah* was fulfilled.

Seeing that all it took was a *berachah* from this *tzaddik*, the wife felt very frustrated. "What were we thinking all this time?" she said to her husband. "We knew about this *tzaddik* even before we were married. Why did we not go to him sooner? Why did we wait for him to come to us? We could have had a 9-year-old child by now, as well as several other children. All those years of aggravation and anxiety could have been avoided!"

The husband explained that she was mistaken. "We were not granted a child because of the *tzaddik*'s blessing," he said. "To the contrary, Hashem sent the *tzaddik* to our doorstep because the time had come for us to have a child. We did not think of it earlier because the time had not yet come for us to have our prayers answered!"

> *"We were not granted a child because of the tzaddik's blessing. To the contrary, Hashem sent the tzaddik to our doorstep because the time had come for us to have a child."*

This is the meaning of עת ללדת. When the Divinely ordained time for a child's birth arrives, Hashem makes it happen.

This lesson applies to all areas of life. We should never have regrets over what we could have or should have done. We need simply to do our *hishtadlus*, and then leave the rest in Hashem's hands. And when things do not work out as we had hoped, we must trust that this was Hashem's decision as to what is best for us.

8

Bitachon Produces Miracles

The Chazon Ish writes that a person's *bitachon* (trust in Hashem) reflects the level of his *emunah* (faith in Hashem). The more one believes that Hashem runs the world, the more this belief will be expressed through his actions and through the extent in which he places his trust in Hashem.

A nephew of the great Rav Nissim Yagen *a"h* related a remarkable story about his illustrious uncle, which he personally witnessed. He had visited his uncle in his office, and Rav Nissim mentioned that he needed to pay the salaries of his kollel that day.

"Do you have the money to pay the salaries?" the nephew asked.

"Actually," Rav Nissim replied, "I am $23,000 short."

"So what are you going to do?" the nephew asked.

"Hashem has never let me down in the past," Rav Nissim said, "and I am sure that today will be no different."

"But even if somebody comes in right now and hands you a check," the nephew persisted, "you'll still need a few days for the funds to be available."

"You don't think Hashem can provide me with cash?" the uncle rhetorically asked.

The nephew described how on that day Rav Nissim conducted his affairs as though everything was perfectly normal. He spent the usual hours learning, he delivered *shiurim*, and he helped people who needed him. There was no worry, no concern, no anxiety. Rav

Nissim went about his business with full confidence that Hashem would provide the funds he needed.

Toward the end of the day, the nephew grew even more curious. After all, there were only a few hours left for Rav Nissim to pay the salaries. Rav Nissim went into his office, and the nephew heard him speak to Hashem: "Hashem, You know that this is Your kollel, not mine. I do not need this for myself, but for You." Rav Nissim then left his room, and assured his nephew that everything would be just fine.

At that very moment, a man ran into the room, dropped a satchel on the table, and left. Rav Nissim opened the satchel, and, sure enough, it contained $23,000 — in cash. He took the money and paid the salaries.

Two years later, Rav Nissim was in Baltimore and came across a fellow who looked vaguely familiar. He introduced himself and asked if perhaps they once met.

"No, we never met," the man said.

Rav Nissim persisted, until finally the man divulged that they indeed saw each other once. He was the mystery man who had dropped the satchel of money on Rav Nissim's desk that day.

The man related that he had been in Eretz Yisrael for his father's first *yahrtzeit,* and after visiting the gravesite, he was feeling down and so he returned to his hotel to take a nap. As he slept, his father came to him in a dream and said, "Why are you sleeping? Rav Yagen needs $23,000!" The man did not even know who Rav Yagen was, and so he immediately went down to the lobby to begin asking around to fulfill his father's instructions. He met a friend who happened to be in Eretz Yisrael on business. The friend mentioned that he had just completed a large, profitable deal, and he now found himself with lots of cash that he did not want to carry around.

"Perfect," the man told his friend. "I need cash. Give me some and I'll pay you back when we get to the U.S."

He took $23,000 in cash, and immediately brought it to Rav Nissim.

ישועת ה' כהרף עין — Hashem's salvation can come suddenly, in the most unexpected ways.

> *He who trusts in Hashem — kindness will surround him.*

The most noteworthy aspect of this story is Rav Nissim's calm, relaxed approach. He did not allow the problem to get him frazzled or upset. He went about his business with complete trust and faith in Hashem. As the *pasuk* says, והבוטח בה' חסד יסובבנו — "He who trusts in Hashem — kindness will surround him" (*Tehillim* 32:10).

9 The Guarantor

A man was carrying one of his small children in a pool. As he approached the deep water, the child shouted in fear that he shouldn't go there. The father described how upset he felt that the child didn't trust him.

Indeed, parents love when their children trust them and feel secure knowing that the parent will care for them and provide them with what they need. And if a child has enough trust in a parent to fall backward, confident that the parent would catch him, the parent will, without doubt, happily rush with open arms to catch the child.

Hashem is our loving Father, and He loves when we trust Him and feel we can depend on Him. And when we do, He'll never let us fall. The Midrash (*Tehillim* 88), commenting on the verse, ה' אלקי ישועתי, writes that if the Jewish people tell Hashem, אין לי ישועה אלא בך ואין עיני מיחלות אלא לך — "You are our only Source of salvation, and our eyes look only to You" — then He responds, הואיל וכן אני מושיעך — "Since this is the case, I am hereby bringing you salvation." When we place our trust in Him, He will be there for us.

"When we place our trust in Him, He will be there for us."

Around forty years ago, a wealthy Jewish philanthropist in London suddenly lost his fortune. He did not tell anyone what had happened, because he did not want those in need to hesitate to approach him to ask for help. He loved giving, and he did not want to stop even after his financial collapse. The man went to a prominent wealthy Jew in Manchester and requested a loan so he could continue helping people. He explained that he had a number of investments that would be maturing in two years, and so he asked for a two-year loan of 2 million British pounds, which was roughly the equivalent of 4 million dollars. The man was prepared to provide the loan but asked if he had a guarantor for the loan. The man from London explained that he did not want anyone to know about his reversal of fortune. He would need to approach at least ten different people in order to find a guarantor, and thus he preferred borrowing without one.

"You are asking me to do the impossible," the man from Manchester said. "How can I lend you so much money without a guarantor?"

"I am doing this *l'shem Shamayim*," the man explained, "in order to help people. I know Hashem can be the Guarantor."

The man from Manchester, with complete faith in Hashem, responded, "You are correct. Because this money is needed *l'shem Shamayim*, we will name Hashem as the Guarantor." And he gave him the sum he requested.

Two years later, the man from London returned to Manchester — without the money. He explained that he did not yet have the funds to repay the loan, and he needed another two months. The man from Manchester began thinking that he would never see the money again, and so he went into his private room and spoke to Hashem. "You are the Guarantor for this loan," he said, "and the time has come for it to be repaid. But I don't want the money. I have a daughter who is already of age and has not been able to find a *shidduch*. Please send her a husband, I will consider this as payment of the loan."

The man's daughter was engaged less than three weeks later. He also closed a profitable business deal that yielded almost the complete sum he had lent.

Two-and-a-half months later, the man from London returned, ready to repay the loan. But the lender refused, explaining that the "Guarantor" had already repaid the debt in full, and the man did not owe him anything. But the man from London insisted, saying that he did not take free gifts and was intent on repaying the money he borrowed. An argument ensued, each party insisting that the other keep the money. Remarkably, they brought the case to a *beis din* in Israel. One of the judges who presided over the case, Rabbi Zickerman, who related this story, said that the judges were all in tears, overcome by emotion upon seeing the honesty and sincerity of these two Jewish men. They ruled that the money should be returned to the "Guarantor," to Hashem. It happened to be a *shemittah* year, and so the money was given to a special fund set up to assist farmers in Israel who observed *shemittah*.

Both these men put their faith in Hashem: the one who borrowed the money in order to continue giving *tzedakah*, and the lender who gave the loan relying on Hashem as the Guarantor. And Hashem did not let them down; He was there ready to catch them. As David HaMelech says (*Tehillim* 25:2), אלקי בך בטחתי אל אבושה — "My Hashem, I trust in You, so I shall not be shamed."

10

Is Hashem's Hand Too Short?

Someone told me that his daughter had been in *shidduchim* for several years, meeting several prospects, but she couldn't find a match. She placed a sticker on her refrigerator that said, היד ה' תקצר (*Bamidbar* 11:23). This remark was made by Hashem when He was asked how He could provide thirty days' worth of meat for *Bnei Yisrael* in the desert. He said, "Am I under any limitations? I can do anything!" This girl made a point of looking at this *pasuk* every day before she davened to give herself encouragement. She did not want to settle; she wanted the very best boy as a husband, and she constantly reinforced her belief that Hashem can give her what she sought. Sure enough, she recently married a boy who had every quality she was seeking.

A person feels that his problems are too big, and so he limits himself in prayer, making only very modest requests of Hashem. This is wrong. We must believe that Hashem can do anything and that He loves when we ask Him for everything we want.

> *"We must believe that Hashem can do anything and that He loves when we ask Him for everything we want."*

I saw the following maxim: "Instead of telling Hashem how big your problems are, tell your problems how big Hashem is."

We never need to settle. We should not pray that the patient is given only a partial recovery, or that he or she should live for another few months. We should pray for nothing less than a full and complete recovery. It's all the same for Hashem; He can just as easily cure a person completely than extend his life for a few months.

Commenting on the *pasuk* (*Tehillim* 81:11), הרחב פיך ואמלאהו, Rashi explains it to mean that Hashem tells us to open our mouths and ask for everything our hearts desire (כל תאות לבך), and He will then grant our requests. The more we ask, the more He will give. Rav Chaim Shmulevitz (*Sichos Mussar, Maamar* 28) remarked in this context that our recognition of Hashem's ability to give us everything we want, and that He is the only One Who can help us, is what makes our prayers so powerful, and Hashem answers this type of *tefillah*.

We should never feel that we are "bothering" Hashem. He loves when we pray to Him and ask Him for what we want. The Gemara (*Taanis* 25a) tells us that Rabbi Elazar ben Pedas was very poor, and one time he fainted. Hashem appeared to him, and he asked Hashem why he was so poor. Hashem answered that he was born under a certain *mazal* of poverty. "But if you want," Hashem continued, "I can destroy the world and build it anew, so that you might then be born under a different *mazal*." The Rabbi said that he did not wish for the world to be destroyed on his account, whereupon Hashem said to him, "In the merit of your not wanting Me to destroy the world so you could be wealthy, I am giving you thirteen rivers of *afarsamon* oil in the Next World."

"Is that all?" Rabbi Elazar asked. "I want more than that!"

Hashem said that He cannot give him more than thirteen rivers, because his peers also deserve this reward, and there needs to be enough for everybody.

Rabbi Elazar did not accept the response. He told Hashem that there are no limits on how much He can give. "You can give me a million rivers," he said to Hashem, "and then a million to each of my friends!"

Hashem told Rabbi Elazar how much He loved that remark, and He gave the Rabbi an affectionate pat on his forehead, as it were, to express His love for him.

Rav Shimshon Pincus (*Nefesh Shimshon — emunah* 244) noted that although Hashem gave Rabbi Elazar a pat, He did not go so far as to give him a kiss. Rav Pincus explained that

Hashem's affection for Rabbi Elazar was not complete, because he did not make a similar comment when Hashem said He could not give him more money. He should not have accepted this response. He should have said, "What do you mean? Regardless of my *mazal*, You can make me wealthy in an instant!"

This is what Hashem wanted to hear, and this should be our attitude toward *tefillah*. We should never limit ourselves when we pray. Channah prayed for a child for nineteen years, and at one point she went into the *Mishkan* and poured her heart out to Hashem, praying for זרע אנשים. Rabbi Yochanan, as we learn in *Berachos* 31b, explains this to mean that she wanted a child as great as Moshe and Aharon combined. She did not just ask for an ordinary child; she did not want to settle for anything less than the very best, and she became the mother of Shmuel HaNavi.

We should pray for as much as we want, knowing that Hashem can give it to us, and only He can give it to us.

11

Hashem Guards Your Life

The *Zohar* (*Parashas Vaeira*) teaches that each person should spend his life strengthening his relationship with Hashem. The closer a person is to Hashem, the more assistance he will receive from Him. Success in life comes from Hashem, and therefore we should not be wasting our time looking elsewhere. The more we look for Hashem in our lives and the more we connect with Him, the more tranquil our lives will be. As the *pasuk* states (*Tehillim* 114:7), משמועה רעה לא יירא נכון לבו בטוח בה' — "He will not fear evil tidings; his heart is firm in trust in Hashem." The Gemara in *Berachos* 60a explains this verse to mean that if a person firmly and confidently trusts in Hashem with all his heart, he will not be afraid of evil tidings.

Another *pasuk* (*Tehillim* 121:7) teaches, ה' ישמרך מכל רע ישמר את נפשך — "Hashem shall protect you from all harm; He shall protect your soul." Hashem is our Guardian Who has the ability to protect us under all circumstances. Human guards are limited in their ability to protect; they cannot protect against illness or death. But Hashem is the ultimate Guardian, Who can protect us from everything and anything that threatens us.

> *"But Hashem is the ultimate Guardian, Who can protect us from everything and anything that threatens us."*

I heard a remarkable story about Hashem's protection from Rav Shlomo Farhi, who is involved in outreach in England. A teenage boy knocked on his door and said, "Rabbi, I know that Hashem loves me, but right now I am facing a difficult situation and I was wondering if you could help me."

Rabbi Farhi asked the boy, "How do you know Hashem loves you?"

"There's no question about that at all," he said.

He proceeded to tell him that during the summer of 2005, he would travel by train to choir practice in London every Thursday morning. It was a long trip from his home, and he needed to be there at 9 a.m. One morning, as the train was just a couple of short stops away from his destination, he looked at his watch and saw it was 8:30. There was a coffee shop across the street and he figured he had plenty of time to get off, get himself a cup of coffee, and relax for a few minutes, before getting back on the train and going to practice. Shortly after he exited the train, he heard a deafening explosion. He turned and saw that the train had blown up. With tears running down his face, he watched the mayhem that ensued, with sirens blaring and fire engines and ambulances rushing to the scene. He tried calling home to inform his family that he was all right, but the cell phone network had crashed.

The boy started walking home, and two hours later, he walked through the door. He found his parents crying and sobbing. As soon as they saw him, they rejoiced.

"You're alive!" they exclaimed. "We can't believe it! You were on that train!" They told him that there was a synchronized terror attack on the London transit system, and multiple explosions took place at 8:50 a.m.

"No," the boy said, "it didn't happen at 8:50, it happened at 8:30!"

"That's wrong," his parents replied. "All the news stations reported that the attack took place at 8:50."

The boy looked at his watch, and his mouth dropped. It still read 8:30. Hashem had made his watch stop so he would think he had enough time to go get a cup of coffee, and this is how his life was saved.

"Do you have a picture of that watch?" the Rabbi asked.

"Rabbi," the boy said, "if you want I will give you the watch to keep." He ran home and brought back the watch. The Rabbi looked at it, and saw that it had stopped at 8:30.

"If I ever experience any doubts in my *emunah* at any point for the rest of my life," the Rabbi said, "I will look at this watch and remind myself that Hashem is controlling the world."

12 Hashem Is Always Watching

The highest level of mitzvah observance is achieved when a mitzvah is observed in private, without fanfare or publicity. The nature of man is such that he always seeks fame and recognition. We must remember that Hashem is always watching and recognizing every ounce of effort we invest in our *avodas Hashem*. When a person performs mitzvos discreetly, this is an exercise not only in humility, but also in *bitachon*.

The *Meshech Chochmah* teaches this concept in explaining the Gemara's comment (*Tamid* 32b) כל העוסק בתורה בלילה השכינה כנגדו — "Whoever learns Torah at night, the *Shechinah* is next to him." When the Sages speak here of לילה (night), the *Meshech Chochmah* explains, they refer to times when no one sees the studying, and he devotes himself to learning in complete privacy, solely for the sake of the mitzvah. Hashem loves the mitzvos that we perform in private.

In the Next World, we will be shown that He watched every mitzvah we perform. Sometimes we are given the privilege of seeing how He watches and is taking note of our good deeds performed sincerely for His sake.

> *"Sometimes we are given the privilege of seeing how He watches and is taking note of our good deeds performed sincerely for His sake."*

Rabbi Pesach Eliyahu Falk told a remarkable story that took place around thirty years ago in Israel. A yeshivah boy took a ride in a taxicab, and he was so engrossed in his learning during the ride that when the driver stopped at his destination, he forgot he was in a cab, and thought he was just being given a lift. He thus exited the cab without paying. The driver realized that the boy did not intentionally fail to pay, and simply made an honest mistake, and so he decided to ignore it and drive away. Just after he took off, however, the boy realized that he had not paid the driver, and started running after the cab as fast as he could. He almost caught up to the car as it stood at a red light, but just then the light turned green, and the cab drove away.

The boy felt terrible. *He is probably thinking that all yeshivah students steal and cheat,* he thought to himself. *I must do whatever I can to pay.* He started running after the cab again, and several times nearly caught it at a red light, only to watch it drive away. Finally, after twenty minutes of frantic running, he caught up to the taxi. He knocked on the window, the driver opened it, and the boy said, "I'm very sorry, I forgot to pay you," and handed him the money.

The driver was stunned. He repeatedly asked the boy, מהו? עד פה? — "What? You ran all the way here?" He simply could not believe it.

Thirty years later, the boy, now a grown man, was walking along a street in Jerusalem and saw a sign announcing a special *derashah* that was being given by a certain Rabbi on the subject of *kiddush Hashem*. This was a topic that was especially dear to this man's heart, and so he wrote down the time and place, and when the time came he attended the *shiur*. He thoroughly enjoyed the lecture, and when it was finished he went up to the Rabbi to thank him.

"I just have one question, though," the man said. "You mentioned in your *shiur* that if somebody creates a real *kiddush Hashem*, then Hashem will see to it that he personally witnesses its outcome. But I once made a *kiddush Hashem*, some thirty years ago, and I never saw anything come of it." He proceeded to tell the Rabbi about the incident with the cabdriver when he was a young yeshivah student.

The Rabbi's face lit up when he heard the story, and he smiled and said, אני הנהג — "I am the driver." He was that cabdriver, and he was so impressed by the yeshivah boy's integrity and the effort he made to pay the money that he decided to become a *baal teshuvah* and study Torah. He eventually became a noted Rav.

"I am the fruits of your *kiddush Hashem*," he said. "Indeed, Hashem showed you the result of your actions, thirty years later."

We must trust that Hashem is watching and taking note of each and every mitzvah we perform, and we will eventually see the fruits of our labor.

13 Recognizing Hashem in Your Life

Hashem is involved in our everyday affairs, at all times. That which appears to us as a coincidence is in truth the Hand of Hashem. This is the concept of *hashgachah pratis* — Hashem's direct providence and involvement in our lives.

> *"That which appears to us as a coincidence is in truth the Hand of Hashem."*

Those who are attuned can discern Hashem in their lives on a daily basis. Sometimes His involvement is very apparent, whereas at other times it is not easily recognizable, but those who look for it can see it. Many individuals record in writing every instance where they see Hashem in their lives. They have all expressed how the more they write, the more they are able to see. And when Hashem's involvement becomes clear, it is a minimiracle, and one is therefore obligated to tell others about it.

A student told his Rabbi of how he was miraculously saved, and the Rabbi reacted with great enthusiasm. Ten minutes later, they were walking and were joined by several other people. The Rabbi turned to the student and said, "So tell me what happened to you."

"But I just told you ten minutes ago," the student replied, puzzled.

The Rabbi answered by citing the *pasuk*, שיחו בכל נפלאותיו — "Speak about all His wonders" (*Tehillim* 105:2). We have to speak about what Hashem does for us, over and over again.

> And thus I feel obliged to share a minimiracle that occurred to me. I needed to prepare a very important speech on the topic of *bitachon*, and I had to find just the right words to say. I was hoping that something from a previous class I had given, which was recorded onto a CD, would be appropriate. I had five CD's of recorded classes, and I did not know which CD had the segment I needed, and I did not have the time to listen to all of the recordings. I put in the first CD and listened to the entire lecture. It wasn't on that one. I then put in the second CD, and after the disc was spinning for twenty seconds, the machine gave an error message. I removed the CD, gently dusted it off, and tried again, but with the same result. And so I put in the third CD, and once again, after twenty seconds I got an error message. I removed and cleaned off the CD, but it still did not work. And so I put in the fourth CD, and it had precisely the words I was seeking.
>
> This was the Hand of Hashem coming to help me. It was so clear to me. I put the second CD back into the machine to see what would happen, and it worked perfectly. I then took it out and put in the third CD — and it, too, worked fine. It was the Hand of Hashem.

גל עיני והביטה (*Tehillim* 119:18) — may Hashem always open our eyes so that we see His guidance and assistance at all times.

14 Hashem Loves Us

It occasionally happens that a person goes through a difficult period, during which he feels dejected and depressed, and does not want to see anybody. The *Orchos Tzaddikim* (*Shaar HaSimchah*) writes that if a person at such moments is able to say to himself, *Who is doing this to me? My loving Father, Who knows what is best for me!* — then he fulfills a mitzvah. Every time a person goes through difficulty and reminds himself that the situation was lovingly brought upon him by his Creator, he fulfills the Biblical command of וידעת עם לבבך כי כאשר ייסר איש את בנו ה' אלקיך מיסרך — "You should know in your heart that Hashem punishes you like a father punishes his child" (*Devarim* 8:5). Hashem deals with us the same way a father deals with his child. But in truth, His love for us is even greater. The Torah uses the example of a parent-child relationship only because it is an experience to which we can relate. But the *Chovos HaLevavos* writes that Hashem grants a parent the ability to love his or her child. He is the Source of parental love. And thus His love for us far exceeds the love of a parent for a child, and is actually unfathomable and beyond our comprehension.

A woman described a near-death experience that she went through. She lost the child she was expecting in her eighth month and needed to undergo emergency surgery. The operation did not go well, and she was losing lots of blood and needed an urgent transfusion. All of a sudden, she described, she saw herself hovering near the ceiling, looking down at those in the room, watching everyone working frantically and seeing the anxious looks on their faces. At that moment she felt such pity for them. She wanted to tell them, "You don't have to worry, I am perfectly fine." She said that she felt such an overpowering love for every single person in that room, a love too deep to describe. She felt like she wanted to hug every person there, and tell them that everything was going to be just fine.

> *"You don't have to worry, I am perfectly fine."*

I told her that she felt this way because at that moment she was a pure *neshamah*, a piece of Hashem. And this experience is but a glimpse of the immense love that Hashem feels for each and every one of us.

If a person can think these thoughts during periods of hardship, he will be able to overcome depression and also fulfill a mitzvah. May Hashem grant us all the ability to feel His love for us at all times.

15 Recognize Your Blessings

Appreciating Hashem's kindness brings us more blessing. Rav Avigdor Miller would stress that we must appreciate not only the big things in life, but also the simple, everyday conveniences that we enjoy.

> *"Appreciating Hashem's kindness brings us more blessing."*

I was driving home on a cold winter night at about 10 p.m., and I noticed a store that was still open and crowded with people. As I came closer I realized it was a laundromat. The place was packed with people waiting as their laundry was washed and dried. I thought to myself how fortunate I am that I have a washer and dryer at home, so that I don't have to go out into the cold shlepping heavy bags of laundry. We have so much blessing in our lives that we at times fail to recognize. A person feels a chill in the air, he presses a button on the thermostat, and within minutes he's comfortable. There are so many of us who are dissatisfied with their living conditions, wishing they had a larger home, without appreciating how good their home is. Sometimes as I drive through other neighborhoods I notice the very small apartments often situated on top of the stores. I am filled with gratitude that I do not have such accommodations.

Truly great people consistently say "thank you." In the *Amidah,* many of us daven at great length when asking for health, livelihood, success, and our other needs. But one section that is often shortchanged is *Modim*, toward the end of the *Amidah*, in which we thank Hashem for all we have been given.

> A student approached his Rabbi and asked why it is that the Rabbi's *Amidah* recitation is always so much longer than his.
>
> "I make a point of praying slowly and with concentration," the student said, "but every time, I finish well before you. Why does your *Amidah* prayer take so long?"
>
> "Simple," the Rabbi answered. "Before I begin *Modim*, I first think about the blessings in my life. I think about each and every one of my children and grandchildren, my house, my *parnassah*, my Torah learning, and so on. I think to myself, *Hashem, You have given me so much!* Only after I finish thinking of all this do I proceed to bow and recite *Modim*."

Reciting the *Modim* prayer is of paramount importance. The *Daas Zekeinim* writes (*Devarim* 10:12) that if one recites *Modim* properly, his recitation is considered equivalent to reciting one hundred *berachos*, as the numerical value of the word מודים is 100.

> A convention was once held in a certain hotel in Europe, with many prominent Rabbis in attendance. One of the participants was outside one of the hotel rooms at night and heard a guest talking to Hashem: "Hashem, thank You so much for my health. Hashem, thank You so much for my wife. Hashem, thank You for enabling me to pay

my bills. Hashem, thank You for giving me intelligence." This guest went on and on, listing all his blessings in life for which he was grateful. The next morning, this participant went to the front desk to ask who had stayed in Room 108 the previous night. It turned out that this was the room of the *Chafetz Chaim*. Before going to sleep each night, the *Chafetz Chaim* would express his gratitude to Hashem for all his blessings.

Appreciation is the key to happiness in life. As we say each day (*Tehillim* 100:1), מזמור לתודה...עבדו את ה' בשמחה. When we appreciate all we have, we will be able to serve Hashem with joy, and thus allow Him to shower us with even greater blessing.

16 Why Doesn't Hashem Show Us Why It Is Good?

Some people ask, if everything Hashem does is good, and Hashem is so kind and merciful, then why doesn't He just show us how this is so? Why does He make things happen that seem bad, instead of just showing us how they are good?

> *"Trusting Hashem elevates a person to great spiritual heights and brings blessing and salvation."*

The answer is that sometimes Hashem indeed does show us how seemingly negative events are truly for the best, but in other instances, as the *Lev Simchah* explains, He makes the situation look bad to give us the opportunity to trust in Him and thereby accrue the great benefits of this mitzvah. Trusting Hashem elevates a person to great spiritual heights and brings blessing and salvation, and Hashem therefore makes events appear difficult in order for us to earn these benefits.

The Gemara (*Berachos* 60b) tells of Rabbi Akiva who was traveling and wanted to spend the night in a certain town, but nobody agreed to host him. He was forced to sleep in the forest, and soon a lion came and ate his donkey, a cat ate his rooster, and a gust of wind blew out his candle. Throughout this ordeal, Rabbi Akiva reminded himself that כל מאי דעביד רחמנא לטב עביד; everything Hashem does is for the best. The next morning, he saw that the town had been ransacked and all the residents were killed. If the attackers would have seen his light or heard his animals, he, too, would have been killed.

In a *shmuess,* Rabbi Chaim A. Yamnick raised the question of why Hashem had to resort to such measures to save Rabbi Akiva's life. Certainly, He could have come up with some other way of ensuring that the attackers would not see him. Why did Rabbi Akiva's animals have to perish and his candle blow out?

The Rabbi answered that Rabbi Akiva earned this miraculous salvation by trusting Hashem when the situation looked bleak. It was specifically by insisting that everything was good when it looked bad that Rabbi Akiva earned the merit he needed. Trusting Hashem and believing that everything is good when it looks bad is what earns us great blessing and salvation, and this was how Rabbi Akiva's life was spared.

17 Emunah Brings Blessing

Facing life's challenges with faith brings salvation and blessing, both spiritual and material. Rav Safrin of Kamarna taught that when a person responds to hardship by saying, "I don't know what You're doing, Hashem, but I know You love me, I know this is the best thing for me, and I know You are with me at every step of the way," his soul is elevated as much as it would had he fasted for three hundred years. Such is the spiritual effect of strengthening one's *emunah*.

> *"I know You love me, I know this is the best thing for me, and I know You are with me at every step of the way."*

An example of the salvation earned through *emunah* is a story told of Rav Mendel of Riminov. Rav Mendel had a student named Rav Levi Yitzchak of Vizhnitz, who was destitute to the point of starvation. He would occasionally go to meet with his Rebbe, and each time his wife would beg him to ask the Rebbe for a blessing for *parnassah*. But Rav Levi Yitzchak would say, "A blessing for *gashmiyus* [material wealth]?! No way. I go for guidance and advice in my Torah study and fear of Hashem."

One day, the situation in the home was so dire that his wife demanded that Rav Levi Yitzchak go and ask the Rebbe for a blessing for *parnassah*. "If you don't get us a blessing," she said sternly, "don't bother coming home." Rav Levi Yitzchak had no choice, and so he went to his Rebbe planning to ask for a *berachah*. But once he got there, he started praying, learning and singing, totally forgetting about asking for the blessing. He was about to leave to return home when he remembered what his wife had told him. He was thinking of approaching his Rebbe, but then he asked himself, *How can I ask the Rebbe for something so silly like money?* He decided he would stay a little longer. He returned to the *beis midrash* and remained there for a couple of days until the Rebbe sent somebody to bring him in.

"How are things at home?" the Rebbe asked him.

"*Baruch Hashem*," the student said, "I have everything. Hashem has blessed me with כל טוב וטוב [every kind of goodness]."

The Rebbe laughed and said, "You think I don't know that you and your family are starving? But the words you just said, that you are blessed with כל טוב וטוב, pierced the heavens, and sustained me and the entire world. In this merit, I guarantee that you and your family will be blessed with great wealth for all generations, forever."

These are the benefits of responding to life's hardships with *emunah*.

18 Accepting Hashem's Will

A man came to the Baal Shem Tov and asked, "Please teach me the proper way for me to serve Hashem so I can earn a share in this world and the next. I am not a scholar. I do not have a brilliant mind. What should I do to serve Hashem?"

The Baal Shem Tov answered him:

קבל על עצמך להיות תמיד שמח בחלקך ומרוצה מהנהגת ה' יתברך עמך בכל העניינים

"Take it upon yourself to always be satisfied with your lot, and content with the way Hashem is dealing with you in all matters."

Take it upon yourself to always be satisfied with your lot, and content with the way Hashem is dealing with you in all matters.

When one says, "Hashem, You are in charge, You are directing my life, You know what needs to be done, and You can do anything; I am completely in Your hands," this is the highest level of *avodas Hashem* (service of Hashem). But when a person says this after getting knocked down, and again after getting knocked down a second time, this is such a lofty level of faith that it causes the heavens to tremble.

Rav Yechezkel Abramsky was taken by the authorities in the middle of the night and sent to Siberia, without being allowed to bring along anything, not even his coat. After his release, he met the famous Rabbi, the Maharyatz, who asked him, "How did you do it? How did you keep yourself going throughout the dreadful ordeal?"

Rav Yechezkel answered, "They took me without my coat, and I arrived in just my shirtsleeves. I woke up the first morning and wanted to say *Modeh Ani* and thank Hashem, but I thought to myself, *What can I thank Hashem for? I don't have a coat, I don't have food, I don't have tallis or tefillin, I don't have a single sefer — I have nothing!* I began reciting the prayer and I reached the words רבה אמונתך — 'having faith in You is great.' I then said to myself, *I have my emunah*! I was filled with such joy, knowing that I still had something that has the greatest power and that is the greatest gift in the world, a gift that nobody could ever take away from me."

After hearing the Rabbi's response, the Maharyatz said, "It was worth all the troubles and hardships that you suffered through for you to reach this level and have these thoughts."

When a person maintains such thoughts of *emunah*, he attains an extremely exalted level, and those thoughts become a receptacle for all of Hashem's blessings. The Torah states (*Devarim* 33:23), נפתלי שבע רצון ומלא ברכת ה' — "Naftali was satisfied and content — and filled with the blessing of Hashem." When a person feels satisfied and content, he is then filled with all of Hashem's blessings.

19

Emunah Cures Illness

What should a person's attitude be if he suffers from a serious illness, Heaven forbid?

The *pasuk* states (*Mishlei* 18:14), רוח איש יכלכל מחלהו ורוח נכאה מי ישאנה. The Vilna Gaon explains:

כשהאיש תמיד בשמחה אף שיבא עליו מחלה ח"ו הוא יכלכל מחלהו בשמחתו אבל מי שיש לו רוח נכאה מי יכול לישא זאת

"When a person is always happy, then even when sickness befalls him, Heaven forbid, he will provide [the cure] for his illness with his joy. But one who has a depressed spirit — who can bear it?"

> "He will provide [the cure] for his illness with his joy."

In other words, a person can battle his sickness and overcome it through joy. If a patient is able to clarify in his mind that he is in Hashem's hands, that only Hashem is in control and He could cure his illness in an instant, and through these thoughts he achieves inner peace, this itself can cure the illness.

I was privileged to see this happen with my own eyes. A man I know was diagnosed with cancer, and the doctors told him that his chances of survival were slim. The man did not allow the news to break his spirit. He continued coming to class every morning with a smile on his face, saying, "*Baruch Hashem*, I have another day of life"; "Hashem is so kind to me." He never became depressed. I visited him in the hospital when he was being treated for complications. He was bloated and uncomfortable, but every other word that came from his mouth was "*baruch Hashem*" or "*yishtabach Shemo*." He said, "*Baruch Hashem*, they found the problem and they are going to take care of it immediately."

After undergoing numerous treatments, he came to me a few days before Yom Kippur and told me he was going for another test on Erev Yom Kippur, and would get the results the day after Yom Kippur.

"*Yishtabach Shemo*!" he exclaimed. "Hashem is so kind. He is giving me a chance to pray on Yom Kippur, a chance to change and get better." He was so happy.

After Yom Kippur, he informed me that the doctors told him a miracle happened. The test came out perfectly clean. He was fine.

I told him this *pasuk* — רוח איש יכלכל מחלהו ורוח נכאה מי ישאנה. It was his joyful, upbeat spirit that served to overcome his illness.

20

Open Our Eyes

There is a well-known passage (*Bereishis Rabbah* 53:14) that many people customarily recite when they are looking for something they are unable to locate: אמר רבי בנימין: הכל בחזקת סומין עד שהקדוש ברוך הוא מאיר את עיניהם — "Rabbi Binyamin said: Everyone is presumed blind until the Holy One, Blessed is He, comes and opens their eyes."

The source for this practice is the story of Hagar, who was wandering in the desert with her son Yishmael. He was dying from thirst. The Torah writes (*Bereishis* 21:19), ויפקח אלקים את עיניה ותרא באר מים — "Hashem opened her eyes, and she saw a well of water." Hashem did not create a source of water that had not existed previously; rather, He opened Hagar's eyes so she could see the oasis that had been there the whole time.

The Imrei Pinchas tells of the Baal Shem Tov, who was once journeying with a student through the desert. Their water rations were depleted, and the student dehydrated. Ultimately, he told his Rebbe that if he does not drink immediately, he will die.

The Baal Shem Tov turned to his disciple and said, "Do you believe with all your heart that Hashem knows that you are thirsty and in desperate need of water? And that He has water and can provide it for you in an instant?"

"Yes," the student answered. "I believe."

"Then do not worry," the Rebbe said. "Everything will be fine."

Several minutes later, a man passed by and approached them.

"Have you seen my horses?" he asked. "I've been searching for three days, and I can't find them anywhere."

The Baal Shem Tov and his student told the man that they hadn't seen any horses, and asked him if he by chance had water to spare. He indeed had water with him, and he gave the student water to drink, saving his life.

"You see?" the Baal Shem Tov said to his student. "The solution was here the entire time; we just had to find it."

"But why," asked the student, "was it necessary for this man to spend three days searching for his horses so we could have water now?"

> *"The solution was here the entire time; we just had to find it."*

"Because," the Baal Shem Tov explained, "Hashem provides the solution to the problem even before the problem arises. By the time we face a problem, the solution is already in existence. We just have to find it."

"Ha'kol b'chezkas sumin." The solutions to all our problems are always right in front of us; we need to just ask Hashem to open our eyes so we can see them.

21

Hashem Thinks About Your Problem More Than You Do

We all know that Hashem exerts complete control over the world, but there are times when we feel inclined to despair. Parents need a *shidduch* for their daughter, and for years they do not find the right boy despite all their efforts and prayers. They might naturally begin to wonder, *Is Hashem listening? Does He know that our daughter needs to get married? Is He thinking about this problem?* A person is experiencing financial hardships, and is unable to pay his bills. He starts thinking, *Is Hashem taking care of this for me? He has so many things to deal with — is He paying attention to me and my crisis?* The doctors tell a patient that the treatment has not been successful, and he starts to wonder, *Maybe Hashem is simply too busy to worry about my condition and to pay attention to my heartfelt prayers?*

The answer to these questions is that Hashem not only thinks about, and pays attention to, our problems and concerns, but thinks about them even more than we do. Regardless of what we are going through, we still go to bed each night, and as we sleep our minds are "turned off" and not focused on the crisis at hand. Regarding Hashem, by contrast, it says, הנה לא ינום ולא יישן שומר ישראל — "Behold, the Guardian of Israel neither sleeps nor slumbers" (*Tehillim* 121:4). He is always thinking about us, at each and every moment, even when we are not.

"Behold, the Guardian of Israel neither sleeps nor slumbers."

When one begins to fall into despair, when he sees that his prayers do not seem to be working and begins to have doubts, this is precisely the moment when he should feel great encouragement and hope. It is specifically then, when a person begins to feel despair, that is the most auspicious time for *yeshuah* (salvation).

Channah, the Sages teach us, was childless for nineteen years. Her pain was intolerable and she prayed weeping bitter tears for nineteen years, and even her own husband, Elkanah, despaired, telling her not to worry because he is better than ten children (הלוא אנכי טוב לך מעשרה בנים — *I Shmuel* 1:8). And it was then, at the height of despair, when everyone around her urged her to give up, that Channah prayed with hope and faith. The Gemara (*Berachos* 31b) tells us that Channah prayed a beautiful prayer, speaking to Hashem with such confidence that she even specified the kind of child she wanted: Rav Dimi explains, "Not too smart but not foolish; not too tall and not too short." And when Hashem saw her genuine faith and trust in His Providence, He blessed her with a child who became one of the greatest prophets of all time: Shmuel HaNavi. In the merit of her bolstering her *emunah* just when she felt naturally inclined to despair, her prayers were answered and she was blessed with a child.

David HaMelech exhorts us in *Tehillim* 27:14, קוה אל ה' חזק ויאמץ לבך וקוה אל ה' — "Hope to Hashem; strengthen and fortify your heart, and hope to Hashem." We are bidden to "hope to Hashem," to place our trust and faith in Him, and when it seems like He is not listening and we are driven to despair, that is the time to "strengthen and fortify your heart," to reinforce our *emunah* and trust that He is there and listening to our every prayer.

22 Don't Lose Hope

Hashem is described as מצמיח ישועה — "He Who makes salvation sprout." Occasionally, when a person is confronted by a certain problem, he turns to Hashem in prayer, and sees that the situation worsens. Instinctively he may begin to think to himself, *Why should I bother praying? It only makes things worse!*

At such moments, one must remember that Hashem is מצמיח ישועה; He brings forth salvation like the ground brings forth produce. When a seed is placed in the ground, it first disintegrates before taking root and developing into a plant. An impatient person will be unable to wait for this process to unfold, and will dig up the seed soon after it is planted and see that it has decayed. The person will then despair. He may think this seed will never produce food. But someone who understands how the process works will trust in the ground's ability to develop the decayed remnants of the seed into nourishing and delicious produce. And he will happily invest the effort and labor, watering and tending to his crops to ensure that they grow properly.

Once we understand that Hashem is מצמיח ישועה, that our *yeshuah* from Hashem grows slowly and gradually like vegetation, we will be able to wait patiently, trust that our salvation will come, and invest in the necessary work and effort in heartfelt *tefillah*. There is no reason to despair when we see the situation deteriorating. This is the process of "decay" that ultimately produces the desired result.

All too often, we feel despair the moment before the *yeshuah* arrives. This phenomenon has been compared to an infant who awakens in the middle of the night crying for a bottle. His mother goes downstairs and prepares the bottle, as the baby continues to cry. As the infant grows more and more desperate, his shrieks intensify, reaching their peak the moment before the bottle is inserted into the baby's mouth. His salvation is being prepared, the bottle is right in front of the baby's mouth, but he does not realize it, and so he cries louder and louder.

"Similarly, our most powerful and potent prayers are those recited at the moment when all hope seems lost."

Similarly, our most powerful and potent prayers are those recited at the moment when all hope seems lost, when we find ourselves on the brink of despair. And these are precisely the prayers born of desperation that bring the *yeshuah* we need.

After the sin of the Golden Calf, Hashem tells Moshe, הרף ממני ואשמידם — "Let Me be, and I shall annihilate them" (*Devarim* 9:14). No situation could possibly be as hopeless as this: when Hashem openly declares His decision to destroy *Am Yisrael*. The Gemara (*Berachos* 32a) teaches, מיד נתחזק משה בתפילה — "Moshe immediately strengthened himself in prayer." At that disheartening moment, when it seemed like there was no hope, Moshe "strengthened himself" and prayed on behalf of the people. And this prayer, recited on the brink of despair, was effective in annulling the Divine decree of annihilation.

Just when we totter on the verge of despair, this is precisely the time to redouble our efforts and pray with even greater faith and with greater determination, recognizing that everything can turn around in an instant.

23 Why Worry?

If we truly knew the extent of Hashem's *hashgachah*, His Providence over us, how He cares for us and looks after us, we would have much fewer worries, and we would live a far calmer, more relaxed life.

When Hashem instructed Avraham to grant his wife Sarah's request and send away Hagar and Yishmael, He promised that He would care for Yishmael and that Yishmael would beget a large, powerful nation (וגם את בן האמה לגוי אשימנו — *Bereishis* 21:13). Soon thereafter, as Hagar and Yishmael are wandering through the desert, Yishmael dehydrates and becomes gravely ill. He is so close to death that his mother moves away, unable to look upon his suffering. As we read this episode, we know that everything will turn out fine. We know of Hashem's promise to Avraham, that Yishmael would survive, marry, and have children, and thus we know that there was no reason to fear.

Similarly, we can all look back upon many instances in our own lives where we faced problems that seemed intractable, difficult situations regarding which we had no idea how they could ever be overcome. But when we look now, in retrospect, and we see how things unfolded, we ask ourselves: *What was the big deal? Why were we so worried? Why did this get us so uptight?*

> *"What was the big deal? Why were we so worried? Why did this get us so uptight?"*

Many people face financial difficulties. They are worried, distraught, anxious, and unable to concentrate and focus on what they're doing. The anxiety causes tension in the home and disrupts *shalom bayis*. The proper advice for a person in this situation comes from this *pasuk* (*Mishlei* 31:15): ותקם בעוד לילה ותתן טרף לביתה. Literally, this verse gives praise to the devoted wife and mother who "arises while it is still night and prepares food for her household," who wakes up early in the morning, when it is still dark, to care for her family. There is, however, an additional interpretation of this verse. ותקם בעוד לילה — if one is capable of "arising," of lifting himself out of anxiety and depression, בעוד לילה — while it is still dark, before he sees the light of salvation, when no solution to his problems has begun to appear on the horizon, then ותתן טרף לביתה — Hashem will ensure that he has what he needs for himself and his family. If one girds himself with faith even when things appear "dark," and he says, "I am doing what I can, and I trust that You, Hashem, are caring for me, and therefore I am not worried, I will stay calm, and continue praying and making an effort" — then he will see Hashem's Providence and care, and all his needs will be provided.

24 Need Money? No Problem.

A person with *bitachon* does not worry about money. The *Chovos HaLevavos* (*Shaar HaBitachon*) writes that if one trusts Hashem to provide his *parnassah*, then his livelihood is guaranteed.

People worry about how they will meet their expenses even many years before the money needs to be paid. It is important to remember that Hashem always provides one's needs, but He does not necessarily provide the money well in advance of when it is needed. A man came to Rav Yitzchak Zev Soloveitchik, the Brisker Rav, to ask for a *berachah* before he embarked on a fund-raising trip to the United States. The Brisker Rav asked him why he was traveling abroad to raise money.

"Is there not enough money here in Israel?" the Brisker Rav asked.

"I've been trying to raise money here," the man said, "but it hasn't been working."

"When is the money due?" the Rabbi asked.

"In three weeks," the man replied.

"Three weeks?! You're worried now about a payment due in three weeks? The money for my yeshivah usually comes in only the day before it is due!"

> Rav Yosef Shlomo Kahaneman, the Ponevezher Rav, told that once he wanted to open a school, and there was an available property that was being sold for 100,000 rubles. The Ponevezher Rav did not have anywhere near this amount, but the owner of the property desperately needed cash, so he made the Rabbi an offer. He would sell the property for just 50,000 rubles

if the Rabbi could pay 25,000 rubles up front, and the rest within three weeks. If the Rabbi did not pay the balance within three weeks, the landowner said, the deposit would be forfeited.

The Ponevezher Rav consulted with his wife, and they decided that this school was so vital for the community that it was worth taking the risk. They paid the man the 25,000 rubles they had received from their parents to help them with their expenses, and they assumed that once the word got out about the new school the donations would be forthcoming. Unfortunately, however, these hopes never materialized. The night before the balance was due, on a Motza'ei Shabbos, the Ponevezher Rav turned to Hashem and said, "Hashem, I did my *hishtadlus* [effort]; I leave the rest in Your hands." He then went to the *beis midrash* to learn, and he would later describe the joy he felt during those hours spent engrossed in learning, feeling as though a heavy burden had been lifted from his shoulders.

> *"Hashem, I did my hishtadlus; I leave the rest in Your hands."*

He returned home from the *beis midrash* at 2 a.m., and much to his surprise, two of the town's wealthiest men were standing by his door.

"Sorry for coming so late," they told the Rabbi, "but we just completed making a *shidduch*, and we would like to entrust the money for the young couple — 25,000 rubles — with you."

"Sure," the Rabbi answered, "but do I have your permission to use the money if I need it? I will then pay it back within six months of receiving notice."

The men agreed, and the next day the Rabbi brought the money to the landowner to complete the purchase of the property. When he returned home, he was told that the *shidduch* between the two wealthy families had been broken. Over the next several months, he raised the 25,000 rubles he needed to repay the money.

We have to place our trust in Hashem, and realize that He is capable of providing, often in ways that we would never expect or even imagine.

25 Only Hashem Is in Charge

One of the advantages of *bitachon* mentioned by the *Chovos HaLevavos (Shaar HaBitachon)* was described by Rav Ephraim Wachsman by way of an analogy. Imagine a friend approached you and said that he could arrange for you to be the best friend of an exceedingly wealthy man. Without a doubt, you would be overjoyed and eager to make this acquaintance and establish a relationship with this fellow. Why? Quite obviously, you would be interested in this friendship because you would likely benefit from it, either by earning prestige or wealth.

This mindset compels us to invest inordinate amounts of energy in trying to impress and please many different people, anyone with whom a relationship could be to our advantage. The *Chovos HaLevavos* writes that if we understand that it is only Hashem Who determines whether we gain or lose, we would no longer be a slave to people.

> *"If we understand that it is only Hashem Who determines whether we gain or lose, we would no longer be a slave to people."*

This is the first of the thirteen principles of faith (found in the siddur) articulated by the Rambam, the belief that Hashem מנהיג לכל הברואים — "governs all created beings." Elsewhere, the *Chovos HaLevavos* writes that one of the ten minimum requirements of a Jew is to realize that whenever we receive any form of benefit from another individual, it comes directly from Hashem. Of course, we must express gratitude to the individuals who assist us. But at the same time, we must believe that it is Hashem Who decided that we would receive this benefit, and if this person had not chosen to provide it, Hashem would have arranged for us to receive it through some other means.

We work so hard trying to impress others — employers, clients, and so on — and trying to be connected to the right people, and, as a result, we end up being beholden and obligated to so many different people in our lives. But with *bitachon*, we need to be connected only to Hashem. Once we realize that regardless of whom we know and with whom we're connected, Hashem will provide exactly what we need, then we can free ourselves of this burden of trying to impress and please.

As simple as it sounds, this concept is very difficult to implement in practice. The reason is because this belief must be felt, and not simply known. Having *bitachon* is an emotional task, not an intellectual one. Indeed, the *Chovos HaLevavos* writes that a person "should feel" that only Hashem, and not other people, determines what he gains or loses. This perception needs to be felt and internalized, and not just rationally understood.

Sometimes, we try so hard to impress the buyer or the boss. This is permitted, even admirable, because we are obligated to do our best. But know that they have no say in your income. Even if they say no, Hashem can give you the money from elsewhere. With this understanding, life becomes that much simpler. Instead of working for one hundred people, you only have to work for One!

26

Hashem Has Many Ways

Chovos HaLevavos, in the introduction to *Shaar HaBitachon*, describes ten advantages that the person with *bitachon* has over the alchemist, who claims the ability to transform base metals into gold. One of these advantages is the fact that the alchemist requires raw materials with which to work to earn his fortune. As gifted as he is, he cannot earn anything without a few materials to start with. The person with *bitachon*, by contrast, will always be provided with his *parnassah* even if he is starting with nothing. The *Chovos HaLevavos* draws proof from the story of Eliyahu HaNavi, whom Hashem sustained during a drought by sending ravens to bring him bread and water. Hashem has endless ways of providing a person's needs, and thus even if one has nothing at all, Hashem is able to step in to provide for him.

One might wonder, what does the story of Eliyahu HaNavi have to do with us? We are not prophets, and we do not see ravens bringing us food.

In a *shmuess,* Rabbi Yosef Zalman Bloch explained that episodes in the Tanach are intended to convey practical life lessons, and therefore yes, the story of Eliyahu has a lot to teach us. Even though we do not see ravens bringing food and water, we can nevertheless learn from Eliyahu's experience that Hashem is able to provide our needs in ways that we could never imagine. And therefore even when the situation appears hopeless, and we cannot see from where our *parnassah* will arrive, we must trust that Hashem has a way to provide, and that He will provide.

> A man told me that once his business was going through a difficult period, at the same time that his daughter was to be married. He said that he has always had *bitachon* in Hashem, and during that difficult period, too, he trusted that Hashem would take care of his family's needs. He made a respectable, though not lavish, wedding for his daughter, and then the bills started coming. As he was going through the mail and trying to figure out how to pay the bills, there was one piece of mail that did not seem important and he was about to discard it. But then he decided to open it, and the envelope contained a check for nearly $23,000. The check was from a firm for which he had worked years earlier, in 1995. The firm had recently been audited, and it was found that there was a certain refund due him that had never been paid. The IRS ordered the firm to pay him

the owed money plus eighteen years' worth of interest, which amounted to far more than the principal.

Remarkably, eighteen years before the girl's wedding, when she was just an infant, Hashem was already arranging the means to provide the money for her wedding, and an audit took place eighteen years later so that the money would be there.

"Remarkably, eighteen years before the girl's wedding, Hashem was already arranging the means to provide the money for her wedding."

True, we do not see ravens, but we do see miracles, time and time again. Hashem has an infinite number of ways to provide, and is thus able to care for us even when we cannot see from where the *parnassah* will come.

27 Are You a Slave or a Free Man?

One can regard his boss in two ways. One approach is to think to oneself, *My life is in his hands. If he likes me, then I am set, all is well, and I have security, so I will do anything I need to do to please him*. The second mindset, by contrast, is *He is just a messenger of the real Boss. I will try to please him because I am obligated to try my hardest, and because I am an honest person. Besides, we should be trying to please everyone*.

Both these employees produce the same results. They work hard to please the boss, and he is happy with their work. But there is a fundamental difference between them. The first is a slave. He is entirely bound to his boss' every call. The second, however, while working just as hard, is absolutely free. He does not feel dependent upon his boss, and is therefore a truly free man, not a slave.

The same applies to one's most important clients and customers. The person with *bitachon* understands that they are agents of the Almighty to provide his *parnassah*, but ultimately he is not in their hands, but in Hashem's.

> I know a businessman who lives with sincere *bitachon*. Once he was a bit late shipping an order to a major customer, and the company demanded a $10,000 rebate as a result of the delay. Several days later, the company demanded a further reduction of $86,000. The man explained that he could not grant them such a significant reduction, as this would eliminate his entire profit. But they insisted, and threatened to stop their business with him if he refused.
>
> The man thought to himself, *If I agree to this, that would not be normal hishtadlus [effort]; it would be an act of desperation. But I am not desperate; I place my trust not in my customers, but in Hashem*. He told them he would not accept their demand, and they told him they would no longer be doing business with him.
>
> That night he kept telling himself, *It is only Hashem. It's all up to Him*.
>
> The next day, he called the company C.E.O. to inquire if they could possibly try to work out an arrangement. The person said, "Actually, we were also thinking last night that we would still like to work with you." The company asked if he would be willing to send them 80,000 pieces of a different item at the cost price, and then they would call it even. The man happily agreed, and was then able to renegotiate for a cheaper cost price from his supplier. Thus in the end he not only kept his biggest customer and the $86,000, but made a large profit on this shipment as well.

"But I am not desperate; I place my trust not in my customers, but in Hashem."

This man recognized all along that Hashem is in charge, and he never felt desperate. Sure enough, he saw immediate results and enjoyed Hashem's blessing.

28 Seeing Hashem in Your Daily Life

The Gemara (*Makkos* 24a) comments that the basis of all 613 mitzvos is *emunah*, faith in Hashem, as indicated by the verse (*Habakkuk* 2:4), צדיק באמונתו יחיה — "A righteous person shall live through faith." Similarly, a *pasuk* in *Tehillim* states, כל מצוותיך אמונה — "All Your commandments are [based upon] faith." Accordingly, the Vilna Gaon writes in his commentary to *Mishlei* that the most important thing of all is to have complete trust in Hashem, as this encapsulates all other mitzvos. The stronger one's faith, the better he will be able to serve Hashem.

How does one acquire *emunah*?

A letter signed by two of the leading Sages of the last generation — Rav Moshe Feinstein and Rav Yaakov Kaminetzky — emphasized the importance of internalizing how Hashem oversees the life of each and every individual, and recommends that one reinforce this belief by keeping a journal, a written record of every instance in which he or she sees Hashem's supervision and involvement in his life. The letter concludes by stating, "By strengthening this mitzvah, all 613 mitzvos will be fortified, and then we will experience the words of the prophet Habakkuk, צדיק באמונתו יחיה."

> Mr. Charlie Sultan, ע"ה, lived his life for many years based on this letter. His son discovered fourteen notebooks in which the deceased had written personal stories of *hashgachah* (providence) over the course of two decades, and this letter was kept in one of the notebooks. The letter contained the following message, "Try it, just a few words a day." One of his children scanned all the material, from all fourteen notebooks, and when he finished, he was amazed to discover that there were

precisely 613 pages of material. Just as the letter said, by recording our personal stories of *emunah*, we fortify all 613 mitzvos.

> *By recording our personal stories of emunah, we fortify all 613 mitzvos.*

One prominent Rabbi in the Syrian community was so inspired by this incident that he decided to compile a *hashgachah pratis* journal that includes various quotes on the topic of *emunah* and Divine providence, as well as blank pages to add your own personal stories. The stories don't need to be dramatic; even minor experiences when you felt Divine providence in your life are very meaningful and worthy of being transcribed.

I wanted to conclude with a sample story and I remembered that somebody gave me a book on the topic of *emunah* with a section on *hashgachah pratis*. I thought to myself there will surely be good stories there. The book contains 515 pages, and I randomly opened to page 15. I was amazed to find on that page the *pasuk* צדיק באמונתו יחיה quoted from *Makkos* — the very source with which I began this essay. I am grateful to Hashem for a perfect story of *hashgachah*.

29 Everything Is a Test

Once we recognize Hashem's involvement in every aspect of daily life, we can understand the following comment of the *Mesillas Yesharim* (Chapter 1):

כל עניני העולם בין לטוב בין לרע הרי הן נסיונות לאדם

"All matters in the world — whether good or bad — are tests for a person."

Anything that happens to us, any situation in which we find ourselves, is a handpicked test with which Hashem chose to test us to see if we will respond the proper way. Sometimes we end up in places through unexpected and unforeseen circumstances, or bump into somebody unexpectedly, and it seems as though it happened randomly. But in truth, it is a "setup" orchestrated by Hashem to test us if we will do what we are supposed to do in the given situation.

"All matters in the world — whether good or bad — are tests for a person."

The purpose of a test is to elevate us. The Torah says regarding Avraham's test of *akeidas Yitzchak*, והאלקים **נסה** את אברהם — "G-d tested Avraham" (*Bereishis* 22:1). The Midrash (*Bereishis Rabbah* 55:1) explains the word נסה in light of the *pasuk* (*Tehillim* 60:6), נס להתנוסס — "a banner to be lifted." By reacting properly to tests, we become better, more complete people. For this reason Hashem brings us tests each and every day throughout our lives.

As David HaMelech fled Jerusalem during the rebellion mounted by his own son, Avshalom, he was confronted by Shimi ben Geira, who pelted him with rocks and hurled insults at him. David's servants wanted to kill Shimi, but David instructed them to leave him alone, because Shimi's assault was sent by Hashem. *Chazal* (as quoted in *Chafetz Chaim*, *Shaar HaTerumah* Chapter 8) comments that when David said this to his servants, at that moment he earned the privilege of being the fourth leg of Hashem's chariot, together with the three patriarchs. This was his reward for recognizing that the test he confronted was sent to him by Hashem, rather than losing himself. We must keep this in mind at all times, every day, and realize that all the difficult situations we face are tests from Hashem.

> My relative had an appointment in the city, and as she made her way to the car after the appointment she noticed a ticket on the windshield. At first she was quite upset, as she had made a point of ascertaining that the spot was legal. But then she told herself, "I did my *hishtadlus* [effort], I did what I had to do, and if this happened, then this is a test from Hashem, and I am

not going to let it disturb me." When she got to the car, she read the ticket, and couldn't believe her eyes. It said, "TEST; this is not a ticket do not pay." It was unbelievable; it was as though Hashem was speaking directly to her, informing her that this was really just a test. Since that day, my relative has kept the ticket as a constant reminder that Hashem is behind the scenes testing us and hoping that we will become better people as a result.

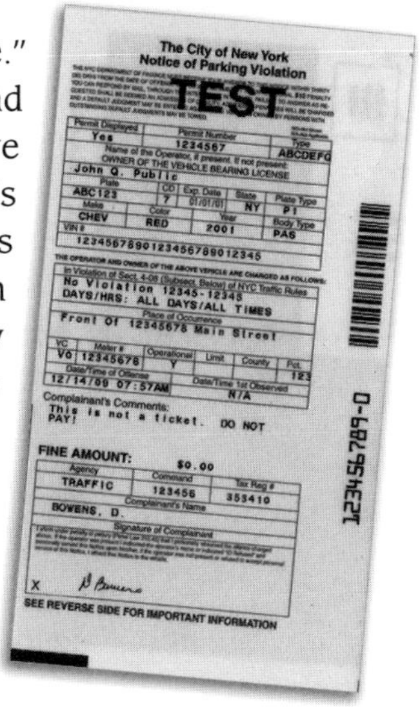

30 Recognizing That It Is Really Hashem

Hashem exerts complete control over our lives, and there is nothing in existence that can prevent His will being done. Nevertheless, He hides behind the scenes in order to allow us free will. Since Hashem conceals His providence behind the veil of the natural order, we have the free will to view everything that happens as either a coincidental effect of nature, or as a manifestation of the Divine will.

A man made a purchase at a grocery store, and forgot to take his change. After he left, the cashier saw the money and said to the storeowner, "Boss, look, he left

> \$1.98 on the counter." The boss told him to put the money back into the register, because it belongs to him.
>
> "Is that honest, Boss?" the employee asked. The boss told him to be quiet and get back to work. Just at that moment, the boss accidentally knocked over a jar of pickles. The worker rushed over to clean the mess, and picked up the broken jar.
>
> "Hey, Boss, this jar cost \$1.98," the worker said. "Maybe someone's trying to tell you something?"
>
> "Well," the boss said, "I guess it's a good thing the guy left his change, so that I wouldn't lose any money from the broken jar."

Some people just don't get it, and insist on viewing everything as coincidence, rather than the Hand of Hashem.

Hashem hides behind the mask of nature, but He wants us to find Him. People who write down their personal stories of *hashgachah* say that once they start this practice, they begin seeing Hashem more overtly in their lives. They discuss these incidents over the Shabbos table, and develop a keen awareness of Hashem's presence in their lives. Once we begin to look for Him, He makes Himself visible, and emerges from behind the mask of nature.

> The Gemara (*Taanis* 25a) relates a story of Rabbi Chanina ben Dosa. He saw that his daughter was upset. She explained that she had inadvertently put vinegar in the Shabbos lamps instead of oil, and had already lit the wicks. She was distraught because the wicks would surely go out and they would not have light for Shabbos. Rabbi Chanina said, "The One Who said that oil shall burn can also make vinegar burn." Sure enough, the wick burned, and remained burning throughout the entire Shabbos. Rabbi Chanina saw right through nature, and understood that Hashem is behind everything. And once he recognized Hashem, Hashem no longer hid behind the ordinary laws of nature.

Many times in life we confront difficult problems and situations, and, as we should, we try to find ways to resolve them. We must remember, though, that while we have an obligation of *hishtadlus*, to make a personal effort, ultimately, everything is caused by Hashem, and therefore, the primary *hishtadlus* is to speak to Him about the problem and seek His assistance. Often, this recognition alone can solve the problem. Once we see Hashem behind the veil of nature, He will come out from behind that veil and make Himself more visible.

Tehillim (92:10) says, כי הנה אויביך ה' כי הנה אויביך יאבדו. Literally, this means, "For behold, Your enemies, O Hashem, Your enemies shall be annihilated." The Baal Shem Tov, however, explained this to mean that once we recognize that אויביך, the enemies, the problems and hardships in life, are ה' — brought about directly from Hashem — then הנה אויביך יאבדו — they will then be eliminated. Once we recognize that the problems come from Hashem, He will step in to solve them.

> *"Once we recognize that the problems and hardships in life are brought about directly from Hashem — they will then be eliminated."*

We must therefore train ourselves in this mode of thinking, in recognizing that everything that happens in our lives is caused by Hashem. And we do this through practice, by looking to see His involvement in our lives, by talking about it and by writing it down. And the more we see Him, the less He will be hidden.

31 In Its Mother's Arms

One of the definitions of the term "*emunah*" given by the *mefarshim* (commentators) relates to the *pasuk*, כאשר ישא **האומן** את היונק — "like a nursemaid carries a suckling baby"

(*Bamidbar* 11:12). *Emunah* is the experience of an infant nursing from his mother. Indeed, David HaMelech described himself as כגמול עלי אמו — "like a suckling infant upon his mother" (*Tehillim* 131:2). What is meant by this comparison? How does *emunah* make a person like a nursing baby?

The Vilna Gaon (*Divrei Eliyahu, Tehillim* 131:2) explained that after a child nurses, he feels completely satisfied and does not worry about his next meal. He is perfectly content, secure, and at ease. An infant is always in his mother's arms, no matter where he finds himself. Whether he is home, in a store, in his mother's friend's home, he is satisfied and secure, because he is in his mother's arms. Rabbi Ephraim Wachsman noted that when Jews were being brought to Auschwitz, they were obviously very frightened, but the babies were perfectly content, secure in their mother's arms, blissfully unaware of any looming danger. Similarly, a person with *emunah*, who sees himself as entirely dependent on Hashem, will never worry. He will always feel the security of being held by Hashem, like an infant in his mother's arms.

This concept was described to me by someone who told how he was walking through a dangerous neighborhood with his 6-year-old daughter. He was very frightened, but his daughter was perfectly at ease. She was holding Daddy's hand, and so nothing could frighten her. As we say in our prayers, ה' לי לא אירא — "Hashem is mine — I shall not fear" (*Tehillim* 115:6).

This feeling, of knowing that Someone is always looking out for us, is priceless. Not only is there Someone taking care of us, but this "Someone" loves us even more than we love ourselves. We are always taken care of, we are always in our mother's arms.

> *"We are always taken care of, we are always in our mother's arms."*

Many people suffer from anxiety that keeps them up at night. But David HaMelech said at the time when he was forced to flee from his own son, אני שכבתי ואישנה...כי ה' יסמכני — "I lay down and slept ... because G-d supports me" (*Tehillim* 3:6). David was able to sleep even during his life's darkest moments because he was held in Hashem's arms, as it were. A baby falls asleep calmly and soundly in his mother's arms, and it is precisely this feeling of security that David experienced.

There is also another comparison between *emunah* and a nursing baby. A mother's milk is genetically designed to perfectly suit her baby's metabolism; it is exactly what the infant needs. Similarly, a person with *emunah* knows that everything given to him is exactly what he needs to succeed in life. As David HaMelech says, ה' רועי לא אחסר — "Hashem is my shepherd; I lack nothing" (*Tehillim* 23:1). This is the feeling experienced by people with *emunah:* that they lack nothing, because whatever they have is precisely what they are supposed to have. And this is the level that we should be striving to attain.

32 Reliance on Hashem Produces Blessings

The more a person relies on Hashem and looks to Him for His security, the more blessing he will receive.

As we noted, David HaMelech (*Tehillim* 131:2) described himself as כגמול עלי אמו — "like a suckling infant upon his mother." He was entirely dependent on Hashem just as a nursing baby is entirely dependent upon his mother. One of the interesting features of nursing is that the milk supply is dependent upon the child. As long as the infant is interested in nursing, the mother's body produces milk. But once he is no longer interested in his mother's milk, it ceases to be available. The same is true of our reliance on Hashem. The more we place our trust in Hashem, the greater the "supply" of blessing there will be.

The more we place our trust in Hashem, the greater the "supply" of blessing there will be.

It is told that the Baal Shem Tov stayed in the home of a man named Shalom during his travels, and the man was thrilled and honored to host such a distinguished Rabbi. Throughout his stay, the Baal Shem Tov told stories and taught Torah to the members of his household, and Shalom was delighted. Finally, after several days, the Rabbi informed his host that he must leave. The host pleaded with him to stay, but the Baal Shem Tov insisted that he must leave to raise money for his charitable organizations.

"How much money do you expect to raise in a day?" Shalom asked.

"One thousand rubles," the Baal Shem Tov replied.

The man offered to donate one thousand rubles so that the Baal Shem Tov would remain another day, and the Rabbi agreed. The next day, the Baal Shem Tov again prepared to leave, but the man once again insisted that he stay, offering him more money. This continued for several days, until Shalom's funds were nearly depleted. Unwilling to allow the great Rabbi to leave, Shalom sold the precious gems that he had relied on as his "backup" source of money. He sold the gems for four thousand rubles, and the Baal Shem Tov was his guest for another four days. At last, the Baal Shem Tov bid Shalom farewell and left. Afterward, Shalom considered his situation and was stunned. He was left with no money and a large family to care for. How would he feed his family?

Shalom turned to Hashem and said, "Hashem, I need you." Sure enough, that night a few drunkards came by, knowing that Shalom sold top-quality liquor. Desperately seeking a way to indulge their addiction, they asked Shalom for some whiskey.

"I am sorry," he said, "but I have no merchandise to sell you." But the drunkards persisted, explaining that his was the best whiskey available and they desperately wanted it. And even if he had run out, they were willing to purchase his empty barrels so they could pour water into it which would absorb the flavor of the whiskey. He agreed, and they gave him numerous gold coins in exchange for empty barrels.

A few years later, the Baal Shem Tov was again traveling through that region, and he came to Shalom's home in order to visit his former host. He knocked on the door, and the person who opened the door was not Shalom. It turned out that Shalom had moved to the wealthier part of town. The Rabbi found out where he lived, and went to his home. He saw that Shalom now lived in a large palace, with a butler and servants. Shalom ran to greet the Rabbi, and expressed how honored he felt to once again host the great sage.

"However," he added, "there's one thing that's been bothering me over the last few years. How could you have left me with no money? How did you take all that money knowing that I would have nothing left, and I have a large family?"

The Baal Shem Tov explained, "I saw in the heavens that you were destined to attain great wealth, but the pipelines of blessing were blocked because you placed your trust in those precious gems. Once I saw that you were prepared to give away those gems and place your trust in Hashem, I knew that the blessing would soon start pouring in."

It is our trust and confidence in Hashem that generates the blessing, just as a nursing infant causes its milk to be plentiful.

33 It's Not All or Nothing

I was asked the following question: "I thought I had *bitachon* [trust in Hashem]. I am constantly telling people that Hashem is great and is always taking care of us. But when a problem comes up in my own life, I lose it. I become nervous and worried. So of what value are all my lessons in *emunah*? What good are they if they do not help me when I confront a personal problem?"

I answered that each and every lesson in *emunah* that we learn and internalize is valuable beyond estimation. *Emunah* is not an "all or nothing" enterprise. Whatever we accomplish is immensely significant, even if there is more room for us to grow further.

> *"Each and every lesson in emunah that we learn and internalize is valuable beyond estimation."*

I once heard a remarkable story from Rav Fishel Schachter that beautifully illustrates this point. There was once a certain Rabbi who was a towering scholar, spending all his time learning, teaching, and writing. He composed pages upon pages of *chiddushim* (novel Torah insights) which he very much wished to have printed. The nearest printing press was overseas, and so he summoned a student and entrusted him with his precious pages. "Please take this, my life's work, overseas and have it printed. Guard it with every fiber of your being." The student was petrified, being entrusted with such a priceless treasure, but he agreed. Soon after he set sail, a violent storm broke out at sea, and the ship began to capsize. Fortunately, the student somehow managed to survive, but his Rabbi's papers were lost.

He returned home and told his peers what had happened. The students were all very frightened. How could they break such terrible news to their dear

Rabbi? How could they tell him that his life's work was lost forever?

One boy devised a plan. The next day, when the Rabbi entered the classroom, this student raised his hand to ask a question. He mentioned the Mishnah's comment (*Berachos* 60b), כשם שמברכין על הטוב כך מברכין על הרע — "Just as we bless [Hashem] for the good, so do we bless [Hashem] for the bad." The student asked, "How is this possible? How can one bless Hashem over misfortune just as he blesses Hashem for joyous events?"

"What do you mean?" the Rabbi said. "Everything Hashem does is good! There is never anything 'bad'!"

Another student raised his hand and asked, "But what if such and such happens?"

The Rabbi repeated what he had said, this time more emphatically: "Everything Hashem does is good! If something happens, then, of course, this is the best thing for the person."

One by one, the students raised their hands to ask what the Rabbi would say if this calamity struck or that calamity struck. The Rabbi grew red in the face repeating himself with greater and greater emotion that everything Hashem does is good, and we thus can and must bless Him and be grateful for everything, even for that which might initially appear as bad.

Finally, a boy spoke up and informed the Rabbi that his papers were lost at sea. The Rabbi heard the news and promptly fainted.

The boys realized that their plan had failed. They thought they could prepare their Rabbi for the devastating news, but it didn't work.

They revived the Rabbi and then apologized, explaining that they had hoped to prepare him by speaking about this theme of trusting that everything Hashem does is good, but apparently their efforts were inadequate.

"What do you mean?" the Rabbi replied. "At least I

woke up. Who knows what would have happened if you hadn't prepared me!"

There are thousands of levels of *bitachon*, and every lesson we learn and contemplate brings us to a higher level, and is thus immensely meaningful and significant.

34 Learning How to Walk

At times those who experience difficulties or challenges in their lives become angry with Hashem, Heaven forbid. Some will say, "Why are you doing this to me?" but nevertheless continue serving Hashem, while others might decide that they are too upset to go to shul or to learn Torah. It is very difficult to give *mussar* (moral and ethical instruction) to people in this situation, but nevertheless, we must all remember that Hashem is our loving Father Who deeply cares for us, and everything He does is for our benefit. He does not want us to suffer; He wants us to grow in *ahavas Hashem* (love of Hashem) and in *yiras Hashem* (fear of Hashem).

There is a *pasuk* in the chapter we recite as the *Shir Shel Yom* (daily psalm) for Monday (*Tehillim* 48:15): כי זה אלקים אלקינו עולם ועד הוא ינהגנו על מות — "For this is G-d, our G-d forever; He shall lead us above death." This means that even in situations of life-threatening danger, Hashem raises us above the danger and allows us to survive. Our Sages note that the final two words of this verse — על מות — are hyphenated, and should thus be read as one word — עלמות — which means "child." That is to say, Hashem acts toward us as a parent acts toward a young child. The Baal Shem Tov explained that when a child is first learning how to walk, the mother will stand a few steps away and urge the child to walk toward her. Just as the child is about to reach her, she takes a few steps back, to train and encourage the child to walk even further. And then again as the child approaches, she moves back again. This is not cruel. The mother deeply loves her child and wants him to learn to keep his balance, to develop and to grow, and so she moves back to make it a bit more difficult for the child, who must then work harder to reach her. This is precisely how Hashem acts toward us. When we face some kind of challenge or hardship in life, when it seems as though Hashem is moving away from us and abandoning us, He is not being cruel. Rather, He is standing there with open arms like a loving parent, inviting us to come and move forward. He is right there in front of us, saying, "Come on, just a little more, just develop yourself a bit more, and if you fall, then get up and try again." When He sends us challenges, it is for us to persevere and grow from the experience, for us to become great people by overcoming the challenges and obstacles He places in our way. The *pasuk* therefore is teaching us: כי זה אלקים — What looks like *middas hadin* (strict justice) is really אלקינו — our loving G-d; הוא ינהגנו על מות — He is just leading you like a young child learning to walk.

> *"When it seems as though Hashem is moving away from us and abandoning us, He is not being cruel."*

35 No Pain No Gain

We often hear people reflect upon struggles that they had to confront, and say, "Those struggles made me into the person I am today." It is nearly impossible to see the benefit of difficult situations while we experience them, but we must remember that Hashem intends to build us into great people through the struggles He sends our way.

> *"Those struggles made me into the person I am today."*

Someone once asked me, "I don't understand, why does Hashem make it so difficult for me? I desperately want to learn Torah, but it's so hard. There are people around me who are opposed to my doing this, and between work and school, I can barely fit one hour of learning, at most two, into my daily schedule. Why does it have to be so hard?"

I suggested that perhaps Hashem made it this way because it is specifically because of the challenge that he values learning so much. The fact that it is so difficult makes him appreciate and cherish each available second for Torah learning, and thus it is the challenge that is building him into a devoted student of Torah.

I read an essay about a man who saw a cocoon, and noticed the butterfly inside trying to make its way out of the tiny hole. The butterfly struggled mightily to exit the cocoon, and spent several hours trying to force its body through the small opening. Finally, it appeared as though the butterfly had reached an impasse, and could not proceed any further. The man felt sorry for the butterfly, and so he took a pair of scissors and cut a large opening through which the butterfly could leave. Sure enough, the butterfly easily exited the cocoon, but the man noticed that the body was contorted and its wings were shriveled. He kept the butterfly, figuring that eventually, as it grew, its wings would develop and it would be able to fly. But this never happened. The butterfly lived its entire life with small, shriveled wings, and was never able to fly. The man failed to understand that the struggle to exit the cocoon has the effect of transferring fluid from the butterfly's body to its wings, which is how they develop. He thought he was doing the butterfly a favor by ending its struggle, but in reality, he thwarted its growth.

Sometimes, a struggle is precisely what we need in life to develop our "wings" so we can soar and reach great heights.

There is a row of houses in Lakewood, New Jersey in which all the homes have precisely the same landscaping.

Each lawn has a large tree planted in the same location. They had been planted around the same time. During Superstorm Sandy, some of the trees fell, but others did not. The people wondered why, if all the trees were planted and positioned the same way and exposed to the same stormy conditions, some withstood the hurricane and others did not. After some investigation, the mystery was solved. The trees that were watered with automatic sprinkler systems collapsed, but those without automatic sprinklers remained intact. The trees that were not automatically watered had to spread their roots deep into the ground to access the water and nutrients they needed, and thus they were firmly rooted in the ground and able to withstand the hurricane's winds. The other trees received their water easily, without any effort, and were thus not strong enough to survive the storm.

The struggles we endure build us into strong, great people, and are thus ultimately to our benefit.

36 Accepting With Love

After the Jewish people received the Torah at Mount Sinai, they began traveling toward Eretz Yisrael. The journey was to have taken just three days, but as a result of their complaints, they spent forty years wandering before finally entering the Holy Land.

The *Sfas Emes* raised the question of how it would have been possible for the Jewish people to take possession of Eretz Yisrael *after just three days*. After all, the Gemara (*Berachos* 5a) lists three gifts that can be acquired only through *yissurim* (suffering and hardship), and the Land of Israel is one of these three gifts (the other two being Torah knowledge and the World to Come). Indeed, in our generation we see how many wars must be fought, how much blood must be spilled, how many orphans and widows there must be, and how much anguish and sorrow is necessary for the Jews to take possession of their land. If so, the Rebbe asked, then how were *Bnei Yisrael* initially meant to take the land after just three days of travel through the Wilderness? True, traveling through the Wilderness with young children is very difficult, but still, it is a very short period of hardship. How could this period have sufficed as the *yissurim* needed to take possession of the Land of Israel?

Rabbi Shalom Arush explained that if *Bnei Yisrael* had accepted the three days of affliction with love and *emunah*, they would have accomplished in that short time what instead resulted in years of suffering. The *zechus* (merit) of *emunah* is so powerful that those three days of *yissurim* would have sufficed to grant *Bnei Yisrael* possession of Eretz Yisrael. A person who recognizes that all problems in life are sent from Hashem for our benefit, and thus accepts them with complete faith and without complaint, earns incalculable merit and great blessing from Hashem.

"If Bnei Yisrael had accepted the three days of affliction with love and emunah, they would have accomplished in that short time what instead resulted in years of sufferings."

Two centuries ago a severe drought struck the Jewish community in Yemen, and no rain fell for several years. The Rabbi at the time, the Maharitz, assembled the community and announced that it was revealed to him from the heavens that the rain was withheld because they did not accept Hashem's judgment. He explained that the people protested, cried, and complained, insisting that they did not deserve such harsh treatment, rather than trusting that everything Hashem did was for the best, and because of this response the drought continued. The Rabbi told the people that they must be content with whatever Hashem gives them, and they will then be deserving of great blessing.

It must be emphasized that this attitude, of lovingly accepting whatever Hashem gives us, in no way contradicts the concept of prayer and asking Hashem for the situation to change. When a person prays for rain, for example, the mindset should be that he accepts the fact that Hashem has withheld rain until now for a good reason, and this is what is best, but this does not necessarily mean that it is best not to receive rain a moment from now. Hashem allows and commands us to pray for what we want in the future, but with respect to what has transpired in the past, we must accept it all with love and recognize that it must be the best thing for us. And thus, for example, if a person needs a *shidduch*, he should say to Hashem, "Hashem, if I have not found my *zivug* until now, then there must be a good reason for it, and I fully accept that with love. But please, open my eyes and let me find my *zivug* now." In the merit of accepting the past with joy and faith, regardless of how Hashem has dealt with us, we will see much blessing and success in the future.

37 Keep Smiling

We mentioned earlier that when a person accepts the small, minor "afflictions" in his life with love, then they take the place of far greater suffering and misfortune. This perspective can truly change a person's life. The next time you're on your way somewhere and then realize you forgot something at home, and you must therefore turn around and go back to get it, say to Hashem, "Thank You for this minor inconvenience; You're so kind for bringing me *yissurim* [hardship] in such a mild fashion."

The Chazon Ish remarked, "We all need to go through trials in life. Some people will respond to them with a smile, and others will be bitter. It is my experience that the people who smile live happier lives."

There are countless occasions in daily life when this principle can and should be applied. The next time you walk into shul and see someone in your seat, you can either get upset and think to yourself, *Who does this guy think he is, sitting in my seat?!* or you can think, *I know Hashem directed him there so I will experience very mild yissurim. Thank You, Hashem, for letting me get away so easily, with this slight inconvenience; I accept it with love.* After a long, tense day at work, a man comes home in the evening and sees that supper isn't ready, or that dinner is burnt. He should accept this "suffering" with love and be grateful that he is given such a minor challenge to deal with. A child spills a container of milk at the dinner table. People might instinctively become angry and berate the child for ruining the food on the table and making such a mess. But who knows just how much these "*yissurim*" accomplish, what kind of more severe forms of suffering are being avoided as a result of these mishaps? It is all from Hashem, and there are no accidents. So we should accept everything with love and faith.

> *"Thank You, Hashem, for letting me get away so easily, with this slight inconvenience; I accept it with love."*

It is told that a container of milk once spilled in the home of Rav Yisrael Salanter. Rav Yisrael turned to his wife and asked if she has any thoughts as to why this may have happened. What did she think Hashem was telling them through this incident? She said, "Yes, I just remembered that last week I forgot to leave money for the milkman." Hashem was speaking to them directly by way of this spilled container. We might not be on the level where we can always determine precisely why each mishap in our life occurs, but we must remain calm and know that these small inconveniences give us a lot of "mileage." If a person loses $20 and he accepts the loss without worry or complaint, he might be saving himself a loss of $2000.

We customarily read *Tehillim* 107 on Pesach. It cites people who were rescued from some kind of crisis, such as illness, captivity, and dangerous travel. The chapter concludes (107:43), מי חכם וישמר אלה ויתבוננו חסדי ה' — literally, "He who is wise will guard these, and contemplate the kindnesses of Hashem." The Rebbe of Belz explained this to mean that a wise person (חכם)

who wants to protect himself (וישמר אלה) from all these travails will (יתבוננו חסדי ה׳) recognize *chasdei Hashem*, that all the small, minor problems in his life are really expressions of Hashem's kindness. These minor problems are what spare us from more significant forms of suffering, and are thus a great *chesed* shown to us by Hashem.

38 Make Hashem's Will Your Will

Accepting Hashem's will brings blessing and salvation. In *Pirkei Avos* (2:4) our Sages teach, עשה רצונו כרצונך — "Make His will your will," meaning, in any situation one should be happy knowing that whatever happens is Hashem's will. The Mishnah then continues, כדי שיעשה רצונך כרצונו — "So that He will make His will your will." If one accepts His will, Hashem then grants that person all his wishes and does anything he asks of Him.

We've discussed the notion that the joyful acceptance of minor problems spares a person far greater troubles. Rabbeinu Yonah, in *Shaarei Teshuvah* (4), cites as a source of this concept a verse (*Tehillim* 76:11), כי חמת אדם תודך שארית חמות תחגור (literally, "For the rage of man shall thank You; the remnant of fury You shall restrain"). Rabbeinu Yonah explains this to mean that if a person experiences חמת אדם — problems and troubles — and he reacts with תודך, by thanking Hashem, recognizing that He knows what is best, then שארית חמות תחגור — he will prevent far greater troubles. Rabbeinu Yonah writes that if one accepts his problems with love, יהיה זה למגן מן היסורין הרבים הראוין לבוא עליו — "This shall be a shield against the many afflictions that were meant to befall him."

Similarly, Rav Chaim Palagi (*Zechirah L'Chaim* 8:2) writes that if a person sees that things are not going his way, he should not feel depressed. Instead, he should accept his situation with joy, and then, as the verse states, הבוטח בה' חסד יסובבנו — "He who trusts in Hashem, kindness shall surround him" (*Tehillim* 32:10). Rav Chaim Palagi writes (6:3) that he guarantees things will change for the better if one accepts his problems with joy, noting that this is a *segulah* for success.

The Midrash *Tanna D'Vei Eliyahu* records Hashem's response to Moshe when Moshe asked to understand why some righteous people suffer while many wicked people prosper. Hashem said to Moshe, "You will never fully understand My ways, but I will tell you that when people bless Me and pray to Me under all circumstances, in all situations, then even if they do not have many good deeds to their credit, I will double their *parnassah* [livelihood]." And the *Likutei Halachos* writes that he guarantees if people would heed the voice of the *tzaddikim* and have faith that everything is good, and thank Hashem in all situations, all problems and troubles would come to an end, and the redemption would arrive. This is the *segulah* that can bring all our troubles in life to an end: realizing that everything that happens is orchestrated by the Almighty, and thanking Him for all that occurs.

"This is the segulah that can bring all our troubles in life to an end."

It must be emphasized that it is worthwhile and valuable to say "thank You" to Hashem for everything that happens even if one does not truly mean it in his heart. After all, practice makes perfect. As the *Sefer HaChinuch* writes, our actions have a profound impact upon our inner feelings. And thus the more we verbally express our gratitude to Hashem, the more we will feel genuine gratitude in our hearts.

So stop complaining and feeling sorry for yourself. Be happy with whatever comes your way, accept Hashem's will as your will, and He will then make your will His.

39 The Highest Level of Love

The *Chovos HaLevavos*, in *Shaar Cheshbon HaNefesh*, writes that Avraham Avinu is praised for passing his ten trials not simply because he did Hashem's will under trying circumstances, but also because he did so willingly and lovingly. As the *pasuk* states (*Nechemiah* 9:8), ומצאת את לבבו נאמן לפניך — "You found his heart loyal to You." Avraham was נאמן, infused with the faith that anything Hashem wants must be good. And even thousands of years later, we are still reaping the benefits of this merit of Avraham Avinu, who happily accepted everything Hashem did, knowing that it must be for the best.

We have been discussing the *berachah* that one earns by accepting everything Hashem does with love. Why is this so? Why does one earn such great reward for accepting everything with love?

There is a positive Torah command to love Hashem: ואהבת את ה' אלקיך בכל לבבך ובכל נפשך ובכל מאדך — "You shall love Hashem your G-d with all your heart, with all your soul, and with all your might" (*Devarim* 6:5). The Rabbis (*Berachos* 54a) explained בכל לבבך ("with all your heart") to mean that we must serve Hashem with not only our *yetzer tov*, our positive inclination, but also with our *yetzer hara,* our evil inclination, by channeling our negative tendencies toward the service of Hashem. The second aspect of this command, ובכל נפשך ("with all your soul"), means that we must love Hashem to the point where we are prepared to make sacrifices on His behalf, and at times a Jew must be prepared to make the ultimate sacrifice — sacrificing His life — for Hashem. The third requirement, ובכל מאדך, as the Mishnah explains (ibid.), means בכל מידה ומידה שהוא מודד לך הוי מודה לו — "regardless of the measure He measures for you, thank Him."

We must thank Hashem for everything He does, even when we do not feel how it is good and beneficial for us. The *Nesivos Shalom* explains that this *pasuk* proceeds in ascending order of difficulty. The first level is בכל לבבך. Channeling our innate negative tendencies toward the service of Hashem is not always easy, but it is not especially difficult, either. The next level of difficulty is בכל נפשך, sacrificing one's life to Hashem. But even more difficult, the *Nesivos Shalom* comments, is the obligation of ובכל מאדך. Sacrificing one's life for Hashem is less difficult than living one's life with a genuine appreciation for everything that occurs, even for the day-to-day inconveniences and problems that we consistently confront. Accepting one's problems and living with the belief that they are for our benefit is the greatest challenge of all, and for this reason, the reward is so immense.

> *"Sacrificing one's life for Hashem is less difficult than living one's life with a genuine appreciation for everything that occurs."*

A chassid traveled far from home in order to see the famous Chassidic master, the Chozeh ("Seer") of Lublin. When he entered the room, the Chozeh took one look at him and immediately told him to return home. The man was dumbfounded, but the Rebbe told him to leave, and so he did. He had no choice but to make the journey back home without even enjoying a few moments in the great Rebbe's presence.

Along the way, he stopped at an inn, where he met a group of chassidim who were traveling to Lublin to see the Chozeh. They invited him to join them, but he explained to them that he had just been there and the Rebbe had told him to leave. As he told the story, the chassidim noticed that he felt dejected because of what had happened.

"Why are you so down?" they asked him. "If this is what the Rebbe told you to do, then it must be Hashem's will. There's no reason to be depressed if you're doing what Hashem wants you to do!" The chassidim proceeded to make a special *seudah* (meal) in this man's honor to celebrate his loving acceptance of Hashem's will. During the meal they sang and danced, and the man's spirits were uplifted, and he was able to feel genuine *simchah* (joy) for his accepting Hashem's will that he return home instead of staying with the Rebbe.

The next morning, the chassidim told the man that now he was able to return with them to the Rebbe, and he did.

When the Rebbe saw him, he was amazed, and asked, "What happened to you?" The chassid told him the story of the celebration in the inn.

"Amazing!" the Rebbe said. "When I saw you yesterday, I noticed there was a heavenly decree of death against you, and so I instructed you to return home so you could die peacefully, surrounded by your family. But because you accepted Hashem's will with such joy, the decree was annulled."

This is how much reward one earns for lovingly accepting everything Hashem does with true joy and happiness.

40

Make Hashem Your Partner

The Midrash (*Shemos Rabbah* 1:8) comments that the period of slavery in Egypt did not begin until all those who had migrated with Yaakov Avinu from Eretz Yisrael to Egypt had passed away. The *Ohr HaChaim* explains that the oppression did not begin during these people's lifetime as a reward for their having accepted Hashem's decree. It was certainly not easy to relocate in Egypt, and they could have felt bitter over having to move away from home rather than purchasing grain and bringing it back to Eretz Yisrael. But they instead recognized that this was what Hashem wanted, and they accepted it with joy. In this merit the period of enslavement was delayed until after their lifetime.

The *Ohr HaChaim* (*Bereishis* 46:7) concludes by stating, סמא דיסורין קיבוליה — "the remedy for affliction is accepting it." Accepting Hashem's will in periods of hardship is the best means of improving the situation. And thus, for example, if a person is finding it difficult to earn a living, and has to struggle to pay his bills, he can either complain and say to Hashem, "Why are You doing this? How come I have to struggle so much while my friends seem to have it so easy?" or thank Hashem for whatever he has and trust that he is given precisely what he needs to be successful in this world. Choosing the second option will help him overcome his troubles and alleviate his difficult situation.

> "*The remedy for affliction is accepting it.*"

The Gemara (*Berachos* 63a) states, כל המשתף שם שמים בצערו כופלין לו פרנסתו — "Whoever makes G-d his partner in distress, his livelihood is doubled." Rashi explains this to mean that if a person willingly accepts Hashem's decrees without complaint, then He doubles his earnings. The Vilna Gaon adds that one establishes a "partnership" with Hashem by recognizing that his problems do not occur coincidentally, by happenstance, but are rather directly brought upon him by Hashem. If the customer decided not to purchase the product, for example, it was because Hashem determined that this should happen. And by realizing and accepting His will, we become partners with Hashem, and thereby earn great merit.

The *Nesivos Shalom* tells of a very poor plumber named Motele Koplovitz. One Thursday night he found himself without any money with which to buy food for Shabbos. He sat at the table, heartbroken, bemoaning the fact that his family will not have any food on Shabbos. For hours he waited, hoping that maybe a job will come his way, but as the hours passed it became clear that it was too late. Around midnight, he decided he would drive the sorrow and depression from his heart. He turned to Hashem and said, "Hashem, I tried everything I could. If it is Your will that we will not have food to eat on Shabbos, then I happily accept it." He felt totally content and at ease, fully accepting his situation, and he went to sleep peacefully.

A few hours later, in the wee hours of the night, there was a knock on his door. A main pipe in the local bathhouse had burst, and it urgently needed to be fixed so that people could bathe before Shabbos. It was a major repair, and Motele was paid handsomely for his work. He earned enough money for Shabbos food with plenty to spare.

By accepting Hashem's decree, he became His "partner," whereupon his *parnassah* was doubled.

41 End the Suffering

The *Sfas Emes* received a letter in which the writer described how he suffers from so many hardships in his life, and how things never seem to go his way. The Rebbe responded, citing the *halachah* of אין מפסיקין בקללות (*Megillah* 31a). This means that on the two occasions during the year when we read the *tochachah* in the Torah, the segment warning of the calamities that will befall the Jewish people if they betray Hashem (once in *Parashas Bechukosai*, and once in *Parashas Ki Savo*), the entire section must be read in the same *aliyah*. A congregation should not interrupt in the middle of the *tochachah*. The reason for this *halachah*, as the Midrash (*Devarim Rabbah* 4:1) explains, is that Hashem says, אין בדין שבני מתקללין ואני אתברך — "It is not proper for My children to be cursed while I am blessed." When a person comes up to the Torah for an *aliyah*, he recites a *berachah*, giving praise to Hashem and describing Him as King of the world. Hashem does not wish to be blessed while dreadful curses are being read about His children, and therefore halachah forbids being called for an *aliyah* during the reading of the *tochachah*. In light of this halachah, the *Sfas Emes* advised this man to praise and thank Hashem at all times, acknowledging that He knows what He is doing. If he praises Hashem, then the *yissurim* (suffering) that he endures will disappear, because Hashem cannot bear to hear His praises while His children are suffering. He will thus have no choice but to bring an end to the man's suffering.

One man faced a grave crisis. Large sums of money which he knew he did not actually owe were being demanded from him. Instead of crying and worrying about the problem, he went to the beach, looked out at the ocean, and began contemplating all his blessings in life and how grateful he is to Hashem. For an entire hour, he thanked Him and affirmed his belief that the people coming after him are just puppets, sent by Hashem for whatever reason, and that they, too, in some way, are an expression of His kindness. The next morning, the claim was dropped. If he had spent an hour crying and fretting over the problem, he would have accomplished nothing. But by using the opportunity to thank and give praise to Hashem, handing the situation over to Him with peace of mind, the problem was solved.

"If only people would bless and praise Hashem more, rather than worry and complain, they would see miracles."

The *sefer Divrei Yisrael* (*Parashas Behar*) writes that anxiety and depression block the pipelines that bring blessing and prosperity; one opens those pipes by recognizing that Hashem is in charge and controls the world. If only people would bless and praise Hashem more, rather than worry and complain, they would see miracles, because, as we have seen, praising Hashem has the effect of eliminating harsh judgments.

It is said in the name of *tzaddikim* that if a person turns to Hashem and says, "You are so kind, You give me so much kindness and I am so grateful for everything," then Hashem says to him, "You think this is good — I will show you what goodness really is!" Let us, therefore, accustom ourselves to constantly thank and praise Hashem in all situations, and we will then fulfill one of our main missions in life, as the *pasuk* (*Yeshayah* 43:21) states, עם זו יצרתי לי תהילתי יספרו — "I have created this nation for Me, that they should speak My praises."

42 Everything Will Be Clear

The *Zohar* (31a) comments (*Parashas Pinchas*) that whenever the Torah uses the word ויהי ("it was," or "there was"), it alludes to some form of calamity or crisis. The *Chasdei David* raises the question of how this principle applies to the *pasuk* in the very beginning of the Torah, ויהי אור — "There was light" (*Bereishis* 1:3). What kind of calamity could possibly be referred to in the context of the creation of light?

The *Chasdei David* answers this question in light of the Gemara's comments (*Niddah* 31a) regarding the *pasuk* (*Yeshayah* 12:1), ואמרת ביום ההוא אודך ה' כי אנפת בי — "You shall say on that day: I thank You, Hashem, for having been angry with me." In the Messianic Era, we will all thank Hashem for what had initially appeared as expressions of anger, for the *yissurim* that He had inflicted upon us, as we will recognize that they were actually for our benefit. The Gemara gives the example of two people who were rushing to catch a boat for their respective business trips. One made it on time, but the other accidentally stepped on a nail and was unable to walk, and thus literally, missed the boat. The man was upset and frustrated, and bemoaned his misfortune. Later, however, he learned that the boat sank. He thereupon turned to Hashem and thanked Him with all his heart for making him step on that nail, whereby his life was saved. In the future, we will all see how every bit of *yissurim* we endured during our lifetime was actually a great blessing, and we will all turn to Hashem with praise and thanksgiving.

"In the future, we will all see how every bit of yissurim we endured during our lifetime was actually a great blessing."

On this basis, the *Chasdei David* explains the *pasuk* ויהי אור. All the ויהי in our lives, all the misfortune and distress, will, in the future, be transformed into אור, into light. It will become perfectly clear why everything happened and why even the seemingly unfortunate events were really the very best things by far that could have happened to us. We will then be filled with joy and overflowing with gratitude to Hashem.

Our challenge is to recognize the אור in the ויהי already now, in this world, before everything becomes clear. One of the greatest sources of merit that we can earn is by recognizing that everything is good even now, before we are shown that this is so.

We state in the *kaddish* prayer that Hashem's Name is praised לעלא מן כל ברכתא שירתא תושבחתא נחמתא דאמירן בעלמא — which literally means, "beyond all the praises that can be recited in this world." However, the word לעלא can also be interpreted to mean "the most," in which case this passage means that the most, or greatest, praise to Hashem is the praise given בעלמא, in this world, when we are as yet unable to clearly see how everything Hashem does is truly good and to our benefit. The highest level of praise is that which we express when things outwardly appear bad, but we nevertheless affirm our belief that it is all good. And by expressing this praise, we earn for ourselves immense physical and spiritual rewards.

The *Midrash Iyov* (*Yalkut Shimoni, remez* 908) writes that if Iyov had not complained about the misfortunes that befell him, and would have instead realized that they were actually good and to his benefit, then we would have included his name in the *Amidah* along with Avraham, Yitzchak, and Yaakov. Meaning, instead of saying at the beginning of the *Amidah* prayer, אלקי אברהם אלקי יצחק ואלקי יעקב — "Hashem of Avraham, Hashem of Yitzchak, and Hashem of Yaakov," we would have instead said, אלקי אברהם אלקי יצחק אלקי יעקב ואלקי איוב — "Hashem of Avraham, Hashem of Yitzchak, Hashem of Yaakov, and Hashem of Iyov." He would have been as great as our holy patriarchs, attaining the same level of spiritual devotion and stature as they. This is the awesome merit of accepting Hashem's will with love.

Let us, therefore, have faith already in this world, before everything becomes clear, and we will then enjoy the great benefits of this merit both in this world and the next.

43 Everything Hashem Does Is Good

The Gemara (*Berachos* 60b) teaches, לעולם יהא אדם רגיל לומר כל דעביד רחמנא לטבא עביד — "A person should always accustom himself to say: Everything that Hashem does is for the best." It is not natural to respond to unfortunate events by saying that they are actually good, and the Gemara therefore teaches that we must train ourselves to say this and react this way to our experiences.

The first and most crucial step to achieve this goal is to realize that everything that happens is brought about by Hashem. The *Ben Yehoyada* commentary notes that the Gemara instructs us to react this way לעולם, "always." We must recognize Hashem not only in the unusual, dramatic events, but even in the ordinary, day-to-day occurrences that appear perfectly normal and natural. Even these are caused directly by Hashem.

As previously noted, the Gemara tells of Rabbi Akiva, who was traveling and requested lodging in a certain town. Not one person in the town granted his request. Still, Rabbi Akiva declared כל דעביד רחמנא לטב עביד, that even though he was forced to spend the night in the woods, this was for the best. At first glance, one might wonder, what does this have to do with Hashem? Each person in the town decided on his own not to let Rabbi Akiva in. It was their decision, not Hashem's! Rabbi Akiva recognized that this is not the case. Even when people say "no," this, too, is from Hashem. When a cat came and ate Rabbi Akiva's rooster that night, he realized that this seemingly "natural" occurrence was also from Hashem, that the cat had no way of touching his rooster unless this was willed by Hashem, and if it was willed by Hashem, then it must be the best thing.

This statement in the Gemara is not disputed by any *Tanna* or *Amora*. There is no dispute among the *Rishonim* concerning this *halachah*, and it is codified by the *Shulchan Aruch*. In fact, the Rambam, in his commentary to the Mishnah, writes about this teaching that any בעל שכל — "intelligent person" — could have figured out on his own that everything Hashem does is for the best. Therefore the agreed-upon response in all situations according to all authorities is to feel that everything Hashem does is good.

> Rabbi Moshe Sherer related that when he was very young, he once came down with a very severe illness and was running a high fever. His mother obtained a prescription for the medication he needed, but she could not afford it. She got together all the money she had and ran to the pharmacist, hoping he would give her the medication even though she could not pay full price. The pharmacist's assistant was running the shop, and she tearfully explained to him that she could not afford the medicine, but was bringing him all the money she had. The assistant graciously agreed to fill the prescription, and so he prepared the bottle, gave it

to her, and took the money. The woman was so frantic that she ran toward her home, and along the way she tripped and dropped the bottle. It fell to the ground and shattered, spilling the medicine on the pavement.

The woman was heartbroken. She thought this was it, there was no longer any possibility of saving her son. She picked up the broken pieces of glass, and returned to the pharmacy. This time, the head pharmacist was present and filling prescriptions. With tears running down her face, she explained to him what had happened. He warmly assured her that he would give her the medicine she needed at no extra charge. He took the broken pieces of glass and smelled them to determine what medication the bottle had contained.

"You must have angels protecting you today," the pharmacist said. "It seems my assistant had given you the wrong medication. This could have seriously endangered your child."

When the bottle broke, the woman thought that her very worst nightmare had come true, and her son would die. In the end, it turned out that her son was saved. Rabbi Sherer said that his mother told him this story and emphasized that this was a lesson for life. When things happen that seem bad, horrifically bad, we must believe that they are really good.

> *"Even when a situation appears devastating, it is actually a blessing in disguise."*

In truth, even the assistant's mistake was from Hashem but it is likely that Hashem makes such incidents happen specifically to teach us this lesson of לטב עביד, that even when a situation appears devastating, it is actually a blessing in disguise. We must believe that even when we face difficult and dire situations, it is really for the best, and a great blessing from Hashem.

44

It's Really Hashem's Mercy

We say each day, שמע ישראל ה' אלקינו ה' אחד — "Hear, O Israel, Hashem our G-d — Hashem is One" (*Devarim* 6:4). The *She'eiris Menachem* explains that the Name of הוי"ה represents the Divine attribute of mercy (רחמים), whereas the Name אלקים (or אלקינו, as it appears in this *pasuk*) signifies the Divine attribute of judgment (דין). In this *pasuk*, we proclaim that ה' אלקינו — these two different attributes — are essentially ה' אחד — one single attribute, the attribute of mercy. Even that which appears to us as דין, strict justice, is in truth רחמים, a manifestation of Hashem's loving kindness and compassion. We cover our eyes while reciting this *pasuk* as if to tell Hashem, "Even though we cannot see it, we believe that everything You do is an expression of mercy."

> *"Even that which appears to us as din, strict judgment, is in truth rachamim, a manifestation of Hashem's loving kindness and compassion."*

When do we experience Hashem's attribute of mercy in our daily lives, and when do we experience what appears as judgment?

Rabbi Fishel Schachter said that when a man is getting dressed in the morning to go to work, and he looks through the window and notices that it's a beautiful, sunny day, he reads that the stocks are on the rise and the market is looking good, his children are happy, smiling, and all dressed ready for school, and during the day he gets a call from the teacher describing how well the child is doing — this is the מידת הרחמים, Hashem's attribute of mercy. But on days when the stocks are down, the reports from Wall Street are gloomy, the kids are kicking and screaming and refusing to go to school, and during the day the principal calls and asks you to pick up your child who has been suspended for misconduct — this is when Hashem's רחמים takes the form of דין, when we see "judgment" but must believe that it, too, is an expression of Hashem's compassion. We do not know why each inconvenience must befall us, but we can derive immense benefit from the belief that they are all expressions of Hashem's mercy and love for us.

The Gemara teaches (*Taanis* 8a): כל השמח ביסורין הבאין עליו מביא ישועה לעולם — "Whoever rejoices in the afflictions that befall him brings salvation to the world." What are יסורין ("afflictions")? This term refers even to the slight inconveniences that we "suffer" in daily life, such as when we mistakenly put on our shirt backward, when we miss a turn or have to wait in line longer than we wanted to. Once we have been compelled to endure these inconveniences, we might as well rejoice and contemplate that they are expressions of Hashem's mercy, and that way we bring salvation to the world.

The *pasuk* (*Tehillim* 73:1) states, אך טוב לישראל אלקים לברי לבב. The *Yismach Moshe* explains this verse to mean אך טוב לישראל אלקים — even אלקים, the Divine attribute of judgment, is טוב לישראל — good for the Jewish people, but only לברי לבב, for the pure-hearted ones who accept whatever Hashem does and recognize that it is good. In *Parashas Vayishlach* (*Bereishis* 32:13) it states, ואתה אמרת היטב איטיב עמך — "And you said, 'I will assuredly deal kindly with you.'" The *Divrei Yisrael* explains the double terminology of היטב איטיב to mean that if one accustoms himself to saying היטב, that things are good, then Hashem says איטיב עמך — that He will make things even better for him.

Let us, therefore, practice this beautiful quality of accepting whatever Hashem does. The next time we feel we are about to become upset, let us stop and say, "Hashem, this is an expression of Your kindness, and I accept it wholeheartedly." We will then earn the merit to bring salvation to the entire world.

45 Problems Solved

When a person lives with *emunah*, with the knowledge that Hashem always deals favorably with him, even when this does not appear to be the case, he is content and satisfied. And when a person is content and satisfied, he earns Hashem's blessing, as the *pasuk (Devarim* 33:23) states, נפתלי שבע רצון ומלא ברכת ה' — "Naftali is filled with satisfaction, and filled with the blessing of Hashem." When a person feels content, he earns Hashem's blessings.

A man called and told me of a conversation he had when he went to pray Minchah in the middle of the workday. He arrived a few minutes early and was speaking with another man about the Emunah Daily series. In particular they discussed the notion that although we should firmly believe that everything that has happened until now is the best thing for us, we are still allowed and urged to pray that things should change, that our lives going forward will be different, the way we want them to be. Speaking about this lesson encouraged him to apply it to his own situation.

He was encountering three difficult issues: one personal problem, and two significant problems in his business. One problem he had was that the warehouse where he stored his merchandise demanded an additional $200,000 a year, and he had two days left to sign the new deal before having all his assets frozen. He had tried other options, but none came through. The second problem was that he had just leased a new showroom and was prepared to begin construction, but the landlord told him that he could not start before obtaining certain special permits. The permits would take at least a month to obtain, and the process would cost him significant amounts of money.

In the face of all these problems, the man related, he turned to Hashem that day before Minchah and said, "Hashem, I fully accept that everything that has happened until now is the best thing for me." But when he prayed Minchah, he prayed very hard, asking Hashem to give him the results he wants going forward.

The moment he completed Minchah, the person with whom he had the personal issue approached him and invited him for a walk to talk over the problem. They walked for a short while and the issue was completely sorted out. The man then returned to his office, and found his staff celebrating. While he was gone, a warehouse they had contacted six months earlier called and agree to a deal, at a price $100,000 less than what they had been paying. Not only did he avoid a loss, but he would now be spending $100,000 less every year. Less than an hour later, the new landlord of the showroom called and agreed to resolve the issue with the permits so he could begin construction immediately. Just like that, all three problems disappeared.

"Just like that, all three problems disappeared."

This must be our approach: to tell Hashem, "I know You always do only what is best for me, and I accept everything that has happened until now." And when we pray with this mindset, our prayers for the future are then answered. Let us live our lives with שבע רצון, with contentment and joy, and we will then be מלא ברכת ה' — filled with Hashem's blessings.

46 Remember the Kindness of Hashem

The *Chovos HaLevavos* writes at the end of the *Shaar HaBitachon* section that a person's level of *bitachon* (trust in Hashem) depends on the extent to which he realizes how much Hashem is involved in his life, and of how loving and merciful He is. We are to realize that every bit of enjoyment we experience in life is given to us directly from Hashem. Many of us recognize that our ability to think, see, walk, and talk is granted to us by Hashem, but often, when we experience pleasure, such as by eating a food we enjoy or donning nice clothing, we do not attribute this enjoyment to Hashem. Our level of *bitachon* will be elevated the more we recognize that everything we enjoy in life is given to us by Hashem.

The Gemara (*Berachos* 58a) says that there are two types of guests. The good guest says, "Look, everything the host did, all the foods and drinks that were prepared and served, it was all done for me. I am so grateful." The bad guest looks at all the food and drinks and says, "What's the big deal? He was preparing it anyway. He didn't do anything for me."

The Vilna Gaon (*Beurei Aggados,* ad loc.) commented that we are all guests in this world, and we must strive to be "good guests," appreciating all that the "Host" has done for us. Whenever one walks out the door into a beautiful, sunny day, he should say, "Thank You, Hashem, this is just what I needed. Thank You for doing this just for me." Every dollar that we have is given to us by Hashem, and this, too, must be appreciated. Rabbi Yosef Zalman Bloch noted that when a person walks into a store and orders the exact coffee that he enjoys, he should thank Hashem for giving him just what he wants. When we view his coffee from the perspective of nature, it appears that this coffee was available because the product is in demand and the shop wants to earn money. But in truth, Hashem loves us and this is why He provides us with the coffee we want. Nature is the mask that makes it seem as though it happens by chance, when in truth it is all done by Hashem.

The *Sefer HaChareidim* (9:23) writes that there is a Torah command to remember the kindness performed by Hashem for our ancestors in the Wilderness, as indicated by the *pasuk*, וזכרת את כל הדרך אשר הולכך ה' אלקיך — "You shall remember the entire route along which Hashem, your G-d, led you" (*Devarim* 8:2). During that period Hashem fed *Bnei Yisrael* the miraculous manna, their clothing did not wear out, and their feet did not swell. If a person is credited with a mitzvah for remembering the kindness performed for our ancestors millennia ago, it is certainly an even greater mitzvah to be mindful of and express gratitude for the kindnesses that a person himself experienced. We experience hundreds of small pleasures each day, such as eating food we enjoy, driving the car we want, using the phone we want, living in a nice house, and so on. If we would pay attention to all the blessings given to us by Hashem and express our gratitude, our lives would be so much happier.

> *"If we would pay attention to all the blessings given to us by Hashem and express our gratitude, our lives would be so much happier."*

Someone commented that it's relatively easy to see the blessings in other people's lives, but it takes genius to see the blessings in one's own life. As the *pasuk* states, מי חכם וישמר אלה ויתבוננו חסדי ה' — "Whoever is wise will guard these, and contemplate the kindnesses of Hashem" (*Tehillim* 107:43). Only one who is "wise" has the ability to truly contemplate and recognize all the kindnesses Hashem performs for us. Let us be wise enough to realize how all our enjoyment in life comes from Hashem, and let us constantly thank Hashem for His blessings. We will then increase our love for Hashem and increase our *bitachon* manifold.

47 Say Thank You

The *Yesod VeShoresh HaAvodah* in his will describes a certain *tzaddik* who would make a point of thanking Hashem for every bit of goodness he experienced in his life. If he dropped a glass bottle and it didn't break, he would thank Hashem. If he passed through a dangerous area and emerged without harm, he would thank Hashem. He realized that everything that happened was caused directly by Hashem, and thus constantly expressed his gratitude for all things, both big and small.

The Chozeh of Lublin said that he was shown from the heavens how significant and valuable this quality is, the quality of thanking Hashem for all the goodness one experiences in his life. There are countless ways in which we can apply this to our daily lives. If one forgets to set the alarm but somehow manages to wake up in time for work, he should thank Hashem. If one is late for the train but somehow manages to make it, he should thank Hashem. If a businessman lands a big order from a customer, he should thank Hashem. By thanking Him, we acknowledge that He is fully in control of the world and of our lives.

The *Midrash Tehillim* comments that one who thanks Hashem for his good fortune is considered as though he brought a *korban todah* (thanksgiving offering), which brings an abundance of kindness upon him. The *Pele Yoetz* (*Erech Hillul*) remarks that if one experiences a miracle and sings praise to Hashem, he is rewarded with yet another miracle. And *Chazal* (*Midrash Tehillim, mizmor* 18) teach us, כל מי שנעשה לו נס ואמר שירה בידוע שמוחלין לו על כל עוונותיו — "Anyone who experiences a miracle and sings praise — it is certain that his sins are forgiven." If this is the reward for someone who thanks Hashem for a major miracle he experiences, we can only imagine the kind of reward one earns for making a point of expressing gratitude for even the small, seemingly trivial miracles that occur each and every day.

The final *pasuk* (150:6) in *Tehillim* reads, כל הנשמה תהלל י־ה — "Every soul shall give praise to Hashem." Our Sages interpreted this to mean that we must give praise to Hashem על כל נשימה ונשימה — "for each and every breath." We have what to thank Hashem for at every moment, because at every moment we are breathing and our bodies are functioning. Moreover, at any moment, Hashem is performing countless miracles and kindnesses of which we are totally unaware. As the verse (*Tehillim* 136:4) describes, Hashem is עושה נפלאות גדולות **לבדו** — "makes great wonders by Himself." Hashem performs miracles לבדו, alone, without anybody watching or noticing. We must therefore constantly be praising and giving thanks to Hashem, Who is always performing "great wonders," under all circumstances. Even if we did not make the train, or if the long-awaited order did not arrive, we still have much for which to be thankful.

> I was recently told about a certain businessman who receives a large order of seasonal goods each year. There is always a lot of stress involved in preparing and shipping the large order in time. Therefore, this year he decided to order the merchandise well in advance to have everything ready. As it turned out, the customer let them know that this year he would not be placing an order. This man was now stuck with 180,000 pieces of merchandise for which he had paid. He accepted the loss with equanimity, knowing that whatever occurs, occurs only through Hashem's will. Just a few days later, a different company, with which he had always wanted to do business, called and said they would enter into a long-term contract if they could arrange a large shipment of that exact merchandise on short notice. The man informed them that the merchandise was all ready for them, and the deal was made. He thus found himself with a new satisfied customer, and, in the interim, he learned that the former customer went out of business.

We pray in our *tefillah*, הראנו ה' חסדך, that Hashem show us His kindness. And later we say, לה' הישועה על עמך ברכתך — "Salvation is G-d's; Your blessing is upon Your nation." Hashem's job is to care for us, and our job is to bless Him and thank Him for all He does for us.

48

Hashem Talks to Us All the Time

Shlomo HaMelech teaches (*Mishlei* 20:24), מה' מצעדי גבר ואדם מה יבין דרכו — "A man's steps are from Hashem; what does a person know about his way?" So often, we set out to do something but end up doing something entirely different. Hashem places us in various situations that we had never intended to be in, and we believe that everything is directed by Him. Often, this occurs in a concealed manner, בדרך הטבע, through what appears to be natural means. But the word הטבע ("nature") has the same numerical value as אלקים, the Divine Name that signifies Hashem's power. Hashem uses the forces of nature to communicate with us and direct us to where we are supposed to go. As the Chazon Ish teaches in his work *Emunah U'Bitachon* (Chapter 2), the obligation of *bitachon* includes the belief that there is no coincidence, nothing happens by chance, and everything is set and directed by the Almighty.

Many people desire to see Hashem in their lives. The truth is, He is in their lives, but they simply need to open their eyes and look more carefully. He communicates with us regularly to let us know that He is here, but generally in concealed ways.

"Many people desire to see Hashem in their lives. The truth is, He is in their lives, but they simply need to open their eyes and look more carefully."

I read a book that tells of a *tzaddik* who made a point of thanking Hashem for everything, for even the minor, everyday blessings in his life. The example mentioned in the book was a situation where a glass bottle fell but did not break. When this happened, the man made a point of saying "thank you" to Hashem. I wrote up a lesson mentioning other examples of similar situations, including where one is late for the train but manages to get on because it was delayed. When this happens, one should thank Hashem and acknowledge that this occurred because Hashem wanted it to occur. Shortly thereafter I taught a Gemara class, and one of the men asked to share his experiences that day. He had to fly that day for a business meeting, and had a ticket for the return flight immediately after the meeting. However, his first flight was delayed, and he had no choice but to reschedule his meeting for several hours later than its original time. He realized there was no chance of making his return flight, and as the airline had only one return flight a day, he would not be able to return home that day. He did not want to stay overnight, but it seemed like there was no alternative. After the meeting, however, he thought to himself how everything is in Hashem's hands, and Hashem could find a way to get him home. He went to the airport and discovered that, sure enough, his return flight was delayed by two hours. He got on the flight and thanked Hashem for His kindness.

Upon hearing the story, I said to the man, "That's unbelievable! Just two hours ago I recorded this exact example, where somebody was late for the train but it was delayed."

The very next day, I was carrying a few goblets in my home, and one slipped out of my hands. It landed safely on my foot and did not break. I thanked Hashem, and then said to myself, *This is amazing — I just gave this exact example!*

When things like this happen, it is Hashem communicating with us, letting us know that He is with us. Incidents like these occur all the time; we need only to open our eyes and recognize that everything is from Hashem.

49 Found Money

The *pasuk* (*Mishlei* 20:24), מה' מצעדי גבר — "A man's steps are from Hashem," teaches that Hashem controls our footsteps and guides us along the path we are meant to follow.

> I read a story in the book *Two Halves of a Whole* of a 35-year-old man who was on a business trip in the Far East, and was scheduled to fly home from Bangkok and arrive in New York on Erev Rosh Hashanah. When he arrived at the airport in Bangkok, however, he was told that there was a problem with his ticket, and he could not board the flight. The next available flight would not get him home in time for Rosh Hashanah, and so the man had no choice but to spend the holiday in the Far East. Knowing there is a Jewish community in Hong Kong, he boarded a flight to Hong Kong and contacted some people he knew to find hospitality. In the end, he spent Rosh Hashanah in the home of a family he had never met before. As it turned out, that family was the family of the woman he married soon thereafter.

There was no mistake on the ticket. Everything was exactly the way it was supposed to be, as planned by Hashem.

> Someone recently told me that one day his baby was cranky and his wife asked him to put the infant into a car seat and go for a drive to help him fall asleep. The man happily agreed, and as he was driving he remembered he needed to make a deposit at the bank. He went to the drive-thru and made his deposit, and while he was there the baby's pacifier fell out, causing him to cry. And so the man got out of his car, put the pacifier back in the baby's mouth, and then continued driving. He drove for about another half-hour and then returned

home. At home, he noticed something missing from his pocket. He had been carrying $2000 in cash, and now it was gone. He looked around the house, and went back outside to check in the car and in the driveway. The money was nowhere to be found. He returned to the bank and searched all over the area of the drive-thru where he had been with the baby. No money in sight.

Suddenly, a Jewish man drives up and approaches him.

"Are you missing something?" he asked.

"Yes, I lost a substantial amount of money here."

The stranger pulls $2000 out of his pocket and gives it to him. He explained that he had come with his wife to the drive thru about an hour earlier, and they saw money scattered all over the ground. They figured somebody must have dropped it, and so they gathered it together and waited, expecting that the person who lost the money would come looking for it. No one came, and so they went off to run a couple of quick errands. They completed their errands and returned to the drive-thru to check again — and just as they arrived they saw the man searching for the lost money.

"I couldn't believe it," the man told me. "Brooklyn is a big place, and at the exact moment I went back to look, this couple happened to come back after their errands looking for me."

This is מה' מצעדי גבר. Hashem directs our path toward where we need to go.

The couple who returned the money performed a truly heroic act, taking the time to gather the scattered money and making an effort to find the owner. We were able to find out who they were, and there are numerous valuable lessons to be learned from what they did.

The couple said that when they found the $2000, they immediately understood that Hashem was giving them the special opportunity to do a great mitzvah that would help them and save them in the future. They were so excited to do the mitzvah that they happily disregarded the inconvenience of driving back to the bank hoping they could earn this valuable *zechus* (merit). After they returned the money, they called their rabbi to discuss what had happened and how they had handled the situation. The rabbi complimented them, saying that this was indeed a beautiful way to look at the situation, and assured them that they received great *zechus* that day.

Two days later, the couple's daughter, who was expecting a baby shortly, experienced severe stomach pains. Her doctor sent her to the hospital. It turned out that her appendix had become infected and was about to burst. She underwent surgery, and, *baruch Hashem*, both she and the baby are perfectly healthy. The couple called their rabbi again to tell him what had happened, and said, "We were confident the whole time that everything would be fine, because we had the *zechus* of this mitzvah."

The *pasuk* states (*Tehillim* 41:2), אשרי משכיל אל דל ביום רעה ימלטהו ה' — "Fortunate is he who is wise toward the pauper; on the day of evil, Hashem will rescue him." One who uses his intelligence to see the needs of a poor man and helps him, earns merit that will protect him in dangerous situations.

"We were confident the whole time that everything would be fine, because we had the zechus of this mitzvah."

This concept, that Hashem sends us opportunities to perform mitzvos so we can earn merit to protect us from future danger, is taught to us by the Gemara (*Shabbos* 156b), where we read about Rabbi Akiva's daughter. Rabbi Akiva was informed by astrologers that his daughter would die on her wedding day. Following the marriage ceremony, she removed her headpiece and stuck the pin into the wall, unknowingly killing a poisonous snake hidden inside the wall. The next morning, when she took her headpiece from the wall, she saw the dead snake and realized what had happened. She told her father how she had been saved, and Rabbi Akiva asked her if she had done any special mitzvah that made her worthy of such a miracle. She thought for a moment and recalled that at the wedding celebration, there was a pauper asking for some food, and she fed him her portion. Rabbi Akiva told his daughter that Hashem gave her this opportunity to accrue merit and protect herself from the danger that lurked.

This is a beautiful way to approach life: to view situations to help people as special opportunities graciously given to us by Hashem to earn protection. Hashem knows the future and knows of the dangers that threaten us, and so He sends us opportunities to perform mitzvos and protect ourselves.

> Someone told me a story he read in one of Rabbi Paysach Krohn's books about a man who was driving to the mountains and stopped off at a restaurant to get a quick bite to eat. A poor man approached him and said he was very hungry and needed some money for food. The beggar was shabbily dressed and smelled, but the man nevertheless agreed to care for him. He invited him to sit down next to him and to order whatever he wanted. The pauper said he wanted just a baked apple and tea, and this is what the man ordered for him.
>
> After they finished eating, the man continued on his way. As he was driving, the car skidded and flipped over three times. Miraculously, he emerged unscathed from the accident. Another Jew saw him on the side of the road and offered to help, bringing him to his home and giving him something to eat and drink ... a baked apple and a cup of tea.
>
> *Wow*, the man thought to himself. *It was because of the baked apple and tea I gave that poor man that I was saved. Hashem sent me the cure before the illness; I was given the opportunity to earn protection even before the accident happened.*

This is how we must view the situations in which Hashem places us. Sometimes it is difficult, unpleasant or inconvenient to help people. But these are opportunities that Hashem sends us to earn merit, and hopefully we will all be משכיל אל דל, wise enough to seize these opportunities, so that Hashem will protect us from harm.

50 Is It You or Hashem?

The Ramban writes in his commentary to *Parashas Bo* that the objective of all the mitzvos is for us to believe and recognize that Hashem created us, and that all He wants is for us to know that we are His creations. Similarly, Rav Yerucham Levovitz (*Daas Torah, Parashas Behar*) writes that the underlying purpose of life is the recognition that כי לי כל הארץ, that Hashem runs the world (*Shemos* 19:5).

One mitzvah that expresses and exemplifies this concept most clearly is the mitzvah of *shemittah*, requiring a landowner to let all his fields lie fallow for an entire year. Numerous landowners in Eretz Yisrael observe this mitzvah. They collectively own hundreds of thousands of dollars' worth of agricultural land, and for an entire year they watch it all just wither away in order to comply with this mitzvah. The Midrash (*Shemos Rabbah* 18:5) refers to these people as גבורי כח, mighty heroes. Normally, when we have a mitzvah to do, it takes us a brief moment, or perhaps a day, maybe a week or a bit more. But the mitzvah of *shemittah* obligates the landowner for an entire year. Some of us find it difficult to close our businesses just for Shabbos and Yom Tov; these people close their enterprises for an entire year!

A Rabbi once told of a conversation he had with one of these landowners in Eretz Yisrael during *shemittah*. He asked the man how he has the fortitude to abandon his livelihood for an entire year, and the man answered by citing the *pasuk*, רוח והצלה יעמוד ליהודים ממקום אחר — "Respite and salvation shall arise for the Jews from elsewhere" (*Esther* 4:14). He had full faith that Hashem would provide his livelihood through some other means if he complied with the mitzvah's demand to let his lands lie fallow. If someone knows that even when he works it is actually Hashem Who is providing his livelihood, then he has no trouble at all abstaining from work when Hashem tells him to. If he realizes that his planting and harvesting is not what brings him success, then he will have no concerns at all when Hashem tells him to stop planting and harvesting.

People generally think that they are the ones who secure their livelihood through their industry and hard work, by making the right investments and the right decisions. Rav Ephraim Wachsman noted that if a farmer thinks he produced food through his hard work, he should ask himself: Who provided the sunlight? Who brought the rain? Who supplied the nutrients in the ground? Who performed the photosynthesis and all the other miracles of the agricultural process? A person feels pride over the money he earned by making a smart investment. He should realize that more neurological data is needed for his finger to press the button on his phone to call his broker than all the human actions that have been performed since the beginning of time. The human brain contains 100 billion neurons, which form more combinations of circuitry than the elementary particles in the entire universe. But we credit ourselves for having an idea? Could we even pick up the telephone without Hashem?

There was a Rabbi in France named Rabbi Gershon Liebman, who is credited with leading 80,000 Jews to becoming *baalei teshuvah*. His students compiled his lectures into a book and presented him with a copy. They saw him read through the book and express his amazement. "Wow, what beautiful *chiddushim*!" "This is really good!" The students were very surprised. They knew their Rabbi was very humble and not one to boast about his brilliance. They approached him and asked why he was praising his own work.

"Just because Hashem put this chiddush into my mind," he answered, "does that mean I did anything?"

"Just because Hashem put this *chiddush* into my mind," he answered, "does that mean I did anything?"

The more we understand the message of כי לי כל הארץ, that everything that happens is because Hashem wanted it to happen, the easier it will be for us to perform the mitzvos, and, in addition, by performing the mitzvos we will enhance our recognition of Hashem's control over the world and over our lives.

51 Talk to Hashem

Hashem governs the world and exerts absolute control over everything that exists, from the tiniest insects to the millions of enormous galaxies that lie well beyond the earth. We would think that no entity could possibly have any say on how He does things, and how He runs the world's affairs. But while this is generally true, there is one remarkable exception: prayer. Hashem granted us the unique power of *tefillah*, through which we can have an impact upon the way He governs the world and the way He deals with us.

In a letter, the Chazon Ish noted how wondrous it is that a person can discuss all his problems and concerns with Hashem. Whenever we have any sort of issue, when there is something on our mind, we can talk about it with Him, and we'll then feel better. The Chazon Ish further notes that this privilege is not limited to the "big things," to major concerns such as health and *parnassah*. Even with regard to the small things in life, such as if a person is looking for a new pair of shoes, one can bring the matter to Hashem. Nothing is too small for Him to listen. What a great *chesed* this is. We don't have to wait in line, and we don't even have to pick up a phone. We don't have to pay a fee to speak to Him, and to the contrary, we can profit from it. Anything can be accomplished through *tefillah*.

Tefillah offers us a golden opportunity at every moment of every day. When someone wants to speak to an important person, he has to put in considerable effort: wake up early, travel, and wait in the office, and then perhaps he'll get a few minutes with the person. Even when one wants to meet with an esteemed Rabbi, he needs to go to the Rabbi's office; often he can only schedule a meeting if he has the right connections, and he then has to wait his turn and ends up speaking for just a minute or two with the Rabbi. But we can speak to Hashem, the

King of the universe, whenever we want, wherever we want, and for as long as we want.

Furthermore, we are able to speak to Hashem about anything, even matters about which we would feel too ashamed to speak with anybody else. Shlomo HaMelech writes (*Mishlei* 12:25), דאגה בלב איש ישחנה — "If there is worry in a person's heart, he should speak about it." The Gemara (*Yoma* 8a) explains that often a person feels too embarrassed to talk about a specific problem or concern that he has. But we never have to be embarrassed when speaking to Hashem.

> *"We can speak to Hashem, the King of universe, whenever we want, wherever we want, and for as long as we want."*

Nobody loves you more than Hashem. Let us imagine the person who loves us more than anybody else in the world, and we approach that person to discuss a specific problem. The person kindly reassures us that he will help. But the issue weighs heavily on our minds, so we go back to the person to talk it over again. Once again, he patiently assures us that it will be taken care of. But we're still concerned and upset, so we return yet a third time to speak to him. At a certain point, the person will lose patience and tell us to stop pressuring him. But this will never happen with Hashem. We come to Him during Shacharis with our problems, and then again during the day, and we speak to Him about it again at Minchah and Maariv. He does not mind. To the contrary, He wants us to keep coming back to Him, and the more we ask, the more He is willing to help.

דרשו ה' ועזו בקשו פניו תמיד — "Seek out Hashem and His strength; beseech Him always" (*Tehillim* 105:4). We should utilize this beautiful gift of prayer and take advantage of this opportunity תמיד, always, turning to Hashem whenever we have a problem on our minds, and then He will provide us with all our needs.

52 Hashem Is Waiting for You to Ask

The *Sefer HaChinuch*, in discussing the mitzvah of *tefillah* (431), writes that Hashem wants to bestow goodness upon us, and so He provided a means whereby we can obtain all forms of goodness, and that is prayer. He describes prayer as follows:

שיבקשו ממנו ברוך הוא אשר בידו ההסתפקות והיכולת כל חסרונן כי הוא יענה את השמים לכל אשר יקראוהו באמת

"They should ask Him, blessed is He, Who has the capacity and ability, for all their needs, for He will answer from the heavens to all who call out to Him with sincerity."

There is so much good waiting for us, but Hashem wants us to first ask for it, in order that we develop a relationship with Him. The source for this concept is in *Bereishis*, where the Torah relates that even after the vegetation was created Hashem did not immediately allow it to grow, because אדם אין לעבוד את האדמה — "there was as yet no human being to cultivate the earth." Rashi explains this to mean that Hashem waited for the creation of Adam, who would recognize the need for vegetation and pray for it. Rav Yerucham Levovitz (*Daas Torah,* Vol. 2) commented in light of Rashi's explanation that there is an abundance of blessing at the edge of the heavens waiting for us, but Hashem created a system whereby prayer is required to bring forth that blessing.

This answers the question that many people ask as to the purpose of prayer if everything has already been decreed on Rosh Hashanah. Just as we obviously cannot sit around at home all day waiting for Hashem to miraculously send us a check, and we must instead do our *hishtadlus* (personal effort)

to earn a living, similarly, we must pray for our blessings to arrive. Prayer is also part of our *hishtadlus*, because it is part of the system through which the world operates. In fact, prayer is the primary *hishtadlus*. Our livelihood derives mainly from our recitation of *bareich aleinu*, and only secondarily from our input. Our health derives primarily from our recitation of *refa'einu*, and only secondarily from our medical treatments. Hashem is our Provider and Healer, but He created the world in such a way that we must ask Him for His blessings. If we do not pray with the proper *kavannah* (intent), we deprive ourselves of all the goodness that is waiting for us.

> *"Prayer is the primary hishtadlus."*

We read in *Parashas Shemos* (6:12) that when Hashem first appeared to Moshe and assigned him the task of leading *Bnei Yisrael* out of Egypt, Moshe initially refused. One of the reasons he gave for his refusal is that he suffered from a speech impediment, which compromised his ability to effectively confront Pharaoh. Hashem replied that he should nevertheless approach Pharaoh, and his brother, Aharon, will serve as his spokesman. The Ramban (*Shemos* 4:10) raises the question of why Hashem did not simply cure Moshe's impediment, rather than have Aharon speak in Moshe's place. The answer, the Ramban explains, is that Moshe did not ask to be cured. The Ramban suggests a reason why Moshe did not ask, but what is significant for our purposes is the fact that Hashem was prepared to provide the cure, but He withheld it because the request was not made. Asking is necessary and required to bring down the *berachah*.

Let us utilize this wonderful gift of prayer, and constantly ask Hashem for anything and everything we need and want, so He can bestow upon us all the many *berachos* waiting for us.

53 Living With Hashem

Some people use the gift of *tefillah* to pray to Hashem, and there are others who use this gift to live with Hashem.

Tefillah is not limited to the three formal prayers of Shacharis, Minchah, and Maariv. Hashem is always with us, and one can speak to Him at any time and in any language. The great Rabbi, Reb Simcha Bunim of P'schischa, said (*Beis Yaakov, Parashas Vayeitzei*), "I have the following piece of advice for anyone who never wants to lack anything, and who wants to be connected to Hashem: accustom yourself to pray and ask Hashem for every little thing, wherever you are. Whatever you need, ask Hashem for it, and He will grant your request."

> *"Accustom yourself to pray and ask Hashem for every little thing, wherever you are."*

We should strive to be like David HaMelech, who said about himself (*Tehillim* 109:4), ואני תפילה — "I am prayer."

A man called and told me he was having problems with his business, and had not received a large order in a long time. He was considering cutting down the time he spent learning in order to take a second job to supplement his income. I asked him whether he asks Hashem for help before he speaks to a customer, and he said that he does not. I urged him to bring Hashem into his life and ask Him for help regularly, in his own words and in his own language. Within ten minutes, he called me back to tell me he had received a large order.

❖ ❖ ❖

A man once came to the Lev Simchah of Ger and complained that he felt very alone in the world. He had no friends or family, and there were many problems he needed to deal with and had no one to whom he could turn for help. The Rabbi helped him with some of his problems, and told him, "I have the best friend for you: become friends with Hashem! He is more loving and devoted than any other friend, and can solve every single one of your problems. If you become His friend, you will never feel alone again."

We should try to follow this advice and make Hashem part of our lives by speaking to Him regularly. When someone is planning a trip, he should talk to Hashem and ask Him to help him get to his destination safely. When a person goes to work, He should ask Hashem for success. When a person is on his way to an important meeting, he should ask Hashem to help him get the desired results. When someone is looking to buy a house, and he has difficult decisions to make, he should ask Hashem to guide him in the right direction. When someone is looking to get married, he should ask Hashem to help him or her find the right person. When a woman is making dinner for her family, she should ask Hashem to make sure it turns out right. When the children are misbehaving, the parents should speak to Hashem and ask Him to give them the right words to help the children behave.

Whenever there's anything we want, big or small, we should ask Hashem. No request is too trivial. He wants us to speak to Him and is waiting for our prayers and requests. If somebody has a decision to make, even on a small matter, he should ask Hashem, Who has the right answer for every question and every problem.

Let us bring Hashem into our lives, and we will then see how beautiful life becomes. As David HaMelech said (*Tehillim* 73:28), ואני קרבת אלקים לי טוב — "for me, closeness with G-d is what is good." Nothing is better than being close with Hashem.

54

Let Hashem Figure It Out

When we pray to Hashem for something, it is not our job to figure out how our request can be granted. That is Hashem's responsibility. Our job is to pray sincerely and to realize that Hashem can find a way even when it appears as though there is no possible way for our wish to be fulfilled.

Chazal teach us (*Bava Basra* 123a) that Leah Imeinu had always been told that she would marry Esav. Lavan had two daughters, and Rivkah had two sons, and it was assumed that Lavan's older daughter would marry Rivkah's older son, and Lavan's younger daughter would marry Rivkah's younger son. This meant that Leah would marry Esav and Rachel would marry Yaakov. And then, when Yaakov arrived in Lavan's home, he asked to marry Rachel, and Lavan agreed to allow him and Rachel to marry in exchange for seven years of work. It seemed like there was no possible way for Leah to marry Yaakov, but nevertheless, she continued praying. The *pasuk* (*Bereishis* 29:13) says, ועיני לאה רכות — "Leah's eyes were weary" from crying and praying to Hashem. Even when it looked like all hope was lost, she did not despair. Sure enough, Lavan substituted Leah for Rachel, and Rachel gave Leah the signals she had arranged with Yaakov. In the end, Leah married Yaakov and was the mother of six of the Twelve Tribes of Israel.

"We only need to pray, and leave it to Hashem to figure out how our prayers will be answered."

We only need to pray, and leave it to Hashem to figure out how our prayers will be answered.

I am involved in a yeshivah for post-high school boys

who learn in the morning and then attend college or work in the afternoon. Once a boy came to me toward the end of the summer and said he was hoping to arrange his college schedule in such a way that he could learn in the yeshivah in the mornings. I learned with this young man for the last two weeks of the summer, and I saw that he was an exceptional young man, with outstanding *middos* and a great mind. I very much hoped he would stay and learn in the yeshivah during the upcoming year, but he said he had not been able to schedule his classes in the afternoon. I urged him to see what he could do, and so he went back to the school and spoke to the dean. The dean declined his request, explaining that as a freshman, he needs to take what he can get and there was no room for flexibility.

"Look," the boy said to me, "I did my *hishtadlus* [effort], and it didn't work out."

"Have you been praying to Hashem?" I asked him.

"No," he said, "but it's too late now. There's no way I can schedule my classes for the afternoon."

I explained that he should pray to Hashem and leave it up to Him to find a way. Sure enough, a few days later, he told me that he would be coming to the yeshivah. It turned out that the dean, who had been at the college for forty years, retired, and the new dean allowed him to schedule his classes in the afternoon.

This is the power of *tefillah*.

Someone recently told me that every year he goes to Las Vegas for two different trade shows, and this necessitates a total of four trips a year, twice for each show. He would prefer not to have to go, but has no choice as he has many customers there and needs the business. He prayed to Hashem to work it out so that he would not have to go that often. Just a couple of weeks after he started praying, he learned that one of the shows bought out the other, and now he needs to go only twice a year. It seemed like there was no alternative, but Hashem found a way to make it easier for him.

We need to pray and beg Hashem for whatever we want, and leave the details to Him.

55 Why Didn't You Ask for Help?

The *pasuk* (*Tehillim* 81:11) states, אנכי ה' אלקיך המעלך מארץ מצרים הרחב פיך ואמלאהו — "I am Hashem your G-d Who took you from the land of Egypt; open your mouth wide, and I will fill it." The Gemara (Berachos 50a) interprets הרחב פיך ואמלאהו as a reference to praying for spiritual success. Hashem here invites us to ask for His help in Torah and spirituality.

But what is the connection between the two parts of this *pasuk*? How does the concept of prayer for spiritual success relate to *yetzi'as Mitzrayim* — the fact that Hashem took us from Egypt?

Rav Chaim Shmulevitz (*Sichos Mussar, Maamar* 28) explained that just as Hashem lifted us from the 49th level of impurity in which we were submerged in Egypt, and elevated us to the 49th level of holiness at Mount Sinai, he is similarly capable and willing to assist each and every one of us in our spiritual efforts. The only condition, however, is that we "open our mouth wide," that we ask Hashem for help. And the wider we open our mouth, the more we pray and beseech Hashem for help, the more help He will provide.

> *"The wider we open our mouth, the more we pray and beseech Hashem for help, the more help He will provide."*

As observant Jews, we face many tests. The Gemara teaches (*Kiddushin* 30b) that the *yetzer hara* (evil inclination) is very difficult to overcome, and without

Hashem's help we have no possibility of withstanding the pressure it exerts upon us. A person might feel, Look, what can I do? It's just too hard. My schedule is so busy and makes it too difficult for me to learn Torah. It's too hard to always have to watch what kind of food I eat, what kind of things I look at, and the kind of things I hear. I have pressure from my friends, or from my spouse, not to be so religious. It's just too hard. All these claims are true, but there is one very compelling response: Why don't you ask Hashem for help?

> Rav Shimshon Pincus (*Sichos Elul, Amud* 33) drew an analogy to a department of a hospital with a team of doctors who were giving instructions to the doctor who would be taking the night shift. They told him that all the patients were asleep; should one of them awaken, he should tend to that patient. If several patients awaken, and he cannot handle the workload on his own, he should call other doctors for help, no matter what time it is. Sure enough, a number of patients woke during the night, and the doctor ably took care of them. As time went on, though, more patients woke and required treatment, and the doctor found himself frantically running back and forth in a desperate attempt to treat them all. Eventually, the workload proved too much for him to handle, and, unfortunately, one of the patients died as a result of the doctor's failure to meet all his needs.
>
> The next morning, when the other team members arrived at the hospital, they reprimanded the doctor for allowing a patient to die. He explained to them that there were just too many patients to treat, and he couldn't get to them all.
>
> "You fool!" they exclaimed. "We told you to call us if the situation became too much for you to handle. You were supposed to ask us for help, and we would have come and treated the patient!"

This is precisely our situation with respect to spirituality. Hashem knows that the *yetzer hara* is too difficult for us to handle on our own, and He therefore instructs us to "call" Him for help. If we don't call Him and pray for assistance in overcoming our spiritual tests, then we are to blame for our inability to achieve spiritual success.

When a person finds himself struggling in a certain area of religious observance, he should pray, "Hashem, please help me; I want to do the right thing, but I need Your help!" When a person feels he has stopped growing spiritually and does not have the desire to move forward, he should pray to Hashem for that desire. When a person is having difficulty learning or understanding what he learns, he should pray to Hashem for help.

> Recently, I was learning a passage of the Rosh with several students, and we were having a very hard time figuring out what the Rosh was saying. We read it several times, and we just couldn't understand the passage. I told the students that the reason why we couldn't understand the Rosh is because we did not pray to Hashem enough to help us. So we stopped, asked Hashem to help us, and then looked at it again. This time, it clicked. In fact, it was so clear and obvious what the Rosh was saying that we couldn't understand why we had so much trouble initially.

The *Ya'aros Devash* (*Derush* 4) comments that if we see a student who has more success than his peers in Torah study, it is not because he is brighter, but because he asks Hashem for help.

This is true regarding our children, as well. If someone sees that his child is not properly observing the Torah, or does not want to pray or learn, the parents should pray to Hashem and ask for His help to enable the child to improve. This is part of our *hishtadlus*, and the more we ask, the more we receive. הרחב פיך: We must open our mouths wide in prayer; even when we find it difficult to pray, we must ask Hashem to help. Even when we feel our *emunah* (faith) is lacking, we must ask Hashem to give us *emunah*. He is always listening and always ready to help us overcome any personal challenge we confront.

56 Prayer Is for Everyone

A person should never say to himself, *How can I ask Hashem for something, when I'm on such a low spiritual level? Why would He be interested in hearing my requests, let alone granting them?* Hashem always wants to hear from us, no matter what spiritual level we are on.

The Midrash (*Shemos Rabbah*) comments that Hashem caused *Bnei Yisrael* to be trapped against the sea because He wanted to hear their *tefillos*. In Egypt, as they suffered persecution, they prayed to Hashem, as the Torah says, ויזעקו — "and they cried out" (*Shemos* 2:23). Once they left Egypt, however, they no longer prayed. The Midrash says that Hashem desired to hear *Bnei Yisrael* pray as they did in Egypt, and so He brought Pharaoh and his army to pursue them and trap them against the sea, at which point they again prayed: 'ויצעקו בני ישראל אל ה — "the Children of Israel cried out to Hashem" (*Shemos* 14:10). Hashem then said, "This was the voice that I missed — the same voice that I heard when *Bnei Yisrael* were in Egypt!" Rabbi Chaim A. Yomnick (*Ki Atah Imadi,* Volume 2, page 53) notes that Hashem desired to hear the voice that He heard when *Bnei Yisrael* were in Egypt, despite the fact that the people at that time were submerged in the 49th level of impurity. Even though they had fallen to the lowest spiritual depths, Hashem cherished their prayers and even longed to hear them again afterward. This demonstrates that no matter what level a person is on, Hashem very much desires to hear his *tefillos*.

The *Kedushas Levi* (Rav Levi Yitzchak of Berditchev) writes that we have to strengthen and reinforce our belief that Hashem, the King of the universe, wants to hear the prayers of all people, even of those who are on the lowest spiritual levels. In fact,

Rav Tzadok HaKohen of Lublin writes that sometimes those on a low spiritual level have even a greater chance of having their prayers answered than others. These people are keenly aware of their unworthiness, and thus pray with complete trust in, and dependence on, Hashem's mercy and compassion, and these are the greatest prayers of all.

> *"No matter who a person is and what he has done, Hashem anxiously awaits his tefillos."*

The Chafetz Chaim (Rav Yisrael Meir Kagan of Radin) delivered a public address in which he proclaimed, "I promise you Hashem is waiting and longs for the *tefillos* of each and every one of you." One should never think for a moment that because of his wrongdoing Hashem is not interested in hearing from him and listening to his requests. No matter who a person is and what he has done, Hashem anxiously awaits his *tefillos*.

A man told me that when he was 60 years old, he was forced to sell all his stores and suddenly found himself without a source of income for the first time in his adult life. He didn't know how he would support himself, and was thinking that he might have no choice but to sell his home and move into a small residence. The next morning, he remained in the shul after everyone else had left. He got down on his knees and said, "Please, Hashem, I need help. Please give me another job." He then got up, recited a chapter of *Tehillim*, and left.

On his way home, a car pulled up alongside him. A man he knew, who was the president of a large company, noticed him walking home and stopped to ask why he was not at work at that late hour. The man explained to him that he had to sell his stores and was now left without any work.

"Perfect!" the driver exclaimed. "I need a new manager for one of the divisions in my company, and I think you're the perfect man for the job." The man started work the next day, and earned the exact salary he needed. This man is not a great scholar or *tzaddik*, but just a simple Jew whose prayers were lovingly accepted by Hashem.

One should never be discouraged from crying out to Hashem. No matter who he is, Hashem very much wants to hear what he has to say.

57 How Much Does Hashem Love Us?

Some people perceive Hashem as a strict judge Who gave us a set of rules and is ready and waiting to punish those who disobey. Nothing, however, could be further from the truth. Hashem's love and mercy for us extend far beyond our comprehension. Rav Moshe Feinstein is quoted as saying that Hashem's love for the worst sinner is a million times greater than our love for the greatest *tzaddik*.

> *"Hashem's love for the worst sinner is a million times greater than our love for the greatest tzaddik."*

The prophet Malachi begins his prophecy by conveying Hashem's message to the people (*Malachi* 1:2), אהבתי אתכם — "I have loved you." The Malbim explains this to mean that Hashem loves us because of who we are, and not merely because of our righteous ancestors. This message was conveyed during the period of the Second *Beis HaMikdash*, when the people committed the most grievous sins. Even then, Hashem expressed His great love for His people.

The Gemara (*Berachos* 7a) cites the *pasuk*, וחנותי את אשר אחון — "I shall be gracious to those to whom I choose to be gracious" (*Shemos* 33:19) and explains it to mean that Hashem is compassionate even to those who are not worthy of His compassion. The Torah (ibid. 22:26) describes the situation of a poor person who cries out to Hashem, and Hashem responds, ושמעתי כי חנון אני — "I will listen, because I am compassionate." The Ramban explains that Hashem accepts the pleas of all people, regardless of whether or not they are deserving of a favorable response. He writes: כי גזירה היא מלפניו לרחם על כל מי שמתחנן לפניו — "There is a decree that Hashem has compassion upon everyone who pleads to Him." In fact, the Gemara (*Berachos* 63a) relates that if a thief who is about to rob calls to Hashem, even he is answered. Despite the fact that he is about to transgress a grave Torah prohibition, even his prayers are lovingly accepted by Hashem. Rav Tzadok HaKohen (*Harei Tzaddik, Eikev, Os* 19) explains that since the thief shows his faith in Hashem by turning to Him to help, in this merit he earns Hashem's assistance.

> Rav Yisrael Salanter was once invited to meet the queen at the palace, shortly after the queen had given birth to a child, after thirty years of waiting. The queen described to the Rabbi how much she loved and adored her new son, and how her life's goal was now to ensure that he would always be happy and never experience any form of suffering. She would ensure that he would always have servants ready to fill his every wish to ensure that he never suffers.
>
> The Rabbi asked, "But what happens if he wants to remove a tissue from his pocket, and mistakenly puts his hand in the wrong pocket, in which case he would then have to endure the inconvenience of removing his hand and placing it in the other pocket? Who is going to ensure that he avoids this kind of suffering?"
>
> The queen replied, "Well, that's not suffering, that's normal life. It wouldn't bother me if he has to endure that."
>
> When Rav Yisrael left the palace, he looked up to the heavens and said, "This queen has her first child after thirty years, and loves him so much, and yet it wouldn't bother her if he puts his hand in the wrong pocket. But You, Hashem, love Your children so much that You consider this suffering."

Indeed, the Gemara (*Arachim* 16b) comments that if one puts his hand in the wrong pocket and then has to put it into the other, this qualifies as *yissurim* (suffering). Even this bothers Hashem, as it were.

Hashem loves us more than we can imagine. We must never feel discouraged from turning to Him and asking Him for help. And we must never think that He does not want to hear from us. He always wants to hear our voices, and eagerly awaits our prayers.

58 If I Keep Asking, Will I Lose My Merits?

Everything is accomplished through *tefillah*. Rav Shimshon Pincus (*She'arim B'Tefillah*) writes that even if a person is deserving of a certain blessing or *yeshuah* (salvation), he will not receive it unless he asks for it. This is the system that Hashem set in place because He wants us to turn to Him in prayer.

There are several reasons why people do not constantly ask Hashem for what they want. Some people feel that they do not wish to use their limited supply of merits by asking Hashem to give them what they want. This rationale, however, is based on a fundamental misconception. Our Sages teach that a person forfeits merits only when a miracle occurs. Ordinary blessings that come through the natural system are not "charged" to a person's account of merits. And the Maharsha, in his commentary

"Ordinary blessings that come through the natural system are not "charged" to a person's account of merits."

(*Kiddushin* 29b), writes that anything one receives as a result of prayer is not considered a miracle. Therefore, one does not use up any merits by asking Hashem for something. In fact, it is specifically through the merit of his *tefillah* that he will be granted his request.

Another reason why some people do not ask Hashem for what they want is because they do not want to feel indebted to Him. Rabbi Yosef Zalman Bloch noted that this reason is entirely without validity, and, in fact, is ludicrous. We already receive infinitely more from Hashem than we deserve; everything we have, without exception, is from Him. By saying that we do not want to ask too much so we do not feel indebted, we are in essence denying how much we are already indebted to Him.

> Rav Bloch drew an analogy to a very wealthy man who was driving and saw what looked like a pile of rags on the side of the road. He told his driver to pull over, and it turned out that it was a destitute, gravely ill Jew wearing tattered clothes who had collapsed and was freezing. The man brought this person to the hospital, where it was discovered that he suffered from sixteen different maladies. The wealthy man covered all this person's medical expenses and he received the treatment he needed. When he was discharged from the hospital, he thanked the wealthy man and told him that he was homeless and had nowhere to go. The wealthy man gave him a position in his company with a handsome salary, and the man was finally able to buy a home and respectable clothing. He then gave him his daughter in marriage.
>
> At the end of the last *sheva berachos* celebration, the wealthy man turned to his new son-in-law and offered him a cup of tea. The groom politely declined.
>
> "Why not?" the father-in-law asked, curiously. "You always enjoy a cup of tea after your meal."
>
> "I prefer not," the groom said, "because I don't want to feel too indebted to you."
>
> "What?!" the father-in-law bellowed. "You don't

want to feel indebted?! Everything you have is because of me. If I had not taken care of you, you would have died a long time ago. Your job, your house, your car, your wife, your very life — it's all because of me. And you're concerned about a cup of tea?"

This is our situation vis-à-vis Hashem. He gives us everything, and we already owe Him far more than we can ever imagine. If we refrain from asking Him for favors out of fear of being indebted, we are, in effect, being ungrateful, showing that we do not already feel indebted.

When we ask Hashem for a favor, we are asking for His compassion, and this is how we honor Him: by showing Him that we need and rely on Him for everything. This is what He wants, and this is how we achieve everything in life.

59 Who Owes Whom?

Sometimes people feel that Hashem "owes" them. They say, "Look, Hashem, I came to shul today," "I learned Torah," "I do *chesed*," or "I pray," figuring that because they do these mitzvos Hashem is somehow indebted to them. But if we think about it truthfully, we will realize how gravely mistaken this attitude is.

Rabbi Jonathan Rietti expressed this idea with a beautiful parable. A 12-year-old boy was rushing to school, and as he picked up his breakfast, just before running out the door to get his bus, he left a note on the table for his mother. It listed the following:

Mowing the lawn:	$5.00
Making my bed:	$1.00
Playing with my little brother:	.75
Taking out the garbage:	$1.00
Good report card:	$5.00
Raking the leaves:	$2.00
	Total: $14.75

After reading the note, the mother was aghast. "He's charging me for taking out the garbage, and for playing with his little brother?! What an ingrate!" After reflecting upon the situation for a few moments, she came up with an idea. She turned over the paper and wrote the following note for her son:

Carrying you inside me for nine months: No charge

Staying up with you for hours on many nights: No charge

Caring for you when you were ill: No charge

Praying for you: No charge

The time and tears you caused through the years: No charge

The nights filled with dread and the worries ahead: No charge

Sum total of all the love I've shown you: No charge.

The boy came home from school and read his mother's note. With tears running down his face, he turned the page over and wrote underneath his original note: "Paid in full."

> *"For giving you a functioning brain — no charge"; "For giving you healthy organs — no charge"; "For giving you two eyes — no charge."*

People turn to Hashem and say, "I came to shul," or "I helped a poor family in Israel," expecting that He is now obliged to repay them for these deeds. But Hashem can then answer back, "For giving you a functioning brain — no charge"; "For giving you healthy organs — no charge"; "For giving you two eyes — no charge."

We, like the 12-year-old boy, often fail to realize how much kindness is provided for us. Each eye, for example, has 100 million receptors, each of which takes an image, transforms it into an electrical impulse and sends it to the brain where it is deciphered. The message is sent to the brain via 50,000 connectors, and the "pipe" is never clogged. And all this happens at lightning speed. I recently saw that the best digital cameras in the world range from 60 and 80 megapixels, and sell for about $40-$50,000. The human eye has about 600 megapixels — and Hashem gave us each two of them, free of charge.

In the *berachah* of *Asher Yatzar*, which we recite after using the restroom, we describe Hashem as רופא כל בשר ומפליא לעשות — which means that He heals us by removing waste from our bodies in wondrous fashion. Our bodies automatically separate what they need from what they don't need, and expel the waste. Who is paying for this service?

Instead of having the attitude of, "What have You done for me lately?" we should appreciate and be grateful for the infinite kindness that Hashem bestows upon us at every moment.

60 Business Deal of a Lifetime

How much *chesed* does Hashem do for us?

Imagine you apply for a job, and the employer hires you, provides you with a beautiful office, presents you with a list of every major account, and offers you 100 percent commission on sales. When you sell merchandise, it outwardly appears that you're working for the company, whereas in reality you are working for yourself, as you receive 100 percent commission for every sale. This is the dream job: you get to profit as though you're the business owner, but without having to worry about maintenance.

"This is the dream job: you get to profit as though you're the business owner, but without having to worry about maintenance."

Each and every one of us has a dream job, called *avodas Hashem*. Hashem gives us everything we need so we can do our job, and we receive 100 percent commission for each and every good deed we do and each and every positive thought we have. It looks like we're working for Him, but in reality we are working for ourselves. The Torah (*Devarim* 10:12) asks, מה ה' אלקיך שואל מעמך — "What is it that Hashem wants of us" — and answers that He wants us to observe His commands, לטוב לך — "for your own benefit." Ramban explains that Hashem does not need us to serve Him; He has nothing to gain from our mitzvos. He gave us the mitzvos solely for our benefit, so we can accrue reward.

Earlier (*Devarim* 6:24), the Torah writes:

ויצונו ה' לעשות את כל החוקים האלה ליראה את ה' אלקינו לטוב לנו כל הימים לחיותנו כיום הזה. וצדקה תהיה לנו כי נשמור לעשות את כל המצוה הזאת לפני ה' אלקינו כאשר צונו

"Hashem commanded us to perform all these laws, to fear Hashem, our G-d, for our benefit, all the days, to keep us living as on this day. And it will be kindness to ourselves when we observe all these commands before Hashem, our G-d, as He commanded us."

Ibn Ezra explains the first promise — "for our benefit, all the days" — as referring to reward in this world, and the second — "And it will be kindness to ourselves" — as referring to the reward in the Next World. Each and every mitzvah is for our benefit, yielding us reward both in this world and in the eternal world of *Olam Haba*.

Rabbi Chananya ben Akashya famously quotes: רצה הקב"ה לזכות את ישראל לפיכך הרבה להם תורה ומצוות — "The Holy One, Blessed is He, wished to confer merit upon Israel, therefore He gave them much Torah and mitzvos in abundance" (*Yeshayah* 42:21). Hashem gave us so many mitzvos to do so we can earn reward. In His infinite kindness, He made it appear as though we are working for Him, giving us the dignity of feeling as though we earn our reward by providing a service, whereas in truth, He has nothing to gain from our mitzvos, and they are all purely for our benefit.

R' Dovid Hoffman (*Torah Tavlin*) offers the following analogy. There was once a successful contractor who employed an outstanding carpenter to work on his building projects. One day, the carpenter came to the contractor to inform him that he had decided to retire. He explained that he was grateful for all the work he has given him over the years, but his wife very much wants him to retire so he could spend time with the family. The contractor pleaded with him to change his mind, telling him that he was his best worker and he really depended on him.

"Sorry," the carpenter said, "my mind is made up."

The contractor explained that he had just committed to another project, to build a home, and he needed him for that project. He asked if the carpenter would agree to work on this one final project before retiring. The carpenter, knowing that building this home could take a year, went home and talked it over with his wife, who urged him to decline. The carpenter felt torn between his family and his commitment to his employer, and in the end, with a heavy heart, decided he would agree to work on this final project.

He began the work, and proceeded without much patience or eye for detail. Rushing to finish the project so he could retire, the carpenter did his work sloppily, and the project that should have taken a year was completed after seven months. The roof was crooked, there were cracks in the floor and leaks from the windows, and some of the tiles were the wrong size.

He returned to the contractor to inform him that the job was done. The contractor handed him the keys to the house and said, "Here — this is your going-away present."

The carpenter was stunned — and infuriated at himself. Had he known that he was building this house for himself, he would have worked with such diligence and done everything to perfection. But he didn't, and so he ended up with a house with leaks and cracks and mismatched tiles.

If we knew that the mitzvos we perform are for ourselves, and not for Hashem, that we are "building" our own "home" through our *avodas Hashem*, we would invest so much more into our religious observance. The next time we feel that mitzvos are a burden, we must remember that we are building our own home, and we are working not for Hashem, but for ourselves.

61

Why Does Hashem Give Something He Is Going to Take Away?

I heard the following comment cited from the *Zohar*: כשם שלגדולתו אין חקר, כך לרחמנותו אין חקר — "Just as there is no possibility of quantifying Hashem's greatness, there is no possibility of quantifying His kindness and compassion." We can never understand just how kind Hashem truly is.

We all pray for Mashiach. Some people pray for Mashiach to alleviate their financial problems. Others want Mashiach because they or somebody close to them is ill. And there are those who pray for Mashiach to help them with their difficulties in *shalom bayis* (domestic harmony). But the real reason why we should pray for Mashiach is, as we say in our *tefillah*, because we want גאולה שלמה **למען שמך** — "a complete redemption ***for Your Name's sake***." When Mashiach comes, everyone will realize just how kind Hashem is, and that even when events appear to be bad, they are, in truth, demonstrations of Hashem's boundless love and kindness. And this is why we want and pray for Mashiach to come.

Rav Ephraim Wachsman told the story of a man who lost a considerable sum of money, and came to his Rabbi to talk about his loss. "I fully accept the fact that Hashem did not want me to have this money," he told the Rabbi. "But what I don't understand is why He gave it to me in the first place. Why did He give me money just to take it away from me?"

The Rabbi answered by citing the *pasuk* (*Iyov* 1:21), ה' נתן וה' לקח — "G-d has given and G-d has taken." The *Be'er Mayim Chaim* notes that when the *pasuk* speaks of G-d giving, it says simply, ה' נתן, but when it mentions G-d taking away, it says **וה'** לקח. The reason, the *Be'er Mayim Chaim* (*Parashas Vaeira, perek* 6) explains, is because when Hashem gives us something, He gives it personally. But when something is taken away, it is actually the *Beis Din Shel Maalah*, the Heavenly Court, which takes it, in collection of a debt. This is why the *pasuk* uses different formulations in reference to Hashem's giving and taking.

> The *Be'er Mayim Chaim* offers an analogy to a king who had a dear friend who was very poor. The king lent the man a large sum of money, and when the time came for the debt to be repaid, it was clear that the poor man did not have the funds. The king knew that the royal agents would soon be knocking on the man's door and applying pressure on him to repay the debt, and there was nothing he could do to stop them, as this was the law in the kingdom. In order to help his friend, the king clandestinely slipped an envelope with money underneath the man's door, so by the time the agents came to collect the money, the man already had it ready.

We might initially think that Hashem is cruel by giving us money just to then take it away later. But in truth, it's the very opposite: He gives us the money that we will need to pay the debts that will come due.

> *He gives us the money that we will need to pay the debts that will come due.*

About a week after I heard this insight, I received a check for about $1000 for a job for which I had never expected to be paid. Two days later, I received a letter from the IRS informing me that I owed an additional $1000 in taxes. Hashem, in His kindness, gave me exactly the money I needed to pay the debt that would soon have to be repaid.

When Mashiach comes, it will become crystal clear just how kind Hashem is. But what an honor it would be for Hashem if we have already started recognizing His kindness now.

62 We Can't Fathom the Extent of Hashem's Kindness

Chazal teach us (*Niddah* 31b), אין בעל הנס מכיר בנסו, which literally means that a person for whom Hashem has performed a miracle does not even realize what has happened. Similarly, the *Ya'aros Devash* (*Chelek* 1, *derush* 1) writes, בכל יום יקרה לאיש הישראלי נסים רבים ואינו מרגיש — "Every day, many miracles occur for the Jew, but he does not notice." He adds that this is why we recite the *Modim* prayer in the *Amidah* three times a day to thank Hashem for all He does for us, and we recite in that prayer that we thank Hashem על נסיך שבכל יום עמנו — "for the miracles that He performs for us each day." We also recite in our *tefillah* the verse (*Tehillim* 124:2-3), לולי ה' שהיה לנו ... אזי חיים בלעונו — which means that if Hashem wouldn't be helping us, the enemy nations would have long ago "devoured" us. The *Kav HaYashar* (*Perek* 8) writes that this is also the reason why each weekday we recite Psalm 30, *Mizmor L'sodah*, the song that would be sung during the offering of the thanksgiving offering in the *Beis HaMikdash*. We recite this because of the countless offerings we owe Hashem for the countless miracles He performs for us, sparing us from dangerous situations of which we are most often not even aware.

There is, however, an additional explanation of the statement, אין בעל הנס מכיר בנסו. Namely, even when we do recognize that a miracle was performed for us, we do not understand how beneficial it really was. We are not capable of fathoming the extent of Hashem's kindnesses. In *Hallel* we recite the *pasuk* (*Tehillim* 106:1), הודו לה' כי טוב כי לעולם חסדו — "Give thanks to Hashem for He is good; for His kindness is eternal." The *Sfas Emes* (Chanukah, 1899) explains this to mean that even while we thank Hashem, we must recognize that לעולם חסדו, His kindness is boundless, that we, as shortsighted mortals, are capable of seeing only a minuscule portion of His kindness toward us.

> *"Even while we thank Hashem, we must recognize that His kindness is boundless, that we, as shortsighted mortals, are capable of seeing only a minuscule portion of His kindness toward us."*

Rabbi Pesach Eliyahu Falk gave the example of a person who has a newborn infant. Of course, he is overjoyed and filled with gratitude to Hashem for this beautiful *berachah*. Why is he grateful? Because the baby is so cute and playful, and brings abundant joy to the home. But this is only a tiny part of the *chesed* involved in the birth of a new child. This infant will, בעז"ה, grow up and perform millions of mitzvos over the course of his lifetime. The parents, who provided him with his *chinuch,* religious education, will thus receive reward for each and every mitzvah he performs. This child will also have children of his own, and he will, because of his upbringing, provide his children with a religious education. And thus for all generations henceforth, the parents will be continually rewarded for all the mitzvos done as a result of the *chinuch* they gave this cute little baby. And if the baby or any of his children grows up to be a prominent person who benefits the Jewish nation, this, too, will be credited to the parents.

The parents rejoice and thank Hashem for the adorable, healthy 8-lb. infant they were given. But they cannot see beyond the present, into the future, and realize the true extent of this *berachah*. The extent of each of Hashem's gifts to us is far beyond our range of vision, and well beyond the limits of our comprehension.

When Rachel finally had a child after many years of infertility, she named the boy "Yosef" because she said (*Bereishis* 30:23), אסף אלקים את חרפתי — "Hashem has put an end to my shame." Rashi cites the well-known comment of the Midrash that Rachel refers here to the "shame" of being blamed for things that break or go wrong in the home. A childless woman is blamed for all household mishaps, whereas if there are children, they can be blamed. Many commentators raise the question of why Rachel stressed this point in particular. After finally having a child, this is what she is grateful for — that she has a child to blame when dishes break?

Rav Gedaliah Schorr (quoted in ArtScroll *Chumash*, Stone Edition) explained that undoubtedly, Rachel was grateful and thanked Hashem for the birth of a son through whom she secured a share in the destiny of *Klal Yisrael*. But she made a point of telling Hashem that she is also mindful of the smaller, seemingly trivial blessings that come along with the birth of this child. She recognized that this *chesed* extended much further than at first meets the eye, even to less significant matters such as absolving herself of blame for broken dishes.

We recite in our Shabbos prayers, אין אנחנו מספיקים להודות לך ה' — "We can never be able to thank You, Hashem." We should all try to realize the truth of this statement, and recognize the fact that Hashem's kindness toward us extends far more than we are able to recognize.

63 If Hashem Doesn't Help, You Are Toiling in Vain

The *pasuk* (*Tehillim* 127:1) states, שיר המעלות לשלמה אם ה' לא יבנה בית שוא עמלו בוניו בו. In this verse, David HaMelech conveys words of *mussar* to his son, Shlomo, regarding the construction of the first *Beis HaMikdash,* a task later accomplished by Shlomo. David says that אם ה' לא יבנה בית — "If Hashem does not lend His assistance to the building project" — then שוא עמלו בניו בו — "its builders toiled in it for naught." Without Hashem's help, we toil in vain. A person can have all the money in the world, all the manpower he could possibly need, the best architects and the best engineers, but this does not guarantee that the building project will succeed. Shlomo HaMelech had everything available to him, but if he did not have *siyata DiShmaya*, Divine assistance, all the effort would be in vain.

> *"A person can have all the money in the world, all the manpower he could possibly need, the best architects and the best engineers, but this does not guarantee that the building project will succeed."*

We need Hashem's help for everything. A person can have the funds and the property for a new house, but without Hashem's assistance, issues can come up and the house won't be built. Without Hashem on our side, our efforts cannot possibly succeed. There could be a child prodigy who is named high school valedictorian and voted most likely to succeed, after which he goes to college for four years and graduates with a 4.0 average. But when it comes time to obtaining a position, he might very well end up with a mediocre job working for his classmate who was voted least likely to succeed. He has all the right tools, but without Hashem's help these tools are useless — שוא עמלו בוניו בו.

Some people wrongly assume that their success depends on their skill and effort, and that they do not require Hashem's help.

> I heard of a businessman who was fierce and ruthless in his business dealings, but he attended shul each morning and prayed a long *Amidah* with intense concentration. One day, the Rabbi approached the man and said, "I don't understand, if you're so close to Hashem and you realize you need His help, then why are you so ruthless in managing your business?"
>
> "No, Rabbi," the man replied, "you got it all wrong. I don't need Hashem's help; I can do it all myself. I realize, however, that He could ruin it for me, so I pray hard that He stays out of it and lets me run my business."

Of course, this attitude is patently absurd. We need Hashem's help for everything, even just to stand up. In fact, when we rise to begin the *Amidah* prayer, the first thing we say is, אדנ־י שפתי תפתח ופי יגיד תהילתך — "Lord, open my lips and my mouth shall speak Your praise." We begin our prayer by telling Hashem, "I cannot even open my mouth to pray without Your help!"

Hashem loves to help us, but part of our mission in the world is to realize that we need His help even for the smallest, simplest matters.

A man told me recently that he had leased a new car. The dealer didn't have the car in the color he wanted, so he had to wait. Finally, after two weeks, the car in the right color was delivered, but it had a small dent. It had to be sent back, which necessitated another two-week wait. He had the money, he knew exactly which car he wanted, but it didn't work out for a whole month. If Hashem doesn't want you to have it, you're not going to get it until He does.

The more we realize how much we need Hashem's help, the more help He will provide. And so the next time we want to do something, to start some kind of project, to go on vacation, or even just to shop for clothes, let us remember that אם ה' לא יבנה בית שוא עמלו בוניו בו — our efforts will be successful only with *Siyata DiShmaya.*

64 Maintaining Your Blessings

Earlier, we spoke of one of the lessons that David HaMelech taught his son, Shlomo, regarding the construction of the *Beis HaMikdash* which Shlomo would oversee after David's passing. That lesson was that without Hashem's help in the building, all the toiling is done in vain.

David additionally taught his son: אם ה' לא ישמור עיר שוא שקד שומר — "If Hashem does not protect a city, then the guards' efforts are futile" (*Tehillim* 127:2). You can have the best possible army, the greatest strategy, and most advanced weaponry, but if you don't have Hashem's protection, none of this will help.

Rabbi Falk explained that this lesson extends further than the first. People intuitively understand that when they're starting something new they need Hashem's help for it to succeed. When it comes to that which they already have, however, they tend to feel secure. David HaMelech here teaches us not to take anything for granted. Just because we have something, this does not mean that it is secure. If Hashem is not protecting it, there is nothing we can do to retain it.

We train ourselves not to take anything for granted each and every morning by reciting *"Modeh Ani,"* thanking Hashem that we are alive, that we are able to wake up. Just because we had life yesterday does not mean that we're guaranteed to have it again today. By reciting *"Modeh Ani"* each morning, we reinforce our awareness of the fact that we need Hashem to sustain our very lives.

This is also the message underlying the *Birchos HaShachar* — the blessings recited each morning thanking Hashem for things such as wisdom, eyesight, and clothing. By reciting these *berachos*, we show that we do not take these things for granted, and that it cannot be assumed that just because we had them yesterday we will necessarily have them today.

One of the *Birchos HaShachar* that we recite is רוקע הארץ על המים, in which we thank Hashem for giving us ground to walk on. How many people longed to have ground to walk on during Superstorm Sandy! Hospitals were flooded, and a major New York hospital had to be evacuated because all its backup generators failed (even though they were on upper floors). Eight million homes were without electricity, and we had to wait on line for hours on end just to obtain gasoline for our cars. Stores were without food because deliveries couldn't be made. It is almost hard to believe that such a situation could arise in modern times. Hashem was showing us that אם ה' לא ישמור עיר שוא שקד שומר — if He does not want us to have something, we are not going to have it. Nothing we have can ever be taken for granted. Rav Avigdor Miller commented that anytime we see a person with a handicap or disability, it is a direct message from Hashem to appreciate that we are not in this condition.

Some people find security in their money. There were those who converted their money to gold and stored it in the basement of the World Trade Center. It all melted on September 11, 2001. I read of a couple who had spent their lives working as teachers and were ready to retire, having saved a million dollars for retirement. Just then they discovered that their retirement money was in a Ponzi scheme, and it was all lost.

"Anything we have is maintained only because Hashem is protecting it. The moment He decides we shouldn't have it, it will be lost."

Anything we have is maintained only because Hashem is protecting it. The moment He decides we shouldn't have it, it will be lost.

Having children is a great blessing and source of joy, yet we often take it for granted. There is a concept in halachah called *chazakah*, which means that when something happens three times it can be assumed that it will happen again. But this does not allow us to take things for granted. After Leah Imeinu had her fourth child, she exclaimed (*Bereishis* 29:35), הפעם אודה את ה׳ — "This time I shall thank Hashem." Why did she thank Hashem specifically after her fourth child was born? The *Kesav Sofer* (as quoted by Rabbi Falk) explained that Leah wanted to make a point of showing that she did not take it for granted that she would have a fourth child. Notwithstanding the rule of *chazakah*, having three children does not guarantee that there will be a fourth. She therefore made a point of specifically thanking Hashem after the birth of her fourth child.

There are no guarantees. This is why we pray three times every day for our intelligence, health, livelihood, and so on. We pray to Hashem to maintain our money, health, and general well-being because we recognize that אם ה׳ לא ישמור עיר שוא שקד שומר — without Hashem's protection, nothing we have can be guaranteed to remain with us.

65 Everything Is Done With Kindness

Hashem is constantly doing *chesed* for us, at every moment of our lives. *Tehillim* is filled with descriptions of Hashem's boundless kindness, such as:

עולם חסד יבנה (89:3)

חסד ה׳ מלאה הארץ (33:5)

טוב ה׳ לכל ורחמיו על כל מעשיו (145:9)

The more we recognize how kind He is, the happier we will be. Everything that happens to us is a manifestation of Hashem's kindness, but we aren't always capable of understanding how. But if we realize just how small we are in comparison to Hashem, how His plan for us and the world is so far beyond the limits of our understanding, we will be able to trust that everything He does is an act of kindness. And thus David HaMelech says (*Tehillim* 23:1), ה' רועי לא אחסר — "Hashem is my shepherd, I lack nothing." Rabbi Falk explained that a shepherd is a human being who acts with intelligence, while sheep are animals. David here compares the difference between us and Hashem to the difference between the shepherd and his flock. The shepherd has a plan for how he will care for his sheep, and they have no idea at all of what it is, and just follow him. Similarly, David says, Hashem is his "shepherd," He knows how to care for him, and David therefore does not feel he lacks anything. He realizes that Hashem sees the whole picture, while we humans can see only what is right in front of us, and therefore, regardless of what happens, he does not feel that anything is lacking, as he trusts that Hashem is caring for him.

> *"Even when Hashem has to punish us, He does so with abundant kindness."*

Even when Hashem has to punish us, He does so with abundant kindness. The *pasuk* (*Tehillim* 62:13) says, לך ה' חסד כי אתה תשלם לאיש כמעשהו — "You are kind, Hashem, for You repay each person according to his deeds." The Gemara (*Rosh Hashanah* 176) understands this *pasuk* to be saying that Hashem is so kind because He punishes us for our sins. The question is raised there of how the fact that Hashem punishes us according to our deeds expresses His kindness. The Gemara answers that the *pasuk* must be read in reverse: Hashem punishes, and then we see the *chesed*. The *Toras Moshe Nasan* explains this to mean that when a person experiences punishment, and it seems to be all bad, then he must look deeper to reveal the kindness latent within the punishment. The example I once heard to clarify this concept is a case of a person about whom it was decreed on Rosh Hashanah that he would earn around $500,000 during the coming year. If Hashem carries out this decree by giving the man a $40,000 profit each month, then at the end of year he will feel very blessed and grateful to Hashem for such a successful year. If, however, Hashem has him earn a million dollars right at the beginning of the year, and then he loses $40,000 each month, he will feel as though he had a difficult year. The man would earn the same amount of money in both scenarios, but in the second instance, Hashem gave him $500,000 while at the same time eliminating thousands of *aveiros* from his record by taking money away from him. He had to endure suffering on account of his sins, and so Hashem gave him extra money and then took it away, leaving him with the precise amount he was destined to earn.

We do not understand Hashem's ways, but if we recognize the fact that we do not understand His ways, and that חסד ה' מלאה הארץ, the world is constantly filled with Hashem's kindness, it will facilitate our ability to trust in Him.

66 Hashem Knows Best

As we just mentioned, the *pasuk* states (*Tehillim* 23:1), ה' רועי לא אחסר — "Hashem is my shepherd, I lack nothing." Rav Chaim of Volozhin explained that there are times when sheep want to run about freely to the neighboring hills and fields, but the shepherd comes with his rod and does not permit them to do so. The sheep might regard the shepherd as being malicious and cruel by restricting their movement, but this is not the case. The shepherd cares about his flocks, and he knows that there is plenty of grass and water where the sheep are now, whereas if they run for two hours over the hills, they will find themselves famished and thirsty in a place with nothing to eat or drink. He knows something that they do not, and thus although it seems to them that he is heartless, in truth he is extending his kindness to them. David HaMelech describes himself as a sheep shepherded by Hashem, Who knows how to care for us far better than we know how to care for ourselves, and therefore we always know that we are not lacking, that we have precisely what we need. As David continues, בנאות דשא ירביצני, Hashem makes him stay in the meadows, where there is "grass," and does not let him run free to places where he would not have what he needs.

At other times, the sheep are tired and want to rest, but the shepherd forces them to move to a different location. Once again, it seems that he is bothering them and needlessly denying them the rest they crave. In truth, however, the shepherd knows that the sheep had depleted the water resources in their current locale, and they will soon be thirsty. He prods them to move in order to bring them to a place where they have the water they will need. And thus David continues, על מי מנוחות ינהלני — Hashem brings him to tranquil waters, to the place where his needs will be met.

"Hashem brings him to tranquil waters, to the place where his needs will be met."

Later (ibid. 23:4) in this chapter David says, גם כי אלך בגיא צלמות לא אירא רע כי אתה עמדי — "Even as I walk through the valley of the shadow of death, I shall fear no evil, for You are with me." Since he realizes that Hashem is always caring for him as a shepherd cares for his flock, he has no reason to fear when the situation looks bleak, because he knows with certainty that Hashem is looking out for him.

A businessman told me that he had a long-standing account with a large chain store. The store had nine slots for the product that this businessman's company supplied, and his company was given six of them. One day, the store hired a new buyer, and when the man met with the buyer to see what he would be ordering for the upcoming season, the buyer said he was not ordering anything. The man was stunned. He told the buyer that the company had been doing business with them for years, and the product always sold well. When the buyer couldn't be persuaded, the man scheduled a dinner meeting with the buyer's supervisor. He respectfully inquired as to why for years the store had been purchasing $3 million in merchandise and now they're not ordering anything. The supervisor said he'd think it over, and he called back a few days later to say that they are not overturning the decision, in order not to challenge the new buyer. The man then contacted the president of the company, but to no avail.

He turned to Hashem and said, "I don't understand. Why am I going from $3 million dollars to nothing?"

A few months later the news broke that this chain store — Caldor — was filing for bankruptcy and couldn't pay off its debt to its suppliers. The businessman again turned to Hashem and said, "Now I understand. You didn't take away $3 million — You saved me $3 million!"

Even when the situation looks bleak, לא אירא רע כי אתה עמדי — we have no reason to fear, for we know that Hashem is looking out for us.

67 No One Can Touch What's Yours

The Gemara states (*Yoma* 38b), אין אדם נוגע במוכן לחבירו...אפילו כמלא נימא. This means that no one can access that which is assigned to his fellow, not even by a hairsbreadth. If Hashem wants a person to have something, he will have it, and no one in the world can take it from him.

> *If Hashem wants a person to have something, he will have it, and no one in the world can take it from him.*

Similarly, the verse states (*Devarim* 28:2), ובאו עליך הברכות האלה והשיגוך — "These blessings shall come upon you and catch up to you." The Rabbis explain the seemingly peculiar term והשיגוך ("catch up to you") to mean that when Hashem sends a person a certain blessing, the blessing will come even if he has made no attempt to obtain it.

This applies as well to all jobs and positions of authority. The *pasuk* (*I Divrei HaYamim* 29:11) states, לך ה' הממלכה והמתנשא לכל לראש, which the Gemara (*Bava Basra* 91b) explains to mean that all positions of authority, from kingship to the least prestigious positions in the world, are determined by Hashem. And thus David HaMelech thanks Hashem (*Tehillim* 118:2) for making him king. He recalls how אבן מאסו הבונים היתה לראש פינה — he was rejected by everyone, and yet he ascended to the highest position of power. Of all of his father's sons, he was deemed the least worthy of leadership, but he ultimately became the king. How did this happen? David answers in the next *pasuk* (ibid. v. 3), מאת ה' היתה זאת: this happened because this is what Hashem wanted.

A rosh yeshivah was in his final days and his son requested that everyone be informed that he will be assuming the role as head of the yeshivah. The rosh yeshivah responded that there was no need for such an announcement, because he will receive whatever position of authority Hashem wants him to have. He quoted the Gemara (*Yoma* 38a) that states, בשמך יקראוך ובמקומך יושיבוך ומשלך יתנו לך ואין אדם נוגע במוכן לחבירו אפילו כמלא נימא — "They will call you by the name you're supposed to be called, they will have you sit where you're supposed to sit, you will get what you're supposed to have, and no one can touch that which is assigned to his fellow, even a hairsbreadth."

This message also applies to the area of *parnassah*. No one can take away even the smallest amount of money that has been assigned to a person. He will receive precisely what Hashem determined he should have, and not anything less.

A grandson of Rav Yaakov Yagen related that his grandfather learned Torah with a great Kabbalist named Rabbi Sharabi. They began learning at 1 a.m., and they continued until the time for the sunrise prayer service. After prayers, they would continue learning until 11 a.m., at which point Rav Yagen opened his soap and perfume store in the Machane Yehudah market. Rav Yagen was aware that the other merchants in the market opened their stores at 6 a.m., while he did not arrive until 11 a.m. His wife said that it might be a better idea to open up earlier, when people first start coming to the market, so that he would do more business. Rav Yagen decided to consult with Rav Sharabi, who told him, "The same Hashem Who sends you *parnassah* at 6 o'clock will send you your *parnassah* at 11 o'clock. You're not being lazy — you are learning Torah!" Rav Yagen heeded this advice, and continued learning until 11 a.m.

There was a fellow in the market who noticed people already waiting by the door to the Rabbi's shop at 10:30, and saw that it never opened until 11 a.m. He figured that if he opened a store nearby selling the same merchandise, and would open for business earlier in the morning, he could take all the Rabbi's customers and earn a lot of money. And so he rented a space right next to the Rabbi's store. His store was larger and more convenient than the Rabbi's. He sold precisely the same merchandise, and opened early in the morning, assuming that all the customers would make their purchases at his new, fancy shop.

Much to his surprise, on the day of his grand opening, the customers all waited in line at Rav Yagen's store. Not one went into the new store. The shoppers preferred instead to wait until the Rabbi opened his shop. The man sent one of his employees to ask those waiting to explain why they weren't coming to the new store.

The customers all gave the same response. "When we buy from the Rabbi, he says, 'Thank you,' and gives us blessings. And that is worth everything."

We should never worry about other people taking our *parnassah* away from us. We get exactly what's in store for us, and no one can ever take what is coming to us.

68 Being Humble

The *Tomer Devorah* (second chapter) writes that the quality of *anavah*, humility, is כולל את הכל — the key to all good *middos*. Humility is the crown jewel and glory of a Jew. It is a delight being in the presence of a humble person, because, as the *pasuk* (*Mishlei* 3:34) says, לענוים יתן חן — Hashem bestows a special element of grace and charm upon those who are modest.

How does a person acquire this priceless character trait?

The answer is provided by a *pasuk* (*Yirmiyah* 9:22):

אל יתהלל חכם בחכמתו ואל יתהלל הגבור בגבורתו אל יתהלל עשיר בעשרו

The wise man shall not pride himself for his wisdom; the mighty one shall not pride himself for his might; the wealthy man shall not pride himself for his wealth.

A person should not pride himself for his wisdom, because, as the *pasuk* (*Mishlei* 2:6) states, כי ה' יתן חכמה — "For it is Hashem Who grants wisdom." One should not be arrogant on account of his strength, because לך ה' הגבורה — Hashem gives people strength (*I Divrei HaYamim* 29:11). A person should not feel proud about his wealth, because העושר והכבוד מלפניך — it is Hashem Who grants wealth, and ה' מוריש ומעשיר — He makes one poor and one rich. לי הכסף ולי הזהב — all wealth in the world belongs to Hashem, and not to the human "owner."

Everything we have is a gift from Hashem, and the more we acknowledge this fact, the more humble we will be.

Nobody embodied this quality more than David HaMelech, who described himself (*Tehillim* 131:2) as כגמול עלי אמו — like a nursing baby. A baby receives everything from his mother: his food, his clothing, all his needs. An infant cannot even put food in his mouth by himself. David says that despite everything he had — his powerful army, his wisdom, his wealth — he achieved nothing on his own. Like a newborn, he received everything from Hashem. It was Hashem Who granted him the wisdom to become the head of the *Sanhedrin*, and it was Hashem Who made him the king and granted him wealth for the purpose of helping others.

"He achieved nothing on his own. Like a newborn, he received everything from Hashem."

In that same chapter (*Tehillim* 131:1), David says about himself, ה' לא גבה לבי — "Hashem, my heart was not haughty." The Sages explain this as referring to the time when David was anointed king. For 28 years, he was scorned. He was not even allowed to sit at the same table with his brothers because of his questionable lineage. He was sent out with the sheep into the pastures, in the expectation that he would be devoured by a wild animal. And when the prophet Shmuel arrived with Hashem's instruction to anoint one of Yishai's sons as king, the family did not even bother to call David to attend. It was only after Shmuel met all the brothers and said that none of them was chosen as king, that Shmuel asked if there were any other brothers, and David was brought. David had been hounded and rejected for all those years, and now, at this moment, Shmuel took his flask of oil and anointed him king over Israel, proclaiming (*I Shmuel* 5:12), כי זה הוא — "This is the one." We could imagine the thoughts passing through a person's mind in that situation, upon being lifted from the dust, and yet David testifies about himself לא גבה לבי — he felt not even one ounce of pride or arrogance.

David continues and declares, ולא רמו עיני — "my eyes were not lifted high." *Chazal* teach us that this was said in reference to David's triumph over Golyas, the enemy who had been tormenting and intimidating the Jews, and whom David killed singlehandedly. Let us imagine the scene: the people saw their greatest enemy and threat killed, and they burst out in song and dance, praising their new hero, David. And yet, לא רמו עיני — David did not feel any pride or arrogance. He thought to himself, *I did nothing; it was all Hashem.*

The more credit we give Hashem for everything we have and everything we accomplish, the more humble we will become. And the Shelah HaKodesh writes that if a person is humble, then his prayers are accepted, his sins are forgiven, he is privileged to sit in the presence of Hashem, and he is blessed with Torah knowledge and wisdom. Our Sages also teach that those who are humble will be given the privilege of serving as the escorts of *Mashiach*, may he come speedily and in our days.

69 The Money Comes After

Having money is a wonderful blessing. It allows one to learn more Torah, perform a lot of *chesed*, and support many worthy causes and organizations. However, this should never be one's goal in life. The Mishnah (*Avos* 1:15) exhorts, עשה תורתך קבע ומלאכתך עראי — our primary goal should be Torah and mitzvos, and our work should be secondary. We need to invest a normal amount of effort to earn a livelihood, but at the same time we must remember that if Hashem wishes for us to support charitable organizations, He'll find a way to give us the money to do so. The *pasuk* (*Tehillim* 23:6) states, אך טוב וחסד ירדפוני — "Goodness and kindness shall pursue me." If somebody is meant to be wealthy, then the blessing will come.

The *Chovos HaLevavos* (*Shaar HaBitachon*) writes that the obligation of *hishtadlus* (effort) applies only to the work necessary to obtain the basic necessities of life. Beyond that, one's wealth will come or not come regardless of our efforts. Our attitude toward *parnassah* must be one of יגיע כפיך כי תאכל (*Tehillim* 128:2); we work so that we can eat, so we have the basics that we need in life. If this is our approach, then, as the verse continues, אשריך וטוב לך — we will earn blessing both in this world and the Next.

Parnassah is not something we should be thinking or worrying about constantly. The Torah says we need to work for our livelihood, not that we need to worry about our livelihood. Hashem brought us into the world, and it is His job to provide for us. Our job, meanwhile, is to serve Him, and *parnassah* must never get in the way of this job.

> Rabbi Pesach Eliyahu Falk received a phone call from a woman who wanted to have another child (her fifth) but her husband was opposed. He said that he earned just enough money to support four children, and they were thus not in a position to have any more. The husband agreed to listen to the Rabbi, and so they consulted with Rabbi Falk, who quoted the Gemara's comment (*Niddah* 31a), בא זכר בעולם בא ככר בידו — "When a child comes into the world, he comes with a piece of bread in his hand." This means that when Hashem blesses a couple with a child, He provides them with the means of supporting the child. A year and a half later, the woman called back and enthusiastically reported that they had a boy. She further reported the day after the baby was born, they received a phone call from relatives who were elated over the birth, and who were blessed with wealth and wanted to share it with this family. These relatives wired money to their account. Several days after the *bris* she went to the bank and found that $10,000 had been deposited. They saw *yad Hashem* (Hashem's hand) so clearly, the fulfillment of the Gemara's statement that when the child is born, Hashem provides the means of supporting him.

We will not always see Hashem's assistance so clearly, but one way or another, He will ensure to increase a family's *par-*

nassah as it grows. Each child that is born brings more blessing. Our job is to do the רצון ה' (Divine will), and His job is to provide us with our needs.

There are men who are still single because they have not yet secured an adequate source of livelihood to support a family. The Gemara says (*Bava Metzia* 59a), אין ברכה מצויה בתוך ביתו של אדם אלא בשביל אשתו — "Blessing is found in the home only on account of the wife." The source of this statement is the story of Avraham Avinu, who received great wealth in Egypt on account of his wife. If a man of marriageable age does not earn enough to support a family, this might very well be specifically because he does not yet have a family to support. Once he marries and has a family to provide for, Hashem will step in to ensure he is able to do so.

> The Alter of Novaradok was admitting more and more boys to his yeshivah during a period of grave financial hardship. The financial committee objected, telling the Rabbi that the yeshivah could not afford to accommodate so many students. The Rabbi told him that they had it all wrong. They thought that they need to determine how many students they can support, and then accept that number. In truth, he said, it was just the opposite. They bring in as many students as they can, and Hashem will find a way to ensure that they will be adequately supported.

We have to do our job, and then Hashem will do His.

70 Happiness Is Not Dependent on Possessions

The *pasuk* (*Eichah* 3:39) states, מה יתאונן אדם חי — "How can a living person complain?" Rashi explains (*Kiddushin* 80b) that Hashem asks, "How could people complain about situations in their lives after all the *chesed* I perform for them? Is it not enough that I give you life?"

Imagine a group of people who were traveling and became lost in the forest in the dead of winter. It's freezing, snow is falling, and they haven't eaten in days. They all believe that they are about to die. Suddenly, out of nowhere, a wagon drives by, and the driver sees them and immediately stops and distributes whatever food, drinks, and extra clothing he is carrying with him. Could we imagine anyone in the group complaining that they did not receive steak? Or a fur coat? Or that other people received more than they did? Of course not. They are so thrilled to be alive and to receive some sustenance that nothing else matters. The same is true regarding any situation in which we find ourselves. Hashem is keeping us alive. What do we have to complain about?

> *"We all want to be in the city of happiness, but the city of happiness can only be found in the state of mind."*

Everyone has the ability to be happy, no matter what is going on in his or her life. I read a clever line: *We all want to be in the city of happiness, but the city of happiness can only be found in the state of mind.* Possessions don't bring us happiness. A proper attitude does. A story is told of a king who took seriously ill, and the doctors said that the only cure is for him to wear the shirt of the world's happiest person. His servants frantically searched for the happiest person in the world, and finally found him. Unfortunately, they discovered that he didn't own a shirt. It doesn't matter what we have or don't have. We choose whether to be happy or to complain.

One woman I know, who spends virtually all her time doing *chesed*, told me that she vividly remembers the very first *chesed* mission she undertook, and how it changed her entire attitude toward life. She was a young mother and volunteered to visit an elderly woman who was confined to her fourth-floor apartment. As the woman was making her way to the apartment with her two young children, she was complaining almost without stop. The weather was brutally cold, the children weren't cooperating, and so on. She finally reached the apartment, and this 97-year-old woman extended the warmest greeting imaginable. As they spoke, every other pair of words that emerged from this older woman's lips was "*baruch Hashem*." She said, "*Baruch Hashem*, you are so nice that you came to visit me. I'm the luckiest woman in the world. My son calls me every day at 10 o'clock, and never forgets." It turned out that this woman had only one child, and he was adopted. The visitor then complained about the cold weather, and the elderly woman said, "Beautiful! I love cold weather. It makes you feel like you're alive." This woman had no complaints. Everything in her life was great.

Today, forty years later, this woman who visited the elderly woman still has those countless "*baruch Hashem*'s" resonating in her head. No matter what happens, Hashem gives us the ability to be happy.

❖ ❖ ❖

One of the masters of this ideal was the Chafetz Chaim. In 1903, a fire broke out in the Jewish area of his town, Radin, destroying an entire section of the neighborhood, and stopping just before the Chafetz Chaim's home. One year later, in 1904, a fire broke out at the opposite end of the town, burning all the homes until and including the Chafetz Chaim's. At that point the fire was extinguished. Chaim Sinai, one of the young men participating in the effort to put out the blaze, saw the great sage standing with his family outside his home, watching it burn down. Desperately wanting to know what the Chafetz Chaim was saying at those moments, he found someone to take his place and stood near where the Chafetz Chaim was standing. He heard the Rabbi say, "Hashem, You're so kind. There was a decree on our town that all the houses would burn down, but in Your infinite mercy, You carried out this decree in two stages. Last year, you burned down half the town, so they could stay with us on the other side while their homes were rebuilt. Then You burned down the other houses, so we can stay in the other homes while ours are being rebuilt." This was the Chafetz Chaim's reaction upon seeing his house burn down.

We all have this ability. May Hashem give us the strength to access this ability and remain happy at all times, regardless of what is happening around us.

71 Hashem Controls the Temperature

Hashem controls every little detail of nature. Nothing just happens; everything is controlled directly by Him.

In *Shir La'maalos*, we read of the promise given to those who look to Hashem for help (*Tehillim* 121:6): יומם השמש לא יככה וירח בלילה — "The sun will not strike you by day, nor the moon by night." The sun and the moon provide great benefits to the world, but are also potentially harmful. The sun is the source of heat, and the moon controls the tides and thus the winds which in turn bring cooling breezes. The sun's ultraviolet rays can cause melanoma, dehydration, and sunstroke, Heaven forbid, but Hashem promises that if we place our trust in Him, לא יככה — we will be spared the harmful effects of sunlight. The Hebrew word for sun, *shemesh*, relates to the word *shamash*, which means "servant." The sun is just a servant of Hashem, carrying out the will of Hashem. And thus in the future, our Sages teach, the sun will be a source of healing for the righteous and a source of calamity for the wicked. The very same sun will have two opposite effects on people, because the sun is only a servant bound to do what Hashem instructs it to do.

Regarding the cold, Rabbi Pesach Eliyahu Falk cites a remarkable comment made by Rashi concerning the *pasuk* (*Tehillim* 147:17) that says, משליך קרחו כפתים — "He casts His ice 'like פתים.'" Rashi explains the word פתים as referring to the material used to stuff blankets. Hashem sends down cold and icy weather כפתים, in accordance with the amount of material one has with which to keep himself warm. He ensures that the poor man, who cannot afford to purchase warm garments and blankets, will be less affected by the cold than those with adequate protection. The *Chiddushei HaRim* makes a similar comment on the *pasuk* (ibid. 147:16) הנותן שלג כצמר — "He provides snow like wool." He explains that Hashem sends harsh wintry weather in accordance with the amount of wool a person has, and proportional to his ability to withstand and tolerate the cold. Hashem not only controls the temperature in the world, but also controls the effect it has on each and every individual. Each person experiences the hot or cold weather differently. At the same time that Hashem is controlling the universe, He is also adjusting the temperature for billions of people.

"Hashem not only controls the temperature in the world, but also controls the effect it has on each and every individual."

This is something to think about the next time we are standing in the hot sun and see the people around us suffering and sweating from the heat while we feel comfortable. Or when we are out in the cold and experience little or no discomfort while the others are shivering. We should thank Hashem for taking care of us and ensuring that we are able to tolerate the temperature.

> Rav Yechezkel Abramsky related that he was always very sensitive to the cold, and would frequently become sick whenever he was exposed to even moderately cold temperatures. His mother, he recalled, had to send him to school wearing several layers in order to protect him. Later in life, he was sent to Siberia, where the weather can be so frigid that one has to keep moving nonstop to avoid freezing to death. Rav Abramsky turned to Hashem and said, "Hashem, I have no way of protecting myself here. I have to walk in the unbearable cold without clothing and with bare feet. I need Your protection." He would later testify that for the year and a half that he spent in Siberia, he never felt cold.

Everything about nature is controlled by Hashem, including the wind and the rain. The Gemara (*Bava Basra* 16a) teaches us that Hashem not only creates every drop of rain in the clouds, but also creates a separate channel for each drop. If two drops would fall through the same channel, it would damage the crops. And thus when it rains, Hashem is controlling trillions of tiny raindrops to ensure that they provide the maximum benefit to agriculture. The extent of His control over the world is simply mind boggling. We need to know that if we look to Him for help, then (ibid. 121:6) יומם השמש לא יככה, He will protect us from all harm posed by nature.

72 Who Is Feeding All the Animals?

The *pasuk* says (*Tehillim* 147:9), נותן לבהמה לחמה — "[Hashem] gives animals their food." The Gemara (*Shabbos* 107b) comments that Hashem feeds all the animals in the world, מקרני ראמים ועד ביצי כינים — from the largest, most majestic creatures, to the tiniest insects. The verse (in *Avodah Zarah* 3b) describes how Hashem hunts for the elderly lion and satiates the appetite of the young cubs, and also provides food for the ravens. The Gemara explains that when a raven is born, its parents abandon the young bird, because it has different coloring. Hashem makes a point of feeding and supporting the young ravens that have no one else to care for them. Even though they have been abandoned, they survive because Hashem takes care of them.

A study was once done at a zoo and it was determined that it costs $5,000 a month — $60,000 a year — to feed and take care of just one elephant in the zoo. Who is paying to care for all the countless elephants running wild in the jungles of Africa? Only Hashem.

Why are there so many *pesukim* describing how Hashem feeds and cares for animals? What difference does it make to us?

The Gemara (*Kiddushin* 82b) explains that if Hashem is so concerned about caring for the animals, who are in this world to serve us, then certainly He is concerned about caring for us, who are here to serve Him. A person should never worry about money. Our Father has all the money in the world, and He can easily give it to us if He deems it to our benefit.

Imagine you are standing over an ant farm, watching the flurry of activity as the ants feverishly go about their work gathering food. You notice that some ants are carrying large amounts of food, while others have next to nothing, and you feel very bad for the poor ants that do not have enough food. What would it take for you to help them? You could just throw them some of your leftover crumbs from lunch, and they will then be the "wealthiest" ants around. That's how easy it is for Hashem to grant us wealth. And the more we look to Hashem for our livelihood, the more He will give us. The *pasuk* (*Yirmiyah* 17:7) states, ברוך הגבר אשר יבטח בה' והיה ה' מבטחו; the more we rely on Hashem, the more He will come through for us. It often happens that we find ourselves in a difficult situation that we do not know how to solve. But when we look back in retrospect, we realize that in truth it was not all that difficult. This happens because Hashem brought us through the hardship and took care of us. This should be our attitude toward *parnassah*, as well. Making a living should be the least of our concerns. Hashem can take care of that for us in less than a second.

> *"The more we rely on Hashem, the more He will come through for us."*

Rabbi Ephraim Wachsman gave an analogy of a struggling businessman who was working very hard to get his business on its feet, and never allowed himself a vacation, as he was worried about the company. One day, his uncle called from Eretz Yisrael and said that the doctors had given him only a few more days to live. As the nephew was his only relative, he asked that he come immediately so he can take care of the funeral arrangements. The man obviously felt very bad about his uncle, and thus despite his anxiety about the struggling business, he left for Eretz Yisrael. Before he left, he gave his main employee strict instructions: "Don't make any decisions on your own. I want you to call me for everything."

The man arrived in Eretz Yisrael and proceeded directly to the hospital to see his uncle. The uncle emotionally thanked him for coming, and said, "I need to tell you something. You don't know this, but I am a billionaire. And I am leaving everything to you."

At that moment, the nephew received a call from his employee, who was very distraught. He received an order for 40 boxes, but they only had 38, and the company said that if they do not receive 40 they will place their order elsewhere.

"Who cares?" the man said. "I'm a billionaire. What difference does it make?"

We should always walk around knowing that whenever we need something, we have to simply go to our Father, and He will take care of it for us. ה' צלך על יד ימינך (*Tehillim* 121:5) — the more we turn to Him for help, the more assistance He will provide for us.

73 Feeling Satisfied

The Torah commands (*Devarim* 18:13), תמים תהיה עם ה' אלקיך, which the Maharal explains to mean that one must feel "whole" and complete, that he lacks nothing, that Hashem has given him everything he needs. Human nature is to feel perpetually dissatisfied, to always want more. As the Sages taught (*Koheles Rabbah* 1:32), ...יש לו מנה רוצה מאתיים — "A person who has one hundred wants two hundred, and a person who has two hundred wants four hundred."

A Rabbi was close with a very wealthy man. The Rabbi noticed that the man worked tirelessly, never allowing himself a break, to the point where he barely had time for anything besides his work. Finally, one day the Rabbi asked the man, "Tell me, how much money do you need to be able to take a break and feel content with what you have?"

The man thought for a few moments and then said, "$100 million."

"And how much do you have now?" the Rabbi asked.

"$50 million."

Exactly as *Chazal* said — a person always feels he needs twice as much as he already has.

This is human nature, but we have the ability to overcome it, to be תמים, to recognize that we already have enough and do not need anymore, and that we will *b'ezras Hashem* always have what we need. Instead of always worrying about the future, we can enjoy the present, feeling content with what we have.

> A story is told of a businessman who was vacationing on an island and saw the fishermen fishing every day. There was one fisherman who headed for home early in the day, several hours before the others, and so the businessman approached him to ask why he stopped working so early.
>
> "When I catch enough fish to support my family," the man explained, "I go for a stroll with the senora along the beach, and then I go home to play with my children, and then we enjoy a family barbeque together."
>
> "But I see you are a very skilled fisherman," the vacationing businessman said, "and if you continued for another few hours every day, you could catch twice as many fish."
>
> "Yes," the fisherman acknowledged, "but what would I do then?"
>
> "You could sell the fish and make extra money."
>
> "What would I do then?"
>
> "You could use the extra money to buy a small boat and sail into the ocean, where you can catch even more fish."
>
> "O.K., but what would I do then?"
>
> "You could sell all that fish and have enough money to buy a large ship. I will be your partner, and we can go deep into the ocean and catch very large fish and sell them for a lot of money."
>
> "And then what?"
>
> "You could open stores all over the island selling your fish."
>
> "And then what?"

"Eventually, you'll catch so many fish that you could ship them overseas and become very wealthy."

"And what would I do then, when I'm very wealthy?"

"You'd be able to retire, so every day you can take nice strolls with your wife along the beach, go home early to play with your children, and enjoy family barbeques."

Everything that you are looking for you might already have.

"Everything that you are looking for you might already have."

Let us recognize all the blessings that Hashem has already bestowed upon us so we can take advantage of them now, feeling happy and content, and living life to its very fullest without always worrying about what tomorrow will bring.

74

You Never Lose By Doing What Is Right

The *pasuk* says (*Koheles* 8:5), שומר מצוה לא ידע דבר רע, when a person performs a mitzvah, no harm will ever result from it. The Gemara (*Shabbos* 63a) cites this *pasuk* and comments that a mitzvah actually serves as a shield protecting a person and negating harsh decrees. Even if it appears that one lost something as a result of a mitzvah he performed, he must realize that this is not the case. He needs just to wait and see how he will ultimately gain from the mitzvah.

A beautiful example of this principle is Rachel Imeinu. When she was to marry Yaakov, she gave Leah the signs that she had arranged with Yaakov, anticipating that Lavan would bring Leah to Yaakov instead of her. They had planned that Yaakov would question the bride to verify that it was Rachel, and Rachel thus knew that Leah would be embarrassed. In order to spare her sister shame, Rachel courageously gave her the signs, effectively sacrificing her marriage for her sister, and running the risk of having to marry Esav. Rachel said to herself, *I can't worry about myself, I need to save my sister from embarrassment.* It seemed at that point that she had sacrificed everything for the sake of doing this mitzvah. But in truth, she did not sacrifice anything. Rachel also married Yaakov. However, she was barren for many years, until finally, as the *pasuk* (*Bereishis* 30:24) says, ויזכור אלקים את רחל — "Hashem remembered Rachel" and blessed her with a child. Rashi explains this *pasuk* to mean that Hashem remembered the signs that Rachel gave to her sister years earlier to save her from embarrassment. He remembered the great compassion and selflessness she exhibited, and in that merit He granted her a child. At the time it seemed she forfeited her entire future by doing this heroic deed, but it was precisely that act that enabled her to have children.

You will never lose by doing the right thing; Hashem is always watching and is sure to repay you.

> *"You will never lose by doing the right thing; Hashem is sure to repay you."*

A woman recently told me that her husband had accepted an offer for their daughter from a *shadchan*, and a meeting was scheduled. The father was unaware, however, that his daughter was strongly opposed to marrying somebody with the same name as her father, and this boy happened to have her father's name. She said she did not want to meet him, but her father explained to her that although he had made a mistake that he regretted, canceling the meeting would hurt the feelings of both the boy and his family. The girl agreed that she did not want to hurt anybody's feelings, and that she wanted to honor her father's wishes, so she consented.

Later that same day, a different *shadchan* called with another suggestion, an outstanding young man who was a perfect match for his daughter. The father accepted the offer, but explained the situation and said that the date would have to be scheduled later in the week. The girl went on a date with the first boy, and as it so happened, the family of the second boy saw her. Enraged, they contacted the *shadchan* and called off the proposed meeting. They were furious that the girl was out with another boy when she was being set up with their son. The *shadchan* tried explaining the circumstances to them, emphasizing that she went out only to avoid hurting someone's feelings. But the family did not accept the explanation, and firmly insisted that their son would not be dating that girl.

The girl heard what had happened, and was devastated. She was pained by the fact that her decision to be nice and to do the right thing caused her to lose an excellent *shidduch*. Her parents reassured her by citing the aforementioned *pasuk* in *Koheles*, שומר מצוה לא ידע דבר רע. "Hashem saw what you did," they said, "and you will only gain from the mitzvah. Don't worry."

Over the next several months, she met several boys, but nothing worked. Finally, they received a phone call from a *shadchan* who told them about an extraordinary boy who had just entered *shidduchim*. People were waiting in line to go out with him, and this *shadchan* had presented him with a long list of girls. He told the *shadchan* that the most important quality for him was compassion; he needed a girl who was exceptionally compassionate and sensitive. The *shadchan* immediately thought of this girl, and told him the story of how she decided to go out with somebody in order not to hurt his or his family's feelings. The boy was very impressed, and decided that she was the one.

Sure enough, they met, got married, and couldn't be happier. At first it appeared that the mitzvah caused her to lose a great opportunity, but in the end it turned out that this was precisely what brought her to the *chuppah*.

שומר מצוה לא ידע דבר רע. Hashem guarantees us that even when it looks like we are losing out by performing a mitzvah, eventually we will see how we have gained.

75 Fear No Man

The *Chovos HaLevavos (Shaar HaBitachon*) writes that everything that happens in life is caused directly by Hashem, and no one can give a person anything or take anything away from him unless it had been decreed by Hashem. This point is also made by the *Sefer HaChinuch* (241), who adds that for this reason, there is no sense in one taking revenge against those who have wronged him, as they are but messengers of Hashem.

> *No one can give a person anything or take anything away from him unless it had been decreed by Hashem.*

Likewise, the *Beis HaLevi* comments that if Hashem wants a person to have something, then no one can give it to him earlier than the time Hashem decided he should have it, or delay his receiving it by even one moment. The *Beis HaLevi* cites in this context the *pasuk* (*Iyov* 23:13), והוא באחד ומי ישיבנו, which means that Hashem is the only One in charge, and no one can oppose Him or prevent His decrees from being carried out.

Once we internalize this concept, we will never experience fear of any person. The *pasuk* (*Mishlei* 29:25) says, חרדת אדם יתן מוקש. Rabbeinu Bachya (*Bamidbar* 14:9) explains this to mean that חרדת אדם — if a person fears another human being, then יתן מוקש — this itself will be his downfall; he will bring upon himself that which he fears. The verse continues, ובוטח בה' ישגב, which Rabbeinu Yonah explains to mean that even if it was decreed that a person would suffer harm, he will be saved in the merit of not being afraid of the person who threatens him. There is no reason to fear any human being. We should fear Hashem, and no one else.

> It is told that when the Lubavitcher Rebbe was arrested, and the secret police were bringing him to prison, one of the policemen held a gun to him. The Rabbi said to him, "That little toy can only frighten a person who has one world and many gods. I have One Hashem and two worlds. Put it away, you don't scare me."

ה' לי לא אירא מה יעשה לי אדם — "Hashem is with me, I have no fear; how can man affect me?" *(Tehillim* 118:6). A person who does not fear other people, and fears only Hashem, standing up for his principles and for what he believes in without surrendering to intimidation, can become a much greater person.

> Rav Ephraim Wachsman relates an episode involving Rav Yitzchak Elchanan Spektor that took place the day he assumed his first rabbinical post in a small town. The very first day, a poor man in the community approached him and said he had been cheated by one of the wealthiest and most prominent members of the community. The Rabbi immediately sent someone to bring the wealthy man for a *din Torah* (trial). The man sent a message back to the Rabbi, "You don't summon the head of the community to court. Remember, this is your first day on the job."
>
> The Rabbi sent for him again, and the man responded, "Who do you think you are? I've hired and fired many like you. Be careful what you do."
>
> The Rabbi sent for the man a third time, with a warning that if he did not come for a *din Torah* he would place him in *cherem* (excommunication).
>
> Shortly thereafter, the man arrived in the Rabbi's office together with the other heads of the community, carrying a tray of cake and whiskey to celebrate the new Rabbi's appointment.
>
> "Congratulations," they said. "We were testing you to see if you were afraid of us or of Hashem."

❖ ❖ ❖

The Rebbe of Nickolsberg kept a stick in the office in which he studied Torah. Somebody once asked him what the stick was for, and he explained, "This is my walking stick. If you ever threaten to fire me, I will take my stick and walk out of here."

We should only have one fear in life: the fear of Hashem. Doing Hashem's will should be the only thing that matters.

76 To Whom Do You Turn for Help?

When a person faces any sort of problem or needs something, his first reaction should be to turn to Hashem for help. The Gemara (*Niddah* 70b) teaches, מה יעשה אדם ויתעשר? יבקש רחמים ממי שהעושר שלו — "What should a person do if he wishes to become rich? He should request mercy from He Who possesses all the wealth." As the *pasuk* (*Chaggai* 2:8) says, לי הכסף ולי הזהב נאם ה' — "Silver and gold are Mine, says Hashem."

Similarly it says (*Tehillim* 146:3), אל תבטחו בנדיבים בבן אדם שאין לו תשועה — "Do not trust in the generous ones, in a human being who cannot even save himself." And the *pasuk* (*Yeshayah* 2:24) teaches, חדלו לכם מן האדם אשר נשמה באפו כי במה נחשב הוא — "Hold yourselves back from the human being ...for of what importance is he?" If we want results, we should trust in Hashem.

> *"If we want results, we should trust in Hashem."*

Rabbi Pesach Eliyahu Falk told of an orphan boy who was studying in a yeshivah in Eretz Yisrael.

All his friends were getting married, but without parents, he did not have the funds he needed to enter into *shidduchim*. His friend assured him that he and others would raise money on his behalf, and sure enough, he was introduced to a fine girl, also an orphan, and they wanted to marry. Unfortunately, they did not have money for a wedding or for an apartment. Once again, his friend reassured him, committing to raise money for them to marry. However, hard as he and his friends tried, they could not raise funds. Nothing worked. They did more than the ordinary amount of *hishtadlus* (effort), but to no avail.

Finally, the orphan said to his friend, "Enough. Don't try anymore. I am going straight to Hashem. I don't want help from anyone else."

He went to the Kosel that Friday morning, and turned to Hashem and said, "Hashem, she and I are both orphans. You are our Father. Please help us get married and start a family." He took out a *Tehillim* and started reading from the beginning. He completed the entire *sefer*, and then he turned to Hashem to wait for His salvation, but nothing happened. "Hashem," he said, "I am not turning to any more human beings. I am turning only to You." And he began reciting *Tehillim* again.

A short while later, he felt a tap on his shoulder, and he turned around.

"You look distressed," a stranger said. "Is there any way I can help you?"

"No, thank you," the young man said. "I am talking to Hashem. He will help me."

For the third time, he looked up and spoke to Hashem. "Please help me," he said. "We are orphans and we want to get married, and I do not want to leave here until I see Your salvation."

Just then, he felt yet another tap on the shoulder. It was the same stranger.

"Your salvation is here," the man said. "I will take care of everything you need. I just arrived in Eretz

Yisrael this morning. I had a major court case relating to taxes, and if I had lost, I would have been left in poverty. I told Hashem that if I win the case, I will find an orphan boy and orphan girl who need help to get married, and pay for their wedding and continue caring for them after their wedding. I won the case, and I came here looking for people I can help. I heard you talking to Hashem, and you're the person I'm looking for."

ישועת ה' כהרף עין — "Hashem's salvation can arrive in an instant" (*Selichos R' Tzadok, Sifsei Raninus*). Hashem arranged the entire court case in order to provide *parnassah* for this young couple.

ברוך הגבר אשר יבטח בה' (*Yirmiyah* 17:7) — "Blessed is the person who places his trust in Hashem," the only One Who is capable of providing all our needs.

77 Hashem Can Handle the Competition

The *pasuk* says, ה' מוריש ומעשיר — "Hashem makes people destitute and makes people wealthy." Of course, we all recognize that our financial status is in Hashem's hands. However, the Chozeh of Lublin commented that this *pasuk* teaches us an additional lesson: that Hashem can make a destitute beggar rich in an instant, and can also make a wealthy tycoon impoverished in an instant.

I recently delivered a *shiur* on this subject, and afterward a wealthy businessman who had attended the class approached to tell me how he had experienced this firsthand. He related that he made his first major profit in a completely unexpected manner, purchasing a large quantity of a certain type of food, intending to sell it at cost price, which was then $1 a pound. Suddenly, before he got a chance to resell the product, the market price rose dramatically, to $5 a pound. Just like that, in an instant, Hashem made him a wealthy man.

The man continued to describe how he has seen Hashem's assistance in his business career. He spent over fifty years building a large corporation, and a couple of years ago it nearly came crashing down. Somebody reported to the FDA (Food and Drug Administration) a suspicion of a certain problem with the food, and an investigation was conducted. The FDA told him he had to recall the food and threatened to shut down the business. The man thought to himself, *Look what Hashem can do; in an instant, He can knock down this entire empire that I have built over the last fifty years!* He prayed to Hashem for help, and, sure enough, it was discovered that the accusations were unfounded. In the interim the price had doubled, and so instead of losing a fortune, he gained an enormous profit as a result of this incident.

Another example of Hashem's clear involvement occurred ten years ago, he told, when a competitor tried to put him out of business. The man would purchase the product at cost price, which was approximately $3 a pound, and then sell it for a profit. His competitor purchased numerous farms where this product was grown, and decided he would sell it to stores for just $2.50 a pound, which was cost price or even slightly below cost price. He figured it was worth breaking even or taking a small loss in order to take over the market and eventually raise the price and make a profit. Before the season, this competitor presold millions of pounds of this product at his low price, essentially taking away all of this businessman's customers. The businessman was stuck with millions of pounds of the same product, which he had already purchased for $3 a pound, without anyone buying it. But he reminded himself of the *pasuk* (*Tehillim* 55:23), השלך על ה' יהבך והוא יכלכלך — "Cast your burden onto Hashem, and He will support you." That year a severe drought struck the West Coast, where the competitor's farms were located, and the farms produced only half the anticipated volume. Desperate to fill his orders, the competitor had no choice but to purchase the product from this man. And because of the shortage, the market price rose to $5 a pound. The competitor had set out to run him out of business, but in the end he became his most profitable customer. Amazingly enough, the competitor tried this scheme again two years later, with the exact same outcome. A drought caused low production, and the competitor was forced to buy the product from the corporation he was trying to ruin.

The man told me that he saw the *yad Hashem* — hand of Hashem. There was nothing he could have done himself to stop his competitor from ruining his business. This could be done only by Hashem, Who controls everything in the world, including the weather, and He protected him.

"There was nothing he could have done himself to stop his competitor from ruining his business."

We must always remember that Hashem is the only One in charge, and the only One Who can help us.

78

It's All From Hashem

A person has to believe that Hashem is watching over him and actively involved in everything that happens in his life. The *pasuk* (*Iyov* 34:21) states, כי עיניו על דרכי איש וכל צעדיו יראה — "For His eyes are upon the ways of man, and He sees all his steps." Hashem not only sees what happens, but is directly and actively involved. Another verse (ibid. 31:4) teaches, וכל צעדי יספור — "He counts all my steps." Everything that occurs is precisely calculated. We do not take a single extra step beyond that which we are supposed to take.

Remarkably, Hashem masks His involvement behind the veil of nature, making it appear as though events occur randomly and haphazardly. He does this in order to allow us the free will to decide whether we will look for His involvement in our lives, or just attribute everything to happenstance. Interestingly enough, the Hebrew word for coincidence, מקרה, has the same letters as רק מה' — "solely from Hashem." Those who see through the mask of nature are privileged to see Hashem's active involvement in their lives on a daily basis.

> A woman sent me an email regarding the birth of her oldest daughter twenty years ago. She called the doctor to inform him that she was in labor, and the doctor offered to pick up her and her husband and bring them to the hospital — something he had never offered to do for any other patient. The doctor intended to stop at a gas station on the way, but due to some unexplainable impulse he went directly to their house. As the woman exited the front door, she felt ready to deliver the baby. *Baruch Hashem*, the doctor was right there and delivered the baby, and everything went smoothly.

The doctor repeatedly said, "Look at the *hashgachah*, look at the *hashgachah*!" He noted that he was not even planning on being home that evening, but his plans changed unexpectedly. Once he delivered the baby, it was perfectly clear why his plans changed.

> *It is so comforting to know that Hashem is constantly looking out for our well-being.*

It is so comforting to know that Hashem is constantly looking out for our well-being, and that nothing can happen to us unless Hashem wanted it to happen.

One Thursday, at around 11:40 a.m., I was in shul preparing for a class I would be delivering, when I realized that I had forgotten to bring a *sefer* I needed. I rarely call my wife at that hour, but that day I called her cell phone to ask if she would be able to read the passage I needed from that *sefer.* She was running an errand and had planned to then go to the park with the children, but since she was not too far from home, she would first stop at the house to get me the information. Ten minutes later, she called from home. As she began speaking, I heard a lot of pent-up tension in her voice, and asked what was going on. She explained that she had gone home after completing the errand. When she walked in, she saw a burglar in the dining room. He was wearing black gloves and a hat, and held a bag with our *menorah* in it. As soon as my wife saw him, he became frightened and ran out the side door. Nothing was taken, and *baruch Hashem* no one was hurt.

At first there did not seem to be any important reason for why I had forgotten my book at home that day. But in truth, Hashem was protecting us. There are no accidents, and there are no coincidences. Everything in life is רק מה', only from Hashem.

79 Stick to Your Route

The *sefer Ki Atah Imadi* relates the story of a man who always wanted to be a bus driver. He took lessons, obtained a license, and finally secured his first job. The man excitedly arrived on the first morning to receive his bus route, and was dismayed to discover that he had been given the quietest route. Most of the stops had only one or two passengers, and he found the experience boring and uneventful. He had fantasized about driving a full bus, with lots of commotion, and having to tell the passengers to move to the back to make room. At the end of the day, he drove the bus back to the station, feeling depressed, and brought into the office the small sum of money he made for the company by driving this route.

The next day, he saw another bus filled to capacity, and felt jealous. He decided he would take a different route that would collect many more passengers and bring in much more money for the company. He went off onto his own route, and he thoroughly enjoyed himself; it was everything he had dreamed of. Crowds of passengers waited by the bus stops, and he had to tell them not to push. Throngs of people boarded and got off the bus, and he collected an enormous amount of money for the company. At the end of the day, he gleefully marched into the office, and placed the huge bag of money on the table.

The next day, the owner of the company called the new driver into his office.

"We've been driving that route for over twenty

years," the owner said, "and we never even came close to making this kind of money. How did you earn so much doing that route?"

The man explained that he decided he could do more for the company by driving a busier route, and that's how he earned all that money.

"You did what?!" the owner bellowed. "You ruined the entire system. We don't need more customers on your route. Your job is to drive the route we give you. Every driver gets paid for doing his job, regardless of how many passengers he picks up. If you want to succeed here, just do your job properly."

The same is true in life. Each person comes into this world with a certain job to do, just like every bus driver in the company is given a route to drive. And the only way to live a successful life is by doing one's assigned job properly. Sometimes, other people's jobs appear more glamorous and appealing. A schoolteacher, for example, might look at the principal and think, *Wow, he is impacting hundreds of lives, while I just have my one class of fifteen students. What is all my hard work worth compared to his?* This perspective is fundamentally mistaken. Hashem assigned a different task to each person. Every individual has his own potential, and is given a task based upon that potential. If we do our task properly to the very best of our ability, then we will be paid our full "salary," which is the same as that of everyone else. There could be a boy who grew up in Bnei Brak and learns Torah fifteen hours a day, and another boy who grew up in Oklahoma and learns Torah two hours a day. Both are reaching their maximum potential, and both will receive their full reward in the Next World.

It often happens that when people are going through stress-laden periods in their lives, such as difficulty earning a living, problems with *shalom bayis* or childrearing issues, they see other people who enjoy financial security and are raising beautiful families, and they feel jealous. They might think to themselves, *If only I wouldn't have these problems I'd have so much more peace of mind and I'd be able to serve Hashem so much better. I'd be able to concentrate more fully on my prayers and learning, and everything would be so much better.* One must realize that when we face a difficult situation, our job at that moment is to deal with the situation to the best of our ability. Our job is not to be like somebody else, but to work with the circumstances in which Hashem placed us. Commenting on the *pasuk* (*Shemos* 3:5), המקום אשר אתה עומד עליו אדמת קודש הוא — "The place where you are standing is sacred ground," the Chafetz Chaim (*Al HaTorah* there) said that the place where Hashem puts a person is "sacred ground," his especially assigned mission given to him by Hashem. We must serve Hashem to the best of our ability in every situation in which He has placed us, recognizing that each situation is אדמת קודש, a sacred opportunity.

> *"The place where Hashem puts a person is "sacred ground."*"

Our Sages famously teach (Mishnah *Menachos* 11:11), אחד המרבה ואחד הממעיט; what matters is not quantity, but rather our effort. Our job is to stick to the "route" assigned to us, and to recognize that life is a גלגל החוזר, *a revolving wheel.* Sometimes Hashem will want a person to serve Him without a secure livelihood, and then later He will want him to serve Him with a comfortable livelihood. We must not waste the opportunity given to us right now. In the situation in which we find ourselves at any given moment, we are bidden to serve Hashem to the best of our ability, without looking around enviously at others. And if we do this, and make the most of every situation, then we will have lived life to its very fullest.

80 Life Is Like a Play

Rabbi Ephraim Wachsman once said, "Life is like a play."

Imagine a show where the two main characters are a very wealthy man and a very poor man. The wealthy man is played by a new actor who is still learning the profession, and who is earning just a few thousand dollars to perform. The poor man, however, is being played by a world-renowned actor who is receiving millions of dollars for the role. People in the audience might look at the wealthy character and think to themselves, *Wow, this fellow has everything he can ever want,* while feeling sorry for the pauper who lives such a difficult life and suffers abject poverty. Of course, nothing is further from the truth; the truth is that the person playing the poor man is a millionaire, and he earns his millions by playing the role assigned to him.

In life, it does not matter what a person's role is. What's important is that he plays the role correctly, and if he does, then he will be a millionaire.

> *"Play your part correctly and you will be a millionaire."*

How does one play the role of a poor man, if this is the role assigned to him by Hashem? One plays this role by recognizing that Hashem knows what is best for him at that moment, and accepting it lovingly. One plays this role by crying out to Hashem when reciting *barech aleinu* in the *Amidah* prayer, begging for a better livelihood. One plays this role by responding when he is approached with a request for *tzedakah,* "I would love to help you more, but this is all I can afford to give you right now."

How does one play the role of a wealthy man, if this is the role assigned to him by Hashem? One plays this role by recognizing that all his blessings have been bestowed upon him by Hashem, and are not the product of his smart business strategies. One plays this role by feeling genuine gratitude to Hashem for all he has been given, and having this in mind as he recites *Modim* in the *Amidah*. One plays this role by responding generously when he is approached with a request for *tzedakah*.

It doesn't matter what role we are given; if we play it properly, we will be rewarded.

Imagine a man sitting with his family at the Shabbos table and sadly observing the children fighting and shouting at each other incessantly. He feels very depressed, thinking to himself, *I always imagined a Shabbos table where the children sit happily, share words of Torah, sing beautiful songs, and enjoy each other's company. I don't understand, Hashem. All I want is a nice Shabbos meal, some oneg Shabbos. Is that too much to ask?* A person in this situation must understand that his job is to play the role he is given at that moment: the role of a father with unruly children at a Shabbos table. This means he has to be calm, think of ways to engage all those at the table, and maintain a pleasant atmosphere. If he fills this role, then he is a millionaire.

> A man once went to his Rabbi complaining about his experience the previous night trying to light the Chanukah *menorah*. He said that he could not even complete the *berachah* without having to break up a fight among his children. The man contrasted that experience with his beautiful memories of lighting the *menorah* in the yeshivah with such peace and serenity, concentrating intently on every word of the *berachos*. Now as an adult, he said, he has an even deeper understanding of the mitzvah and could recite the *berachos* with even greater concentration and feeling, but this is impossible because of his children.
>
> The Rabbi replied, "Who said that Hashem gave you more wisdom and understanding for the purpose of having better *kavannah* [concentration] as you recite the *berachos*? Maybe He gave you more wisdom and understanding so that you can figure out how to light the Chanukah *menorah* with bickering children? If you do that, then you've done exactly what you were supposed to do."

A woman might be trying to recite the *Amidah* prayer with her toddler pulling at her leg and nagging, and she'll be thinking to herself, *If I had more peace and quiet, I'd be able to pray with so much more concentration and feeling!* She must know that her job in life at that moment is to pray the best *Amidah* she can under the circumstances.

How does a person know which role he has been assigned? A person's job is determined by the circumstances he finds himself in at that moment. Regardless of the situation, we should not complain, and should instead accept the role assigned to us. If we fill the role happily and to the best of our ability, then our lives are successful and exactly what they are supposed to be.

81 The Best Insurance Policy

The *pasuk* (*Yirmiyah* 17:7) says, ברוך הגבר אשר יבטח בה' והיה ה' מבטחו — "Fortunate is the man who trusts in Hashem, and Hashem will be his guarantor." This means that Hashem will be a person's Guarantor because he places his trust in Him.

Rabbi Pesach Eliyahu Falk, citing the Baal Shem Tov, compared trust in Hashem to an insurance policy. A person can have a policy granting coverage for $1000, $10,000 or $100,000, depending on how much a person is willing to pay. The larger the policy, the more the person is covered. Similarly, the insurance we receive from Hashem depends upon the amount of trust we place in Him. The above-cited *pasuk* thus says that one who places abundant trust in Hashem is fortunate, because he receives the ultimate "coverage."

> *"The insurance we receive from Hashem depends upon the amount of trust we place in Him."*

A wealthy businessman who works in the clothing industry recently told me that he had been licensed to sell clothing with Disney characters, until one day he received a call from Disney informing him that they were taking away his license because they had given it to too many companies. The man was devastated. These products were the staple of his business, and losing the license would deal him a crippling blow. He actually had a meeting scheduled that week with Wal-Mart to discuss the sale of his clothes, and now he had nothing to show them. He was thinking of canceling the meeting, but then decided that he would place his trust in Hashem. He called his Rabbi to receive some encouragement, and his Rabbi told him, "Your *parnassah* comes not from Disney, but from Hashem. Strengthen your trust in Hashem, and everything will be fine." The man was very encouraged, and he made his way to the meeting with the buyer from Wal-Mart relying solely on Hashem's help.

Along the way, he happened "by chance" to meet his brother-in-law, something that had never happened before. His brother-in-law was in the shoe business, and the man told him of his predicament and how he was on the way to meet with Wal-Mart. His brother-in-law told him that he was also trying to strike a deal with Wal-Mart, and he had received a license from Dr. Seuss to sell sneakers with the Cat in the Hat. The brother-in-law suggested that he try to sell clothing with the Cat in the Hat designs, but the man told him that he did not even have a license yet, and had nothing to show them. His brother-in-law said that all of the posters he had with him had pictures of sneakers, but he did have a piece of scrap paper with a picture of the Cat in the Hat, and offered to give it to the man so he could show it to the Wal-Mart representative.

And so the man came into the meeting with nothing but this scrap paper with a picture of the Cat in the Hat. The buyer at the meeting asked him about Disney, and he explained that he no longer possessed a license to sell Disney clothes, but he then took out the picture of the Cat in the Hat. He explained that American kids these days do a lot of reading, and Dr. Seuss' books are wildly popular. And since Wal-Mart was "America's store" it would really be great for them to carry this. The buyer was very impressed, and he called in other Wal-Mart executives to look at this scrap of paper which the man just happened to pick up on his way to the meeting. Everybody loved the idea, and they extended the largest offer this man had ever received. Immediately after the meeting he called Dr. Seuss and obtained the license. Wal-Mart loved the idea so much that they hired someone to stand by the entrance of each of its 2500 stores wearing the hat from the Cat in the Hat.

This man placed his full trust in Hashem, and Hashem came through. This is a clear example of the *pasuk*, ברוך הגבר אשר יבטח בה' והיה ה' מבטחו.

82

Give Your Children the Gift of Emunah

The Steipler Gaon said that many people would come to him to discuss their problems, and he observed that regardless of whether the problem was major or minor, it always fully occupied the person's heart. Everyone encounters many different challenges and tests in life, some big and some small, and the more *emunah* a person has, the easier it is to deal with these hardships.

> *"We must instill within our children the belief and feeling that Hashem is watching over us at all times."*

It is especially important to teach *emunah* to children. Educators have reported that children who are taught *emunah* generally are at a much lower risk, as they feel secure, they know they are never alone, and they know that Hashem is always with them. We must instill within our children the belief and feeling that Hashem is watching over us at all times, that He loves us, and that everything that happens to us is for our ultimate benefit, even if we cannot understand how. Once they are armed with this belief, they are able to accept adverse situations that they do not understand.

The Gemara (*Berachos* 7a) asks the well-known question of why we sometimes see צדיק ורע לו — righteous people who suffer — and רשע וטוב לו — wicked people who enjoy good fortune. The Gemara answers that if we see a *tzaddik* who suffers, it must be that he is a צדיק בן רשע, meaning, that his father was a sinner. Conversely, if we see a *rasha* who enjoys good fortune, he is a רשע בן צדיק — his father was righteous.

The Chasam Sofer (ibid.) asks: Why is this a question at all? How can there be a situation of a *tzaddik* experiencing misfortune? A *tzaddik* understands that everything he experiences in life is what Hashem wants for him and thus must be the very best thing for him. How can the Gemara speak of a situation of צדיק ורע לו? The Chasam Sofer answers that this was precisely the Gemara's question. The Gemara was asking: How can there be a righteous person who feels that רע לו, that bad things are happening to him? And the Gemara answers that if a *tzaddik* feels this way, it must be because he is a צדיק בן רשע, meaning, his father failed to properly train him in *emunah*. Likewise, if we see a רשע וטוב לו, a wicked person who feels happy and content with whatever he has in life, it must be because he is a רשע בן צדיק, because his father trained him to have *emunah*.

The best gift we can give our children is *emunah*, because once a person grows up with faith, he will always experience טוב לו, he will always view his situation in life as the best possible thing for him.

Later (*Berachos* 60a), the Gemara tells of Hillel the Elder who was returning to his town when he heard the sound of people screaming in horror. Hillel said to himself, מובטח אני שאין זה מתוך ביתי — *"I am confident that this is not coming from my house."* The obvious question arises: How could Hillel be so sure that his household was not the household facing a crisis? The *Ya'aros Devash* (*Derush* 7) explains that Hillel had trained his family to accept everything Hashem does with love, and to recognize that He always does what is best for them. He thus knew that his family members would not be screaming if a misfortune befell them. The screams could not be coming from his home, because his family was trained not to shout and cry when things went wrong.

We must constantly tell our children that everything is from Hashem, Hashem loves them, and everything Hashem does is for the best. These are the skills that will enable them to live a happy and peaceful life.

83 Hope Brings Salvation

The Gemara comments (*Shabbos* 31a) that one of the questions each person will be asked in heaven after 120 years is, "*Tzipisa li'shuah*?" — "Did you anticipate salvation?" The simple meaning of this remark is that we will be asked whether we anticipated and longed for the arrival of Mashiach to rescue the Jewish people from our prolonged exile. However, the *Beis HaLevi* (*Al HaTorah* — end) explains that this question also refers to our anticipating salvation from our personal problems. As long as a person has hope, anything is possible. The Gemara comments (*Berachos* 10a), אפילו חרב חדה מונח על צוארו של אדם אל ימנע עצמו מן הרחמים — "Even if a sharp sword rests upon a person's neck, he should not withhold himself from prayer." Nothing is beyond Hashem. The worst thing a person can do is to despair and stop praying.

The *tzaddikim* instruct that if a patient's doctors despair and say he cannot be cured, no one should be informed of this. As long as the people think there is hope for recovery, they will pray intensely and Hashem will respond favorably to their prayers. But if a person has given up hope, they will not pray and then the salvation cannot come. The Gemara (*Kesubos* 104a) tells that when Rabbi Yehudah HaNasi was gravely ill, hovering between life and death, the entire yeshivah was praying on his behalf. One of the Rabbis announced that anyone who reported that Rabbi Yehudah died would be deserving of being stabbed. The commentators ask: Why would it have been so wrong to report Rabbi Yehudah HaNasi's death? The *Shittah Mekubetzes* explains that if the people would think that he died, they would stop praying. As long as they thought he was still alive, they would continue praying and Hashem could still bring him back. It's never too late to pray, no matter how dire the situation.

> *It's never too late to pray, no matter how dire the situation.*

A woman from Great Neck related that in the summer of 2012, her 2-year-old daughter fell into a pool. When she was pulled out, she did not have a pulse, her eyes were open, her face was blue, and her nails were purple. It appeared as though she had already passed away. While her husband performed CPR on the girl, the mother cried out to Hashem. She accepted upon herself from that moment that she would dress modestly and cover her hair. Miraculously, the child's pulse was restored, at which point she was rushed to the hospital in a Hatzalah ambulance. During the time the girl spent in the hospital, *Tehillim* was being recited by Jews across the world. Six of the top neurologists were brought in to examine the girl, and she underwent hours upon hours of testing. When the testing was finally complete, the chief doctor, Dr. Keith Meyer, said to the parents, "Your daughter is a walking miracle."

The doctors obtained a video of the accident taken by a surveillance camera. It showed, to their sheer astonishment, that the girl had been underwater for three minutes and ten seconds. She should have been clinically dead. Yet, there was not even a trace of any brain damage. She was alive and well.

The doctor, who is Jewish, said to the parents, "I don't know what I have believed until now, but now

I clearly see that there is a Hashem in the world." He noted that he had, unfortunately, seen many children who had been underwater for less than a minute and suffered permanent brain damage. It made no medical sense that this girl suffered no damage after being underwater for that long.

Hashem is כל יכול — He can do anything. Nothing is impossible for Him. No matter what the situation is, the problem can always be solved. As long as there is hope and *tefillah*, the salvation will come.

84 It Will All Become Clear

The *pasuk* (*Tehillim* 126:1) says, שיר המעלות בשוב ה' את שיבת ציון היינו כחולמים — "When Hashem redeems us from this exile, it will all feel like a dream." Sometimes, when a person has a dream, the situation looks dreadful and he feels very frightened. But then he wakes up and realizes that there was nothing of which to be afraid. Similarly, the troubles we endure in this world appear dreadful, but one day they will all be "like a dream," we will "wake up" and realize that there was never anything to fear. In fact, as the next verse says, אז ימלא שחוק פינו — "our mouths will then be filled with laughter." We will see not only that our troubles were nothing to fear, but that they weren't troubles at all, and that they were actually the greatest things that could have happened to us. And upon achieving this recognition, ולשוננו רנה — our mouths will exultantly sing praises to Hashem, thanking Him for everything we went through in life. At that time we will understand why that *shidduch* did not work out, why it took that girl so long to get married, why that couple could not have children for so many years, and why that woman miscarried. It will become so clear to us how everything that happened was an expression of Hashem's immense love and compassion for us that we will erupt in joyous song and dance.

> *"We will see not only that our troubles were nothing to fear, but that they were actually the greatest things that could have happened to us."*

The *Yalkut Shimoni* (*Eichah* remez 997) writes that the future redemption will come in reward for our *emunah*; our faith is what will bring Mashiach. What kind of *emunah* will bring our redemption? Rav Elchanan Wasserman (*Kovetz Maamarim V'Aggadata — maamar zecher yemos olam*) describes this faith as follows: לקבוע בדעתנו כי יד ה' היתה בנו ולא מקרה — the belief that Hashem is controlling everything and nothing happens by chance. The *Ya'aros Devash* (1:1) writes that this refers to accepting the way Hashem deals with us lovingly and without complaint.

How does one know if he has succeeded in implanting this firm belief within himself? He knows by his reaction to the challenges in life. A person who believes that Hashem's only interest is to benefit us and He always does the best thing for us will be able to endure painful situations with a smile. If we know someone is doing something beneficial for us, we will even be willing to pay them to do something that causes us pain. I reflect upon this point every time I have my teeth cleaned. The dentist is scraping the teeth, causing discomfort, pain, and bleeding, but I am happy to go through with it and even pay for the experience. People pay to sit with nutritionists who severely restrict their diets, and they're happy to do it, knowing how beneficial this is for them. Weightlifters endure a great deal of pain, but they do so happily, recognizing how it benefits them. I heard a comparison drawn to someone who saw a person leave the courtroom singing and bouncing with joy. He asked the person why he was so happy, and the man told him that he just paid $10,000.

"Why are you so happy if you just paid $10,000?" the man asked.

"Because I was sued for $10 million."

This is precisely the way we should view our *yissurim* (suffering). If there's a leak in the roof and it costs $1,000 to fix it, he should rejoice, knowing that this was caused by Hashem Who always has only our best interests in mind. And he should thus pay the money with joy. We need to have this simple faith that everything Hashem does is for our benefit. A person told me the other day that one of his workers stole a great deal of cash from the store and ran away. The man said that in the past, he would have lost his mind in frustration and anguish, but now, because he has worked on strengthening his *emunah*, he fully accepted that this is what Hashem wanted and it must therefore be the best thing that could have happened to him. If a person stubs his toe, he should realize that it had been decreed in the heavens that this would happen, and there is thus no reason to feel upset.

The *Reishis Chochmah* writes that emotional pain is more severe than physical pain, and the most severe form of emotional pain is humiliation. People will do anything to avoid embarrassment. But if it does happen, we must accept that this was caused by Hashem for our ultimate benefit.

It is difficult for us to imagine the merit we earn by accepting misfortune with love. We don't always have the answers for why things happen the way they do, but if we strengthen our *emunah* then Hashem will bring Mashiach, and אז ימלא שחוק פינו — we will then rejoice and our mouths will be filled with laughter, as we will understand precisely why everything happened as it did.

85 The Merit of Bitachon

The *pasuk* states (*Tehillim* 62:9), בטחו בו בכל עת — "Trust in Him at all times." We are commanded to always look to Hashem for help, at all times and in all situations. No matter what it is we need, nothing is too small or too big to bring it to Hashem. We must strengthen ourselves whenever any sort of problem arises and depend on Hashem for help. And we must recognize that the situation we face was specifically designed by Hashem for a very good reason, and He can easily resolve the problem. Hashem can save a person כהרף עין, in the blink of an eye (*Selichos R' Tzadok, Sifsei Raninus)*.

The *Kad HaKemach* (*Erech Avel*) writes that if a person looked to Hashem for help but the assistance did not yet arrive, he should not feel disheartened. The merit one acquires by seeking Hashem's help is immeasurable. And when the salvation does come, the *Kad HaKemach* writes, the person will not only receive the assistance he needed, but so much more, due to the merit of this great mitzvah of having relied on Hashem.

Many people recognize the concept of *emunah* and truly believe that Hashem can solve their problems, but they fear that they aren't deserving of His assistance. "Maybe I'm not worthy"; "I've committed so many sins that He might not want to look out for me." This fear has the ability to undermine a person's entire *bitachon*. Commenting on the *pasuk* (*Tehillim* 32:10), רבים מכאובים לרשע והבוטח בה' חסד יסובבנהו — "A wicked person has much pain, but one who trusts in Hashem will be surrounded by kindness," the Midrash writes that even if a person is a רשע, an evil individual, but he turns to Hashem, he will be surrounded by kindness. Similarly, the Ramban (*Emunah U'Bitachon*, first chapter) comments on the verse (*Tehillim* 37:3), בטח בה' ועשה טוב

— "Trust in Hashem and perform goodness," that even if a person has not performed any good deeds at all, and he knows he is sinful, he should nevertheless have faith in Hashem's kindness because, after all, Hashem is full of mercy, as the *pasuk* states, ורחמיו על כל מעשיו — "His compassion is upon all His creatures." In fact, the Midrash in *Tehillim* says that if a thief is digging a tunnel to break into a house and calls out to Hashem to save him, even he is helped, because even a wicked person is "surrounded by kindness" if he is בוטח בה', if he puts his trust in Hashem.

Another source to this notion is a remark by Rabbeinu Yonah in his commentary to *Mishlei*, where he writes that *bitachon* has nothing at all to do with a person's merits. David HaMelech writes about himself in *Tehillim*, ואני בחסדך בטחתי — "I have trusted in Your kindness." David trusted not his merits and worthiness, but rather Hashem's infinite kindness. Rabbeinu Yonah also cites in this context the *pasuk* in *Daniel* (9:18) which we also recite in our prayers: לא על צדקותינו אנחנו מפילים תחנונינו לפניך כי על רחמיך הרבים — "We do not pour forth our supplications before You based upon our righteousness, but rather on the basis of Your abundant mercy." The Chafetz Chaim similarly writes in his work *Shem Olam* that *bitachon* does not depend on one's worthiness, and even a person who conducts himself improperly should strengthen his trust in Hashem, and this itself will protect him. Hashem brings a person salvation in the merit of his faith, even if he is otherwise undeserving. When we recognize that Hashem is there waiting to help us, and we seek to tap into that invaluable resource, we earn immeasurable merit and are "surrounded by kindness."

"Hashem brings a person salvation in the merit of his faith, even if he is otherwise undeserving."

And therefore a person should never say to himself, *Who am I to ask Hashem for something? Why should Hashem answer me after the terrible things I've done?* רחמיו על כל מעשיו — Hashem has mercy for all, and we should therefore never feel embarrassed or unworthy to turn to Hashem for anything we need in life.

86

Miracle at the Kosel

The בוטח בה', a person who trusts in Hashem, is always happy. If things don't go his way, he strengthens his faith. He doesn't fall into depression or despair when his prayers aren't answered. He knows the *pasuk* (*Tehillim* 27:14), קוה אל ה' — that one should pray to Hashem, and if he is not answered, חזק ויאמץ לבך — he should strengthen himself וקוה אל ה' — and pray even more. The בוטח בה' has heard hundreds of stories about Hashem's salvation, and knows with confidence that Hashem can save him from his problems in but an instant. He also knows the inestimable value of heartfelt prayer.

"Hashem can save him from his problems in an instant."

I heard of a couple, Yaakov and Miriam Kaplan; both are *baalei teshuvah*. They lived in Eretz Yisrael and were childless for twelve years. They tried every procedure possible, but nothing worked, and the doctors could not figure out the source of the problem. Finally, they reached the mutual decision to divorce, in the hope that they could each remarry and have children with a different spouse. Yaakov's friends pleaded with him to reconsider this decision, noting that since he was a Kohen, he would not be able to remarry his wife once they divorced. But his mind was made up, and he gave her a *get*.

Within a few months, he discovered that his wife was expecting. He was heartbroken. They had tried to have children for twelve years and nothing worked, and now he could not marry her again and raise the child together. It is difficult for us to even begin to imagine the agony he felt.

Devastated, Yaakov went to his Rabbi and showed

him the *get*, hoping that maybe the Rabbi could find something wrong with the document so it could be invalidated. But the Rabbi found nothing wrong. The Rabbi advised Yaakov to bring the *get* to Rav Elyashiv, who was one of the greatest halachic sages of the generation, to see if perhaps he could find a basis for disqualifying the *get*. To Yaakov's dismay, Rav Elyashiv, too, found that the *get* was perfectly valid. There seemed to be no hope of bringing the family back together.

Rav Elyashiv urged him to go to the Kosel to pray. "Go pour your heart out at the Kosel," he said. "Hashem is the only One Who could help you. Many people have received salvation there at the Kosel."

Yaakov went to the Kosel and cried his eyes out. As he was praying, a stranger came over to him and said, "You have to go see your father." Yaakov paid no attention to the man. He had never seen him before, and besides, although he had a father in Dallas, they were not on good terms. He hadn't gone to visit him in a long time. And so Yaakov went back to his prayers. But a few minutes later, the stranger returned and told him he had to go to his father. Yaakov was very perplexed. That night, he thought about this incident for a long time, and finally decided that he should go visit his father. He took a flight to Dallas, and when he walked into his father's home, his father, for the first time in his life, called him by his Jewish name, Yaakov, instead of Jason. "Yaakov!" he said. "It's so great to see you! How's everything? Did you bring your wife?"

Upon hearing this, Yaakov broke down crying. He told his father the entire story, and the painful situation he now faced.

His father listened and kept silent for a number of minutes. Finally he said, "My son, there is something I need to tell you. Your mother swore me to secrecy, but now I must tell you: you are not really my son. We were childless, and your mother wanted a child very badly.

We adopted you, but we never told a soul. Everybody assumed that you were our biological son. And you grew up thinking that you are a Kohen, but you're not." He showed Yaakov the adoption papers, and Yaakov returned home and remarried his wife.

That stranger at the Kosel was Hashem's messenger. This is the power of heartfelt prayer.

The בוטח בה' knows that Hashem can help him in an instant. He also knows that if he hasn't been answered yet, there must be a very good reason for it, and therefore he thanks Hashem, confident that Hashem knows best. And, he knows that Hashem wants him to continue praying, and he always anticipates his salvation the next time he prays.

87 Never Say, "I Should Have"

Someone who truly trusts in Hashem does not live in the past, regretting decisions he had already made. We so often hear people lamenting, "I should have done this" or "I should have done that." This is a dreadful curse — feeling distress and anxious over past mistakes. The Torah in *Parashas Ki Savo* describes 98 curses, Heaven forbid, one of which is שדפון (*Devarim* 28:22), which refers to a kind of damaging wind that ruins vegetation. But it has been pointed that the word שדפון sounds like "should've." There is a curse that we might call the "should've syndrome," where people are constantly thinking of what they "should've" done. A person wants to sell his home, puts it on the market for $1 million, and receives an offer for $900,000, which he refuses. Three years later, when the house is still not sold, he goes around thinking and saying, *I should've sold it.* A person goes to a doctor for treatment which is unsuccessful, and he thinks to himself, *I should've gone to a different doctor.*

This attitude is incorrect. If a person put in his *hishtadlus* (effort), and made what appeared to him as the best decision at the time, then the reason why it did not work out as he wanted is because Hashem, in His infinite wisdom and kindness, did not want it to work out that way. Even if in the end it becomes clear that he could have made a much better decision, it is *min HaShamayim*; the wrong decision was made because that is what Hashem determined would be best. He did not allow the better option to enter the person's mind, because He knows what is best.

> *"He did not allow the better option to enter the person's mind, because He knows what is best."*

The Gemara (*Berachos* 32b) teaches, הכל בידי שמים חוץ מיראת שמים — "Everything is in Hashem's hands except for the fear of Hashem." This means that Hashem gives us free will to decide between right and wrong, between doing mitzvos and *aveiros*, but that is all. All our other decisions are made by Him. The *Sfas Emes* comments that Hashem is involved even in our thought processes, and thus if He wants us to be in a certain place at a certain time for whatever reason, He will put the idea in our mind to get us there.

> A woman recently told me that she was in Manhattan for a business meeting, and after the meeting she decided she wanted to go eat lunch. She passed a pizza shop, but decided she was not in the mood for pizza. She then passed a sushi restaurant, but did not feel like eating sushi. She was thinking of whether she wanted meat for lunch, and decided she was not in the mood for meat. Then, suddenly, she felt a strange craving for a chicken salad. She headed over to Kosher Delight, and as soon as she walked in, she saw her best friend, who very rarely comes to Manhattan. She ran over to her friend to say hello and to ask what she was doing there, but she noticed that her friend was reciting *Tehillim*.

As soon as she finished reciting *Tehillim*, the friend turned to the woman, said hello, and explained that she was praying to Hashem to send her a ride to Brooklyn, because she did not want to take the train. As she was praying, her friend walked in. Hashem sent her to Kosher Delight. He is involved even in our thought process.

And so the בוטח בה', the person who has firm faith in Hashem, knows that once something happens, it is the רצון ה', it is exactly what Hashem wanted to happen. As long as we do our *hishtadlus*, and try our hardest, doing what we genuinely feel is correct, we should not think twice about it. Once it is done, we believe with complete faith that the outcome was Hashem's will. So unless the decision has to do with mitzvos or *aveiros*, we should never say, "I should've," and we should never second-guess ourselves. Everything that happens is precisely what is supposed to happen.

88 Feeling Hashem's Control Brings Blessing

It has been tried and tested: the more a person truly recognizes and feels Hashem's control over the world, the more he is privileged to witness and experience Hashem's help firsthand.

An acquaintance once told me that he recently received a very large order from a company for six different styles of clothing that he distributes. The company's buyer made it very clear that the merchandise was needed by a certain date, and if it arrived even one day late, the distributor would be charged a substantial fine. The man agreed, and a couple of weeks later, the manufacturer called and apologetically notified him that there was a glitch, and all six styles would be shipped late. The man was quite upset, as he would be losing a major portion of his profit due to the fine that he would have to pay. But he managed to calm himself down, reminding himself that everything that happens comes from Hashem, and there was no reason to allow this problem to disturb his peace of mind.

Initially, he was planning to call the buyer and concoct some sort of excuse to avoid paying the fee. But then he said to himself, *Hashem is in charge of my livelihood. I don't have to lie to make money!* Even so, he didn't truly feel the extent of Hashem's control, and so for the next four days he made a concentrated effort to bolster his faith, listening to *shiurim* on *bitachon* and reinforcing his belief that his livelihood depends entirely on Hashem. Four days later, he truly felt confident that Hashem is the only One in charge. And so he calmly called the buyer and spoke very honestly and directly, apologetically informing him that the merchandise would be arriving a bit late. He politely asked that the fee be waived.

"Well," the buyer said, "in your case we gave ourselves a little cushion, and the goods will still make it onto the shelves on time, so don't worry about the fee."

The man smiled and thanked Hashem for this small miracle. The buyer had stated very clearly that a delay of even one day would result in an extra charge, but in the merit of his *emunah* the fee was canceled.

❖ ❖ ❖

Another man told me that his partner was recently in the Orient to meet with a manufacturer, and noticed that their competitor had placed a huge order from this manufacturer for a style that they had designed. They were shocked to discover that their competitor was ordering and selling their product. It turned out that one of their buyers had ordered a small amount of merchandise from them, shown the product to the competitor, and asked them if they could get it for a cheaper price. The competitor promptly placed a very large order with the manufacturer.

"Until recently," the man said, "I would have called the competitor and berated them, and would also call and shout at the buyer. But now I have faith in Hashem, knowing that He is the Only One in charge, and that my competitor cannot take a single dollar away from me. I realized there was no need to call my competitor or get angry at anyone. All I have to do is make my *hishtadlus*."

Armed with the calm and tranquility engendered by *emunah*, the man called the buyer and said, "I understand you made a large order with my competitor. Please, in the future, check with us first, as this is our product and we've been doing business together for a long time. I'd really appreciate that." The buyer was so impressed by the man's calm, pleasant demeanor in handling this adverse situation, that he canceled the order with the competitor and bought the merchandise from this man. Indeed, it was the largest order he ever received from this buyer.

"Hashem is pulling the strings, don't lose your cool."

The formula is simple: live life with an awareness that Hashem is pulling the strings, don't lose your cool, and understand that it was Hashem Who brought you to this situation, and He can just as easily bring you out of it.

89

There's Always a Way Out

When a person is about to despair, he should bear in mind the *pasuk* (*Tehillim* 130:7), יחל ישראל אל ה' כי עם ה' החסד והרבה עמו פדות — "Yisrael shall look to Hashem for hope, for kindness is with Hashem, and He has an abundance of redemption." Hashem has "an abundance of redemption," meaning, He has innumerable ways to help, even ways that we could never have thought of in our wildest dreams. If we find ourselves in a situation that appears bleak without any hope of a solution, whether it is an illness, trouble with the authorities, problems with *shalom bayis*, or any other issue, and it seems the problem can never be solved, this might very well be true — but only within the limits of human capabilities. Hashem, however, has countless ways of solving any problem that ever arises. הרבה עמו פדות — He has solutions that lie well beyond anything we could possibly think of.

> "He has solutions that lie well beyond anything we could possibly think of."

A man recently told me that he was once visiting his friend's office when customs officials arrived and charged the business owner with "trans shipping." They proceeded to put yellow tape around the entire office, and informed the man that as this was his second offense, the business would be shut down and everyone would be going to jail. It was already the end of the day, and the agents told the man that they would be back at 9 a.m. the next morning.

The business owner happened to be hosting a Rabbi in his office at the time, Rabbi Moshe Malka (who has since passed away). The man begged the Rabbi to help him.

"Please, I will commit to be more honest in the future and not to cut any more corners. But please help."

The Rabbi recognized his sincerity and prayed for forty-five minutes. Afterward, he told everyone to go home and to come back to work on time in the morning. "The problem is solved," he assured them. "They aren't coming back."

The man was hopeful but skeptical. He came to the office at 9 a.m. the next morning, very anxious and concerned. There was no sign of customs officials. Then 10 a.m. came, 11 a.m., and there was still no sign of any government official. At 11:30, Rabbi Malka came into the office, and saw that the yellow tape was still up. He cut the tape and said, "What's wrong? I said you can go back to work as usual. They're not coming back, you have nothing to worry about."

"Rabbi," the man asked, "what did you pray for?"

"I prayed that the authorities should forget your names, forget your business, and forget that you did anything wrong."

The man told me that it's now been eighteen years, and no customs agents have ever come. This was a clear ישועת ה'. Hashem saved him in a way which he could never have imagined would be possible.

❖ ❖ ❖

I recently spoke with a Holocaust survivor named Rabbi Kornreich. He told me he was the only person from his entire family who survived, and after the war he had nothing and nowhere to go, yet he was determined to rebuild his life. He eventually got married, but after eight years of marriage, still had not had children. The couple consulted with a doctor who spoke to the wife about her experiences during the war, and it turned out that the Nazis *y"sh* had given her something that ruined her reproductive faculties. The doctor informed the couple that there was no way she could conceive.

They were devastated. Their only hope to rebuild their future was to bear children, and it was not going to happen. But they still didn't give up. He prayed and prayed, and went to *tzaddikim* to receive blessings. Not long after that, miraculously, his wife conceived. The man said he now has over one hundred grandchildren and great-grandchildren.

הרבה עמו פדות — even when it seems there is no solution, Hashem has a way to help.

90 Kiddush Hashem Brings Yeshuah

We have all experienced and heard stories of *yeshuas Hashem* (Hashem's salvation). Hashem can help in any situation. No problem is too big or too small, and no solution is too costly or too difficult. Hashem can solve any and every problem that arises.

What can we do to bring *yeshuah* when we are faced with a problem?

Certainly, having faith in Hashem and praying intensely are effective means of earning Hashem's assistance. Additionally, as Rabbi Pesach Eliyahu Falk notes, we earn Hashem's salvation by making a *kiddush Hashem*, by glorifying the Name of Hashem in this world through our conduct. Our Sages comment (*Toras Kohanim, Parashas Acharei Mos*: אם מקדשים אתם את שמי אף אני אקדש את שמי על ידכם — "If you glorify My Name, then I, in turn, will cause My Name to be glorified through you." If we make a *kiddush Hashem*, then Hashem will provide us with a means of creating yet another *kiddush Hashem*. If a person was sick and the doctors had despaired, but through the heartfelt prayers of the Jewish people the patient miraculously recovers, this is a *kiddush*

Hashem. And one can earn this kind of *yeshuah* by creating a *kiddush Hashem*. By displaying *middos* that reflect the qualities expected of the nation chosen by Hashem to represent Him in the world, we earn the privilege of being vehicles for further *kiddush Hashem*.

> *"By making a kiddush Hashem we earn the privilege of being vehicles for further kiddush Hashem."*

Mr. Ruby Schron is a well-known philanthropist. Some forty years ago, Mr. Schron purchased a home on East 9th Street. One day his children were jumping on the bed, and they heard a crash underneath. They discovered a safe containing jewelry and bonds worth approximately $40,000. The sale contract clearly stipulated that the purchase of the home applied to everything in the home including all of the furniture and any belongings left behind. The Schrons wanted to do what was proper so they consulted with Rav Moshe Feinstein. Rav Moshe in fact told them that they were correct and definitely should return everything, as people do not usually include valuables in a sale. And so Mr. Schron phoned the house's previous owner, who said, "Our parents left us money in the house, but we were never able to find it. We knew that a religious Jew like yourself would return it to us if he found it" (the previous owners were Jewish but totally unaffiliated).

This was a remarkable *kiddush Hashem*. At the time, Mr. Schron was just starting out in real estate, and Hashem has blessed him with great wealth, allowing him to perform many more קדושי השם with all of his charitable endeavors.

The verse says in *Tehillim* (20:3), ישלח עזרך מקדש — "Hashem sends us His assistance מקדש" — because of the *kiddush Hashem* that we create through our honest, proper, upstanding conduct. *Kiddush Hashem*, very often, is not planned. It results naturally from living life the way Hashem wants us to.

> Rabbi Falk told of a *talmid chacham* in Eretz Yisrael who did not have much money, and whose son took seriously ill one Shabbos. He desperately needed a doctor, and there was an excellent doctor, a secular Jew, who lived down the block. The doctor agreed to treat the boy, but demanded that he be given a check immediately.

"I don't trust religious Jews," he said. "I will tend to your son only if you give me a 500-shekel check right now."

Halachah clearly establishes that the concern for human life overrides Torah law, and so the father wrote a check כלאחר יד (in an unusual manner), and handed it to the doctor. The doctor looked at the check, and noticed that it was for 1,000 shekels.

"Maybe you didn't hear me," the doctor said. "I asked for 500 shekels, not 1,000. Looking around your apartment it does not appear as though you can afford to pay me extra."

The *talmid chacham* explained that to write a 500-shekel check, he would have to write three words: חמש מאות שקל, whereas giving 1,000 shekels required writing just two words: אלף שקל. In order to minimize the Shabbos desecration, he was prepared to double the amount.

The doctor was amazed. He had never seen anything like this in his life: a poor person paying an extra 500 shekels in order to write one less word on Shabbos. He gave the man 500-shekels change, and brought the check home to show it to his wife. After Shabbos, he returned to the man's home and said, "I was so moved by what you did today, I decided I wanted to learn more about Shabbos and Judaism." The Rabbi began studying with him. The doctor ultimately became a *baal teshuvah*.

This is a *kiddush Hashem* at the very highest level. This *talmid chacham* did not plan on making a *kiddush Hashem*, and was just living life the way Hashem wanted him to. And in this merit, this doctor, and his children and grandchildren, observe the mitzvos.

If we conduct our lives the way Hashem wants us to, we will make a *kiddush Hashem*, and then ישלח עזרך מקדש — He will send us the help and salvation that we need.

91 The Missing Shoes

In the previous essay, we cited *Chazal's* comment, אם מקדשים אתם את שמי אף אני מקדש את שמי על ידכם (*Toras Kohanim — Acharei Mos perek* 13). Hashem tells us, "If you glorify My Name, then, in turn, I will cause My Name to be glorified through you." Rabbi Pesach Eliyahu Falk explained that if people see someone who was in a harsh predicament being saved from his crisis, this glorifies Hashem's Name. If we make a *kiddush Hashem* by acting in an honest, refined manner, then Hashem will bring us salvation that will cause His Name to be glorified even more. This is alluded to in the verse (*Tehillim* 20:3), ישלח עזרך מקדש — "Hashem sends us His assistance מקדש," in the merit of the *kiddush Hashem* that we make.

Very often, as we discussed, a *kiddush Hashem* is not planned. Many times we can create a *kiddush Hashem* simply by conducting ourselves the way the Almighty wants us to, without actively seeking to bring glory to His Name, and this effect will occur automatically.

> In this context Rabbi Pesach Eliyahu Falk related a beautiful incident that took place just a few years ago. Rabbi Meisels, a renowned lecturer, was once invited to deliver a lecture in Melbourne, Australia at a Rabbi Meir Baal HaNess function. He was flying to Australia from Los Angeles, and while he was very pleased to deliver a speech, he was concerned about the twenty-hour flight to the other side of the world. The travel agent told him that there was a Jew from Eretz Yisrael on his flight, and Rabbi Meisels was looking forward to meeting him and having a travel companion. The two men met in the airport in Los Angeles, and Rabbi Meisels learned that the man was flying to Australia to raise money to marry off his eleventh child. He had

tried collecting in the United States, but due to the financial crisis he was unable to raise the funds he needed. Someone advised him to travel to Australia, where fewer people go to collect charity.

As the men passed through security, they were told to remove their shoes and put them through the conveyor belt, in accordance with standard security procedures. After they passed through the metal detectors, they went to retrieve their shoes. Rabbi Meisels found his shoes and put them on, but his new friend could not find his shoes. He looked all around, but could not find them. He started getting a bit agitated, but he was nevertheless able to stay calm, and he respectfully asked one of the security staff if they could find his shoes. They looked around, and found a pair of shoes in a corner, but they were two sizes too small.

"Apparently there was a mix-up," they said, "and somebody mistakenly took your shoes." They offered him a $100 voucher to purchase new shoes in Melbourne, but there was nothing else they could do. The man remained perfectly calm, said "Thank you," and continued toward the gate without shoes. He accepted the fact that he'd have to fly across the world in his stockinged feet, and would not have shoes until he got to Melbourne.

On the flight, there was an area on the plane where passengers could go and stretch. Rabbi Meisels was there with this man, and they noticed another man, a non-Jew, standing near them, who kept looking at the man's stockinged feet and then at his face. Finally, this non-Jew said to the man, "I want to tell you, I was right behind you in the airport when your shoes went missing. I must say, I've never in my life seen such refinement, such self-control. If that were me, I'd be shouting and screaming, 'Get me shoes! I don't care if you have to hold up the entire plane until you get me a new pair of shoes — I am not going to

"I've never in my life seen such refinement, such self-control."

Australia barefoot!' But you just accepted the situation with a smile, I couldn't believe it."

The man, whose English was far from fluent, did not understand exactly what this passenger said to him, so the Rabbi translated for him. The passenger then asked Rabbi Meisels who this man was and why he was traveling to Melbourne, and the Rabbi explained that he was going to raise money for his daughter's wedding.

"What?" the man said. "That's not right. Such a refined person should go knocking on doors asking for money? He's far too aristocratic for that. How much does he need?"

The Rabbi replied that he needed $25,000. Right there on the spot, the non-Jewish passenger wrote the man a check for €25,000, the equivalent of $33,000. They couldn't believe it. When they arrived in Melbourne, they went to the bank to cash the check, and the entire amount was covered. The man thanked Hashem for His help, and took the next flight home to Eretz Yisrael.

This was a beautiful example of a *kiddush Hashem* that brought in its wake an immediate salvation. ישלח עזרך מקדש — Hashem lends His assistance in the merit of our creating a *kiddush Hashem*.

92 Go Straight to the Boss

The *pasuk* (*Tehillim* 120:1) says, שיר המעלות אל ה' בצרתה לי קראתי ויענני. David HaMelech proclaims that when he found himself in crisis situations, he called out to Hashem, and Hashem answered his prayers. Rabbi Pesach Eliyahu Falk explained this to mean that David knew from experience that he had just one address to turn to when in dire straits: Hashem. Most people, when confronted with difficulties, consult with many different people for help, and only when all else fails do they turn to Hashem and pour their hearts out, begging for His assistance. But David went directly אל ה', straight to Hashem, right away, and his prayers were answered.

> Someone told me that several months ago, his business unexpectedly started going dry. His buyers were canceling their orders, and new orders were not forthcoming. He felt anxious and concerned, but made a firm decision that being aggravated and uptight will do nothing to help the situation. Instead, he reasoned, he should work on strengthening his *emunah*. He attended numerous classes on the subject of faith, and one morning during Shacharis he thought to himself, *I don't need to beg buyers to buy my product. They have less say in my income than an ant does. I'm going straight to the Source*. He then turned to Hashem and said, "I know that You are the only One Who counts!" The man then cried out to Hashem for help.
>
> Just a few hours later, one of his buyers called and informed him that he had changed his mind, and wanted to place a very large order with the business. This buyer also recommended another firm who likewise placed an order. In the end, the business made triple the profit they had ever imagined they could receive from this customer.

When a problem arises, the only address we need is Hashem. We should go directly to Him.

> Another man told me that he recently married, and he and his wife are, *baruch Hashem*, expecting their first child. As he was not earning as much as he figured he would need once the baby was born, he prayed to Hashem for help. "I learned," he said, "that when a person needs more money, the money will be there. Hashem, I need it now, so please help me."

One day, someone told him about a job opening in a very successful company for which he was perfectly suited. He interviewed for the position, and he received a job offer with a salary twice what he was earning in his current job. The man was a bit hesitant, however, as the new position demanded much longer hours than he was accustomed to, and he was concerned that this work schedule may adversely affect his *shalom bayis*. He sat down with his wife to discuss the options, and they both agreed that Hashem had answered his prayers with this job offer, and so he should accept it.

The man told his current employer about his new offer, and they said that although they were happy with his work and did not wish to see him leave, they could not match the salary offered by the other company. They then asked him if he could stay another two weeks in order to train his replacement, and he agreed. It very quickly became clear that none of the potential replacements were nearly as qualified as he was, and so the employer decided to offer the man a salary that came near the huge increase he had been offered by the other company. The man explained that the new job also offered growth opportunities that he did not have in his current job, and so the company offered him a five-year plan with growth and a salary increase at every stage.

Thus, the man was able to keep the same job and enjoy the convenient work hours without losing money. Hashem can give us exactly what we need without requiring us to make extra *hishtadlus* (personal effort).

❖ ❖ ❖

Someone else approached me last Shabbos and told me that he recently made a bar mitzvah, and finances were extremely tight. He turned to Hashem for help. One day at work, his wife called him and said, "You won't believe it; we just received a check in the mail for $18,000." It turned out that a class-action suit had been filed involving their health insurance company, and they were awarded this huge sum of money. "I couldn't believe it," the man said. "In the past I never got more than $1.50 from these kinds of things! Just when we needed the money, Hashem provided it."

We must look to Hashem for salvation, rather than waste our time dealing with the messengers.

"We must look to Hashem for salvation, rather than waste our time dealing with the messengers."

93 It's All for the Best

A person who trusts in Hashem is always happy. Even when things do not go the way he wanted, he immediately responds by saying *gam zu l'tovah* — "This, too, is for the best." He knows Hashem loves him infinitely and wants only the best for him. Whether it was a job he desperately wanted, or an important position on a committee or in a shul that didn't work out, he knows that גם זו לטובה, in the end this is for the best.

These are not just words of comfort. It is the absolute truth. Today it might not seem that the events are *l'tovah*. The person might think that if he would have received the job he wanted his life would have been perfect and everything would have been ideal. But he has no way of knowing what this job would have entailed long term, what problems would have arisen down the road. We are only able to see the current circumstances, but Hashem sees into the future. He makes decisions based on factors that we could never have fathomed. When a prospective *shidduch* doesn't work out, it can be devastating, and people often become depressed. But the truth is that *gam zu l'tovah*.

We have no way of knowing what the outcome of this *shidduch* would have been many years down the road. Hashem does know the long-term results, and He decided based on this perspective that the *shidduch* should not work out. We must trust Hashem and have full faith in Him that His decisions are always to our ultimate benefit.

Somebody might naturally wonder, *how could it be good not to get that which I so desperately want?*

This is precisely when *emunah* comes into play. We know that Hashem is a loving Father Who does only that which is best for us. At times, we are shown how His decisions were for our benefit, and when this happens, we receive *chizuk* (encouragement) for those occasions when we are not given this information.

> *"We know that Hashem is a loving Father Who does only that which is best for us."*

A woman told me that she once waited an entire year for a certain *shidduch* for her daughter, but the boy ended the courtship after they met six times. The mother was devastated. She had pinned her hopes on this *shidduch*, and it didn't work out. Eventually, however, the girl married this boy's best friend. The friend said that he would never have considered this girl if his friend had not gone out with her first, given the significant differences in their backgrounds. While we are crying over our unfulfilled hopes, Hashem is paving the way for their fulfillment.

Rabbi Pesach Eliyahu Falk tells of a non-observant family in Eretz Yisrael who had a baby who was born with unusually large ears. He looked disfigured, and the mother was distraught. She was so embarrassed by the child's appearance that she never let him leave the house and did not want anyone to see him. One day, her friend recommended that she enroll him in a *cheder* with boys who wear long *peyos* that conceal their ears. As the boy's ears would be hidden by his *peyos*, nobody would notice his deformity and he would not suffer any embarrassment. The parents heeded this advice, and although they were not at all observant, they enrolled this child in a *cheder*. He went through the entire schooling system with boys from very religious families, and he became an outstanding Torah scholar and ultimately built a beautiful family. As it happened, this was the only child from whom the parents had *nachas*. He had one sibling who became a drug addict, and another who went to jail.

This mother had cried many nights worrying about this child, and in the end, this was the child who was her pride and joy.

Sometimes Hashem shows us the benefits of His decisions, but at other times He does not. Either way, we must recognize that *gam zu l'tovah:* everything He does is for the best.

94 Why Pray to Change What's Good for Us?

The question is frequently asked, if everything that happens in life is always for the best, as determined by Hashem, then why do we pray for things to change? Shouldn't we just accept our situation, whatever it is, without ever praying, since we know that everything that happens must be for the best?

We are in this world to do the רצון ה', the will of Hashem. His will is that, on the one hand, we understand and internalize the belief that He always deals mercifully with us and everything He does is for the best. At the same time, however, He wants us to pour our hearts out to Him, to tell Him our problems and to ask Him to deal with us in a way through which we can feel and enjoy His goodness. The two do not necessarily contradict each other, because what is good for me now may not necessarily be good for me tomorrow, and vice versa.

> *"What is good for me now may not necessarily be good for me tomorrow, and vice versa."*

Rabbi Ephraim Wachsman explained this concept by noting that there are two different worlds in which we live: the world of prayer, and the world in which we conduct our lives when we are not praying. When we step into the world of prayer, we can cry all we want and beg Hashem for a different life. But throughout the rest of the day, we must smile and joyously accept the way He runs our lives.

Rabbi Wachsman proved this concept from a curious exchange that took place between Yaakov and Rachel. Rachel was unable to conceive, and she approached Yaakov and said, "Give me children, for if not I might as well die." Yaakov then answered (*Bereishis* 30:2), התחת אלקים אנכי — "Am I instead of Hashem?" This exchange seems very difficult to understand. Where was Rachel's trust in Hashem, her belief that everything He does is for the best? Why didn't she say, "*Baruch Hashem*, this must be what is best for me"? And what is the meaning of Yaakov's response?

Rashi explains that Rachel asked Yaakov why he was not praying for her to conceive the way his father, Yitzchak, prayed that his wife, Rivkah, should conceive. Yaakov responded that his situation is different from his father's, in that he has other wives who did bear children. Yitzchak was childless just as Rivkah was, and thus he felt the pain of not having children. Yaakov, however, did not experience that same pain, and he therefore told Rachel that she must pray herself. קרוב ה' לנשברי לב — "Hashem is close to the brokenhearted" (*Tehillim* 34:19), and thus Rachel should cry to Hashem in pain. The phrase התחת אלקים אנכי literally means, "I am underneath Hashem." Yaakov was telling Rachel, "I am positioned under the Heavenly Throne, and thus I know what is needed: for you, with your broken heart, to plead before Hashem."

Yaakov did not try reinforcing Rachel's *emunah* because he knew that Rachel's faith was fully intact. She spoke to him the way she did because she was coming to pray, and in prayer, one can say anything, even "or else I might as well die." When a person prays, he can tell Hashem how much he is pained by his situation, how badly he needs Hashem's assistance. After prayer, one returns to his normal state of affairs, and if he sees that Hashem did not grant his request, and the situation has not changed, then he must feel confident that Hashem knows precisely what is best for him and has only his best interests in mind.

Hashem loves to listen to our prayers, and when we approach Him with the proper mindset, they are especially powerful.

The Chazon Ish once noted how remarkable the gift of prayer is, as it allows us to express all our worries and concerns to the Creator of the world, like a person talking over his problems with his friend. Shlomo HaMelech said (*Mishlei* 12:25), דאגה בלב איש ישיחנה — which the Gemara (*Yoma* 75b) explains as meaning if a person has worries in his heart, he should speak about them and he will then feel better. Often, however, we are too ashamed to speak about our personal problems with other people. But even then, we have the opportunity to speak about our problems with Hashem, to pour our hearts out to Him, knowing that He is always listening. This alone should bring us comfort during life's difficult moments.

So throughout the day, we must smile and tell ourselves, *gam zu l'tovah,* everything that happens is for the best. But when it's time to pray, we should tell Hashem everything that's troubling us.

95

You Can Get More

Hashem gives each person certain intellectual capabilities and a specific amount of physical strength, and these determine how much he is capable of achieving during his lifetime. However, the *Chasam Sofer*, based on a verse (*Bamidbar* 6:21), comments that a person who draws close to Hashem is able to receive greater potential than that which was initially assigned to him. The *Chasam Sofer* adds that whatever the person had accomplished until then would be like nothing compared to the newfound strengths and the capabilities with which is he now endowed.

"A person who draws close to Hashem is able to receive greater potential than that which was initially assigned to him."

The *Sedei Chemed* (Rav Chaim Chizkiyah Medini), one of the most illustrious Sephardic Sages, is a prime example of this phenomenon. He wrote a remarkable, ten-volume encyclopedia covering the entire gamut of Halachah. When one browses through just a few pages of the *sefer*, he cannot but be awe-struck by the sheer magnitude of the Rabbi's scholarship, his mastery of Rishonim and Acharonim, including many books that most scholars today have not even heard of. It is mind-boggling to think of how one man accumulated so much knowledge without the help of computers.

The *Sedei Chemed* himself tells the story of how he was able to achieve this towering level of scholarship. As a young man, he studied in kollel and was an average student, though an exceptionally diligent one. There was a man in the community who harbored hostile feelings toward the kollel and wanted to see it shut down. Knowing that the *Sedei Chemed* routinely studied late into the night when everybody else had left the study hall, he bribed the Arab cleaning woman who worked in the yeshivah to accuse the young student of improper conduct toward her. The next day, during the *seder*, the woman stormed into the *beis midrash* and began shouting at the *Sedei Chemed*. He was so shamed by the incident that he left town and disappeared. Meanwhile, the head of the kollel recognized that the accusations were fabricated, and promptly dismissed the cleaning woman.

Several months later, this woman tracked down the young student. "After I was fired," she told him, "I lived on my bribe money, but that money has been all used up. I am broke. If you convince the head of the kollel to rehire me, I will tell everyone the truth of what happened, and I'll save your reputation."

The *Sedei Chemed* later recalled how relieved he felt when he was presented with the opportunity to clear his name. But then he started thinking a bit more about the situation, and realized that if he agreed to this deal, he would add to the *chillul Hashem* that had already been caused. The initial shockwaves triggered by the woman's charges had subsided, and the situation had returned to normal. If she would now confess that the accusations were false, people would begin talking about the incident again, different people would take different sides on the issue as to which story to believe, and the scandal would be reawakened. The *Sedei Chemed* wrote that he made a decision that went against every fiber of his being, agreeing to have the woman reinstated on condition that she never says another word about this incident.

At that moment, the *Sedei Chemed* said, he felt his soul and brain expanding, and felt the heavens revealing themselves to him. He sensed that he was rising above his own essence, and that his mind's capabilities were expanding. From that moment on, his Torah learning was supernatural, as he was capable of absorbing and retaining the entire Torah, everything he learned. And it was through this extraordinary power that he was able to compose the halachic encyclopedia.

The closer we draw to Hashem by sacrificing in order to do the right thing, the more Heavenly assistance we will receive, and we will then be able to accomplish far more than we could with our original allotment of capabilities.

96 Quality of Life

If Hashem wants to bless an individual with financial success, He can do so in an instant. To us, the road to success might seem very long, but Hashem has countless ways of shortening that road and bringing one instant success. Of course, we need to do our *hishtadlus*, to invest effort and to work hard. But our main area of *hishtadlus* upon which we focus must be the area of *avodas Hashem*, raising the standards of our service of Hashem. Wealth is a wonderful blessing, but the pursuit of money should not consume all our time. We need to make an effort, to put in a hard day's work, but without ever forgetting the real purpose of life, which is to serve Hashem. We should be asking Hashem for success, and when He feels the time is right, He will send it to us, in ways we would never have imagined.

> *"We need to put in a hard day's work, but without ever forgetting the real purpose of life, which is to serve Hashem."*

A successful businessman told me that he went to lunch with one of his friends in order to try to direct him toward greater *emunah*, to impress upon him that all success comes from Hashem.

"We don't accomplish anything," he told his friend. "It is all from Hashem."

His friend, however, felt that to the contrary, we need to be investing greater effort. "I think you're too laid back in your business," he said, "and you're not putting in enough effort. You don't have accounts with the big names like Macy's and Kohl's."

The man explained to him that building a relationship with these corporations requires a lot of time and a lot of traveling. To do so, he would have to spend a great deal of time away from his family, and he enjoys the quality of life which he has, being able to learn Torah in the morning until 8:45 and then coming home at 6:30 to be with his family and learn more Torah at night. He then said, "Hashem has blessed me with everything I need. If He wants to bless me with more money, I know that He could bring me any big company right to my doorstep." These were his words.

The man returned to his office, and a short while later he received a friendly phone call from his nephew. His nephew told him of a new job that he had recently started, and mentioned that his company has a salesman with excellent connections with all the major stores, and who had succeeded in creating accounts with many of the big names. The next day, the nephew called back and said, "You won't believe it. Remember that salesman I was telling you about? He just left the company and is looking for a new job."

The businessman immediately contacted the salesman and hired him. The new employee spent the next two weeks on the phone trying to set up accounts with all the major companies. "Don't worry," he told his boss, "I know you don't like traveling, so I will be happy to travel if I get meetings set up." As it turned out, that week was market week, and every store came to them, right to their office. They held very successful meetings, and, as the man had said, Hashem brought all the major stores — such as Kohl's, J.C. Penney, Sears, Kmart and others — right to his doorstep. Sears even requested a follow-up meeting, and they agreed to meet at a show that the businessman was in any event planning to attend.

If Hashem wants, He could bring the business right where we are. We should work very hard, not be lazy, and put in the effort, but we should never compromise our quality of life.

97 If Hashem Could Help, Why Didn't He?

Someone recently told me that she's been listening to every *emunah* class, but she is left with a question. "I know Hashem can help me," she said, "and I know he's listening to me when I pray, but I've been praying for something for a very long time, and He still hasn't helped me. It seems He knows how badly I want this, yet He still chooses not to give it to me. This bothers me very much. If Hashem is so kind, and He knows the pain I am experiencing, then why doesn't He help me?"

> *"Hashem, I cannot believe I doubted You! You were truly looking out for my best interests."*

My response was that it is precisely because Hashem is so loving and kind that He has not granted her request. For reasons we cannot understand right now, He decided it would be the very best thing for her not to receive what she wants. One day, however, she will understand, and when she does find out the reason, she will say, "Hashem, I cannot believe I doubted You! You were truly looking out for my best interests."

Imagine a child walking with his father, who is carrying a large bag of lollipops. The boy asks his father for a lollipop, but the father refuses. The bag is full of lollipops, and the child asks for just one, but the father does not give him any. The boy might think to himself, *My father is so mean. I'm begging for just one lollipop, and he won't give it to me.* The boy does not know that the dentist recently warned that if the boy eats any candy, he will have severe problems with his teeth. Similarly, we ask Hashem for favors, and when He refuses, we don't understand why. But there is always a very good reason, and He always has only our very best interests in mind.

People might still ask: Why doesn't Hashem tell us the reason why we cannot have what we want?

The answer, perhaps, is that the benefit we receive by trusting Him is infinitely greater than the satisfaction of knowing the reason why things are the way they are.

David HaMelech (*Tehillim* 131:2) compared his relationship to Hashem with the relationship between a nursing infant and his mother — כגמל עלי אמו. He always knew that no matter what happened, Hashem was looking out for him and caring for him like a mother cares for her child. The Gemara (*Pesachim* 112a) comments, יותר ממה שהעגל רוצה לינוק הפרה רוצה להניק — "A cow wants to nurse its young calf more than the calf wants to be fed." Rabbi Pesach Eliyahu Falk explained that the pain the mother suffers from being engorged exceeds the discomfort of the hungry calf. When the baby does not nurse, the mother is in greater pain than the child. Hashem, our "Mother," is טוב ומיטיב; all He wants is to bestow kindness. It is painful for Him, as it were, when He cannot give us as much as He wants to. He has so much goodness, He is overflowing with "milk" which He wishes to "feed" us, but sometimes, for reasons we do not understand, He knows that it is not good for us to receive His goodness. And on those occasions, He is in more pain, as it were, than we are. The *pasuk* (*Tehillim* 91:15) says, עמו אנכי בצרה — Hashem shares our distress during troubled times. Hashem loves us so much that He goes through the pain of denying us what we want when He knows that this is the best thing for us.

Nevertheless, He wants us to continue praying. Even if it is not in our best interest to receive what we want today, it might be in our best interest to receive it tomorrow, and a person can change himself through *tefillah*.

We must never feel that Hashem is simply choosing not to help us. He is always helping us: when He grants our requests, and when He turns down our requests. Our job is to have faith and remain strong, and, *be'ezras Hashem*, we will all be worthy of recognizing just how kind and loving Hashem truly is.

98 Never Underestimate the Power of Tefillah

We must never underestimate the power of *tefillah*.

When the *Kesav Sofer* was the Rabbi of the city of Pressburg, a Jew was sentenced to hang for a crime he did not commit. The *Kesav Sofer* did everything he possibly could to save the condemned man, but to no avail. The night before the hanging was scheduled, the *Kesav Sofer* was at home, out of ideas of what to do, and cried himself to sleep.

As he slept, his father, the *Chasam Sofer*, appeared to him in a dream with an angry face.

"How are you able to sleep," the *Chasam Sofer* said, "when an innocent man with a wife and children is going to be put to death?"

"But what should I do?" the *Kesav Sofer* asked his father in his dream. "I've already tried everything."

"Why aren't you praying?" his father asked. "You have to pray, pray, and pray some more."

> *You have to pray, pray and pray some more.*

The *Kesav Sofer* immediately arose and gathered the community to the shul for prayer. They prayed throughout the night, and in the morning, miraculously, the judge agreed to investigate the case further. The man's life was saved.

Indeed, *tefillah* is effective, especially when a person cries out in pain, as the *pasuk* (*Tehillim* 34:19) states, קרוב ה' לנשברי לב — "Hashem is close to the brokenhearted."

I read a story of a woman — we'll call her Esther — who had gone through several very difficult childbirths and was now scheduled to have a C-section. She was very concerned and anxious, and so she called her friend, who had also gone through very complicated births, to receive some encouragement. After this friend's second birth, which was a C-section, she was diagnosed with stage 4 ovarian cancer, לא עלינו. *Baruch Hashem*, after many tearful prayers and years of difficult treatments, she was eventually proclaimed cancer-free. Unfortunately, however, the drugs she took during that period were so strong that she was told she had only a 10 percent chance of conceiving again.

When Esther called her to receive encouragement, she asked her, "What are you planning to do when you experience pain during and after the delivery?"

"I don't know," Esther replied. "I suppose I'll just have to bear it."

"No," her friend said. "Every time you feel pain, I want you to pray for me that I can have more children."

After their conversation, Esther thought to herself, *Who am I to pray for somebody else?* But during the operation and its aftermath, when the pain became intense, she heard her dear friend's words echoing in her mind, and she figured she might as well use this harsh pain for something meaningful and worthwhile.

And so she prayed that her friend should be able to bear more children.

Just three weeks later, her friend informed her that she was expecting.

❖ ❖ ❖

A man I know works as a contractor, and he put in a bid for a certain job which he really wanted. He was disappointed when his bid was rejected. One month later, he was davening Shacharis and asked Hashem for a job to come his way. "I know You can do anything," the man prayed, "and You can even give me the job for which I was turned down last month." Just 20 minutes later he received a call. The man who had turned him down said that he has since reconsidered and wants to give him the job.

קרוב ה' לכל קוראיו לכל אשר יקראוהו באמת — "Hashem is close to everyone who cries out to Him, as long as one turns to Him with sincerity."

99 Trust the Driver

The Rosh (*Orchos Chaim, Os* 69) used to instruct his students, רצה באשר ירצה יוצריך — "Want that which Hashem wants for you." If you wanted something, such as to purchase a certain house, and in the end it did not work out, you should say, "If this is what Hashem wanted, then I am happy."

"Want that which Hashem wants for you."

People who accept the way Hashem treats them enjoy much more peace of mind. If we recognize that our lives are led by Hashem, and He always knows what He is doing, then we will be much happier.

> I once heard an analogy of two men who board a bus for an eight-hour ride, both of whom are traveling for important business meetings. The first gets on the bus and looks anxiously at the bus driver, wondering if he really knows the route. *This is such an important meeting,* the fellow thinks to himself, *I really hope he gets me there on time.* From the moment the bus pulls out, he is worried. *Why did he turn left? Wasn't he supposed to turn right? Why is he going this way — there is traffic on this highway!* The entire ride he is at the edge of his seat, concerned whether the driver knows what he's doing. Eventually, the bus arrives at its destination with fifteen minutes to spare. The man arrives at his meeting all stressed out and bent out of shape.
>
> The second fellow, meanwhile, boards the bus, smiles at the bus driver and thinks to himself, *He looks like a good man.* He sits comfortably in his seat, pulls out his headphones, and spends the time listening to pleasant music, learning some Torah, taking a nap, and enjoying the beautiful scenery outside the window. The bus arrives fifteen minutes early, and the man thanks the bus driver and arrives at his meeting calm, relaxed, and happy.
>
> Both men paid the same fare and reached the same destination. The first fellow suffered through nearly eight hours of unnecessary anxiety and stress because he didn't trust the driver, whereas the second man enjoyed a relaxing, pleasant ride because he did trust the driver.

If we trust our "Driver" Who leads us along our journey through life, we can avoid so much stress. Even when we appear to take a wrong turn, we must remember that Hashem knows the "back roads," He knows what He's doing, and we are always going the right way.

Rav Avraham Schorr told of a Rabbi in Eretz Yisrael who

was suffering with cancer. He was bitten by a poisonous snake and treated by a specialist in Ramat Gan. Ten days after his initial treatment he returned for a follow-up examination.

After the doctor saw the test results, he said, "I never believed in Hashem until now. The poison injected by the snake burned up the cancer in your kidneys. You are completely fine."

Do we know what is good for us? Would we have ever imagined that being bitten by a poisonous snake is a good thing? We have to trust our Driver.

> Rabbi Ephraim Wachsman told of a certain yeshivah in Russia that was on the run, fleeing the Communists who were searching for them. At one point, a car drove by, and the students, thinking it was the police, were terrified. They began racing about frantically fleeing out of fear. The Rabbi was disappointed by their reaction, and decided that they needed to strengthen their *emunah*. He instituted that each day they would recite together the thirteen *Ani Ma'amin* declarations of faith.
>
> One week later, the police found them and arrested the entire yeshivah. They were brought to prison in chains, and all throughout they were humming a song about how Hashem is with them. They were later deported to Siberia, and continued humming the entire time. Three days later, the Germans entered the town where they had been staying, and massacred the entire population. The yeshivah was saved.

Hashem always knows what He's doing.

If we follow the Rosh's advice to his students, and always accept Hashem's will, then we will see the fulfillment of the Mishnah in *Avos* (5:16), "If you make Hashem's will your will, then He will make your will His will."

100 Tzaddik V'Ra Lo

One who believes in Hashem knows that everything that happens in life is for the best, even when he sees צדיק ורע לו — a righteous person suffering — and רשע וטוב לו — a wicked person prospering. Even upon seeing the suffering of the righteous and the success of the wicked, the believing person knows that הצור תמים פעלו כי כל דרכיו משפט (*Devarim* 32:4), that Hashem does not make any mistakes. The suffering experienced by the righteous person must be beneficial for him, and the success of the wicked person must be to his ultimate detriment. The believer never lets questions rattle him. He trusts that Hashem knows what He is doing.

Hashem tells us through the prophet (*Yeshayah* 55:8), לא מחשבותי מחשבותיכם — the human mind is not capable of understanding His ways in this world. Part of being a Jew is knowing that we do not have to know the answers to all questions. *Emunah* means that we do not understand everything. It is belief — belief that Hashem is צדיק וישר (*Devarim* 32:4); everything He does is correct and just.

> *"Part of being a Jew is knowing that we do not have to know the answers to all questions."*

We are in this world to withstand tests. If everyone would immediately receive reward after performing a good deed, there would be no tests in life. If the *tzaddik* was guaranteed a good life, then everyone would be a *tzaddik* without any hesitation. If a person who goes to shul would immediately receive one million dollars, and everyone who learned Torah would immediately receive one million dollars, then who wouldn't do it? Likewise, if people would be immediately punished for every sin, there would be no challenge to avoid sin. Furthermore, if we would understand the reason for every bit of suffering people experience, we would lose all our sensitivity to people's pain; we would understand precisely why the pain is ultimately beneficial for them, and we would not be bothered by it or driven to help. For these reasons, Hashem does not want us to know why He treats people as He does.

Additionally, when a *tzaddik* endures suffering, he knows he is earning his share in the Next World with every iota of pain. The Gemara (*Berachos* 5a) relates that Hashem gave us three precious gifts, but they all are obtained only through suffering: Torah, Eretz Yisrael, and the World to Come. The *tzaddik* knows this, and so he is able to handle *yissurim* (suffering). His soul experiences great inner pleasure during periods of *yissurim*. When Rabbi Akiva's students saw the Roman authorities comb the flesh from his body (ibid. 61a), and they saw Rabbi Akiva reciting *Shema* as this was happening, they asked him, זו תורה וזו שכרה — this is the reward for Torah? How was he able to read *Shema* while he was being tortured? The great Rabbi answered, כל ימי הייתי מצטער מתי יבא פסוק זה ואקיימנו — "My whole life I have been looking forward to glorifying Hashem's Name." He relished the opportunity to make the ultimate sacrifice for the sake of *kiddush Hashem*.

There are hidden, precious jewels within each affliction. If somebody would give a person a $10 million gift, but the wrapping paper was very difficult to remove, it is hard to imagine the recipient complaining about the labor entailed in removing the paper. Similarly, the *tzaddik* does not complain about his suffering because he knows there are hidden jewels deep within each and every ounce of affliction. Sometimes we might think the *tzaddik* is suffering, but in truth, the joy he experiences in his life is immense. He might not have much money, but he receives great joy and satisfaction from his children, or is blessed with a wonderful wife and couldn't be happier. We don't really know what is happening in other people's lives, but we know that Hashem gives each person only what he is able to handle.

Our world is a world of questions. From our vantage point, not everything makes sense, but from Hashem's vantage point, everything is exactly the way it is supposed to be, and it is all an expression of Hashem's mercy and love for us. The *pasuk* (*Tehillim* 48:10) says, דימינו ה׳ חסדך בקרב היכלך. The *Arizal* explained this to mean that דימינו אלקים — to us it appears as though the world is being run with Hashem's attribute of strict justice (אלקים), but in truth, חסדך — everything that happens is a manifestation of Hashem's kindness, and can be recognized as such when it is viewed בקרב היכלך, from Hashem's vantage point.

Our job is to continue strengthening our belief that Hashem always knows what He is doing, and one day He will explain it to us. In the meantime, we have to have faith.

101 Help Is on the Way

The tests of life are not easy. There are many people waiting for a *yeshuah* (salvation), and they keep waiting and waiting, and it seems that it will never come. Some are getting older and have still not found a marriage partner; couples wait for years to have children; patients wait to be cured. The days pass, and nothing changes. And the people begin wondering whether things will ever change.

We must never despair, under any circumstances. ישועת ה' כהרף עין — Hashem's salvation can arrive in the blink of an eye. We are not bound by the ordinary rules of nature.

> *Hashem's salvation can arrive in the blink of an eye.*

The *pasuk* states (*Tehillim* 121:1), שיר למעלות אשא עיני אל ההרים מאין יבא עזרי. The Radak explains that this psalm speaks of a person in need of salvation, who climbs to a mountaintop and looks down as far as his eye can see, looking for help. But he sees מאין יבא עזרי — there is no one who could help him, there is no way out of his predicament.

He then declares in the very next *pasuk*, עזרי מעם ה' עושה שמים וארץ — "My help is from Hashem, Maker of heaven and earth." Although by the rules of nature he has no solution to his problem, he knows he has Hashem, Maker of heaven and earth, Who works beyond the rules of nature. No matter what the problem is, Hashem can find a solution.

Rabbi Schorr told a story involving an observant Jew who—undeservedly—was sentenced to be imprisoned on Rikers Island, which would have been devastating both spiritually and physically. Many people intervened to try to have him acquitted, but to no avail. The judge was adamant. There was a certain non-Jewish man with a lot of influence over these matters, but he refused to get involved. One day, this non-Jew was returning from a funeral in North Carolina, and was standing outside Penn Station with his two suitcases in the searing summer heat, waiting for a taxicab. No taxis stopped for him. Two yeshivah boys — no one knows who they were — happened to pass by and saw a man waiting in the hot sun with two suitcases. They graciously approached the man and offered to help him home with his suitcases. He told them that he lived four blocks away, but they said they would be happy to help. And so the two boys carried his suitcases to his apartment building, and when they arrived at the building he thanked them and bid them farewell.

"Wait," they said, "we'll take your bags to your apartment." The man told them he lived on the third floor, but they insisted. When they reached his apartment with the luggage, he pulled out two $20 bills and handed them to the boys.

"No, thank you," they said, "we don't want money. We just like to help."

As soon as he walked into his apartment, he called the lawyer and assured him that the defendant would not be going to jail. "I've never seen such a thing in my life," he said. "I never imagined that Orthodox Jews are such beautiful people."

What would two yeshivah boys be doing walking outside Penn Station in Manhattan on a hot summer day? These were the angels sent by Hashem to save this Jew.

> Recently, a 47-year-old Jewish man collapsed on the tennis courts in Monmouth University. Hatzalah was called, and there was, *baruch Hashem*, a paramedic right down the block. CPR began less than 90 seconds from the moment the phone call was made. Others came and continued CPR, and the man was fully revived in the ambulance on the way to the hospital. The doctor who tended to the patient later said that the kind of cardiac arrest suffered by this man has only a five percent survival rate.
>
> It is a miracle that the Hatzalah member was in the area, but it is even a greater miracle that this fellow knew where the tennis courts are located. The Monmouth University campus covers 156 acres, and very few people — even those living in Deal — know where the tennis courts are located.

Hashem can send his *yeshuah* at any time. Our job is to continue drawing closer to Him and praying.

May we all have the merit to see Hashem's *yeshuah* whenever we need it.

102 The Blessing of a Tzaddik

The Gemara (*Taanis* 23a) says, צדיק גוזר והקב"ה מקיים — "When a *tzaddik* prays for something, Hashem answers him right away." The more a person purifies himself, the more powerful his words become. This is why we go to *tzaddikim* to receive blessings. Because they are so holy, their blessings are especially powerful.

> *When a tzaddik prays, Hashem answers him right away.*

Rabbi Pesach Eliyahu Falk related that over thirty years ago, there was a boy in Gateshead who became seriously ill and was paralyzed from the waist down. He was diagnosed with a brain tumor, and the tumor was located on the part of the brain that controls the lower part of the body. Rabbi Falk told the boy's father that he was going to Eretz Yisrael, and offered to try to get a *berachah* from a *tzaddik*. The boy's father was pleased by the offer and asked Rabbi Falk to go to the Steipler Gaon and ask him three questions: if he could pray on the boy's behalf; if they should change the boy's name; if they should publicize it.

Rabbi Falk waited a long time to be able to see the Steipler Gaon, and when he finally went in, he handed him the piece of paper with the three questions. The Steipler looked at the boy's name and said, "Oh, Hashem should have compassion and heal this boy." He then instructed that the name "Chaim" should be added to the boy's name, and that this should *not* be publicized.

Rabbi Falk sent a letter to Gateshead with the Sage's responses. When he arrived back in Gateshead, as soon as the father saw him from across the room, he ran over to him with a huge smile and thanked him.

"Tell me," he said, "when did you see the Steipler Gaon?"

The rabbi thought for a moment, and said that it was the previous Sunday, at around 2 p.m.

"Unbelievable!" the father exuberantly exclaimed. "That's exactly when my son was healed." He explained that the doctors could not operate on the tumor because it was embedded too deeply in the brain, and they thus figured it was a lost cause. But at that time on Sunday, they looked again and saw that the tumor had dissolved. One word from the Gaon, and Hashem brought the salvation. *Baruch Hashem*, this boy is now a grandfather.

❖ ❖ ❖

A famous story is told of the time when Rav Aharon Kotler went with Mr. Irving Bunim to the head of the Italian mafia, Joe Bonanno, to try to save the Italian Rabbis who were imprisoned by the Nazis. Mr. Bonanno turned to Mr. Bunim and asked about the Rabbi. "Who is the old gentleman sitting next to you?" he asked.

Mr. Bunim said, "He is the godfather of the entire Jewish nation."

The mafia chief was very impressed, and asked for a blessing. Rav Aharon Kotler told him, "You will merit a long life and die in your bed." Mr. Bonanno was very pleased and said that the Italian Rabbis would be freed within two weeks.

Some 25 years later, a black stretch limousine pulled up in front of the Lakewood Yeshivah, and two well-dressed men, with their hair slicked back and wearing sunglasses, emerged and entered the building, asking to speak to the dean. The "dean" at the time was Rav Aharon Kotler's son. They came to the Rabbi and identified themselves as the sons of Mr. Joe Bonanno.

"Recently our father retired," they said, "and told us to take over. He is still healthy and well, even though he is already quite old. Most of his contemporaries have been murdered. He attributes his long life to the blessing he received from the dean of this school many years ago, and we, too, would like to receive a blessing."

This is the power of the words spoken by a *tzaddik*.

Each of us can become a "*tzaddik*" in his own way. The closer we get to Hashem, the more powerful our *tefillos* will become.

103 You Are Being Answered

Sometimes people say to themselves, *I've been praying and praying, but Hashem is not answering. Doesn't the pasuk (Tehillim 145:18) say,* קרוב ה' לכל קוראיו *— Hashem is close to all who call out to Him? And doesn't it say (Berachos 32b),* שערי דמעה לא ננעלו *— the gates of tears are never closed? So why aren't I being answered?*

> *"When it seems that Hashem is not answering our prayers, it may very well be that He is, but it's taking time for us to recognize how."*

When it seems that Hashem is not answering our prayers, it may very well be that He is, but it's taking time for us to recognize how. If a person is praying for a job, it could be that many different things need to happen and to fall into place before he actually begins the new job, and his *tefillos* bring him closer and closer to that eventual goal. If a person is praying for a *shidduch* and he is still not married, it might be that the intended marriage partner is not yet ready, or perhaps she is not quite yet at the level where she needs to be, and his prayers are effective in moving the process along.

There was a young man who was in *shidduchim* for several years, but nothing worked. Finally, one day he decided to travel to Eretz Yisrael and pray at the Kosel. One year later, he married. As it turned out, the young woman he married had not been very religious. At the time he was praying at the Kosel, she suddenly decided, out of the blue, to go to Eretz Yisrael and study for a year. This man's *tefillos* were effective immediately, but he did not realize it until much later.

❖ ❖ ❖

Rabbi Pesach Eliyahu Falk tells of a girl in Eretz Yisrael who graduated high school and was ready to go to seminary. Unfortunately, there was some friction between her father and the head of the seminary that all her friends were attending, and she was not accepted. She applied to other seminaries, but when they discovered that she wasn't accepted into her local seminary, they did not want to admit her, either. The girl was devastated. This was a wonderful young woman, with stellar *middos*, who, through no fault of her own, could not go to seminary to continue her religious studies. She cried and felt miserable. Her father tried all he could to get her accepted, but to no avail.

Finally, he brought his daughter to a certain Torah sage for advice. The Rabbi said to her, "Forget about going to seminary. It's not working out, so drop the idea. Instead, take some classes, maybe learn to be a teacher. Further your education. But additionally, Hashem obviously wants your *tefillos*. Pray very hard." Specifically, he urged her to pray that her future husband, whoever he may be, should be successful in his Torah learning and should enjoy it. The girl wanted to marry a boy who would become a Rav, and so she was advised to pray that her future husband, already then, should succeed in Torah study.

The girl followed the sage's advice. She excelled in her studies, and prayed very hard. Three years later, she graduated from her program and was ready for *shidduchim*. But her parents did not receive a single suggestion for a *shidduch*. Nobody wanted to date a girl who could not get into seminary.

The father realized he needed to make a proactive effort. He decided he would go to a yeshivah which he liked and pray there, three times a day, to observe the students. After a few days, there was one boy who caught his eye. This boy was always there, learning intently, and was respected by his peers. The father decided this was the boy he wanted for his daughter.

He approached the Rosh Yeshivah to inquire about the boy, and the Rosh Yeshivah said, "You hit the jackpot. This is a very special young man, the best boy in the yeshivah."

"Do you think he'll consent to meet my daughter?" the father asked.

"He has a waiting list," the Rosh Yeshivah said, "but you could try talking to his father."

The man went to the boy's father and described his daughter. He emphasized that she had been put through several tests in her life and passed them all.

"Well, we have a lot of options," the father said, "and my son has to choose, so you can go speak to him directly."

And so one night after Maariv, the father went over to the boy, engaged him in conversation, and spoke to him about his daughter. As soon as he mentioned that his daughter did not attend seminary, the boy tried wiggling out of the conversation.

"Just give me a few minutes to explain," the father said. "My daughter has outstanding *middos*, and a great Rabbi told us that she wasn't getting into seminary because of me, and she should therefore do something else and pray that her future husband should get good *chavrusas* [study partners] and have a *geshmak* in learning."

As soon as the young man heard this, his face lit up. "How long ago did the Rabbi tell you this?" he asked.

"Four years ago," the father answered.

"I don't believe it," the boy exclaimed. "When I first came to this yeshivah, I was doing very poorly and strongly considered dropping out. I remember distinctly that it was four years ago when I suddenly felt a desire to improve. I asked for a new *chavrusa*, and from that day on it's been great. I never understood what happened, until now."

The *shidduch* was made, and they married.

Although it appeared that the girl's *tefillos* were not being answered, in truth, they were answered immediately.

We must have faith in our *tefillos*, even when it seems they are not being answered. Hashem is always listening.

104 Hashem Is Protecting Us

The *pasuk* says (*Tehillim* 121:5), ה' שומרך — "Hashem is your guardian." We are so fortunate that Hashem is protecting us all the time. And unlike a human bodyguard, who needs to sleep and rejuvenate, Hashem protects us all the time, 24 hours a day, seven days a week, as the previous *pasuk* (ibid. 121:4) says, הנה לא ינום ולא יישן שומר ישראל — Hashem never sleeps. If we ever find ourselves walking alone and feeling helpless, we have no reason to fear, for Hashem is protecting us. And the more we feel His protection, the more Hashem will show us the extent of His protection.

The *pasuk* continues, ה' צלך — "Hashem is your shadow." Rabbi Pesach Eliyahu Falk explained that Hashem's protection clings to a person like his shadow. As opposed to a human guard, who needs to be alerted and summoned when something happens or when some potential danger presents itself, Hashem is always with us, like our shadow, like a coat of armor, protecting us without our having to ask, and often without us ever even realizing it.

There are, however, times when Hashem shows us how He is protecting us.

I heard of an incident that happened not too long ago involving a passenger on a plane flying from New York to Eretz Yisrael. Approximately ninety minutes before the scheduled landing, the smoke alarm in the lavatory sounded. The flight crew checked out the lavatory and could not find anything wrong. The alarm sounded again fifteen minutes later, and so the plane made an emergency landing in Athens, about one hour away from Eretz Yisrael.

While this was happening, a 39-year-old passenger from Queens, who happened to be a Hatzalah paramedic, was experiencing chest pains. He did not think this was anything to worry about, but when the plane landed in Athens, the pain became severe. The man approached the medic and he was taken to a small medical base where an EKG was performed. When he saw the printout, he turned white; he saw that he was going into cardiac arrest. He was immediately rushed to the hospital, and in the ambulance he indeed suffered a heart attack. The paramedics shocked him twice, and in the hospital the doctors managed to put in a stent. His condition became stable, and now, *baruch Hashem*, he is doing well.

It was later discovered that the fire alarm was activated by a passenger who was illegally smoking in the lavatory. This is how Hashem protected this man. There was no advanced medical equipment on board the aircraft, and thus it is only because of that smoking passenger that this man is still alive.

Sometimes it appears that Hashem is letting us be harmed, when in reality He is protecting us.

"Sometimes it appears that Hashem is letting us be harmed, when in reality He is protecting us."

Someone told me just the other day that he rented office space on the fifth floor of a building, and during construction, the power suddenly went out. He called Con Ed, and they informed him that they could not continue supplying power to the building because he did not have an account with Con Ed like the previous ten-ant did. He told the operator that he wished to open an account, and the person on the phone explained that they needed copies of his lease papers. He immediately contacted his lawyer to get the papers, but the lawyer's staff explained that this would take several weeks.

Although this caused a significant delay in the construction, the man said to himself, *Hashem knows exactly what He's doing. I am not going to get upset over this.*

Nearly two weeks later, the day before Con Ed restored power to the offices, the man received a call while on a business trip. He was told that there had been a small fire in the building and the entire fifth floor was evacuated. Because the fire was so small, no one was hurt and no damage was caused. It turned out that somebody on the sixth floor threw a cigarette through a vent, and it burned condenser units on the fifth floor. If there had been electricity running through these units, a major and potentially disastrous fire would have resulted. (As an aside, it should be noted that both stories I heard around the same time involved fires caused by cigarettes.)

Hashem is always looking out for us. We have to feel that He is protecting us, and we should feel comfort knowing that the only One in charge is always looking out for our best interests.

105 Don't Misjudge Hashem

There are people who are angry at Hashem. They say, "I try so hard to be good. I learn, I go to shul, and I eat only foods with a reliable certification, but I never get what I want. Only bad things happen to me." These people think that Hashem is just "out to get them," Heaven forbid, and feel resentful.

We need to know that even when it appears that Hashem is hurting us, in reality, He is only helping. All He wants is to act for our benefit, regardless of whether we understand how He is benefiting us.

The story is told of a man who was waiting to board his flight from Eretz Yisrael, when he felt hungry. He went to one of the shops near the gate, purchased a box of donuts, and returned to the gate. He put his bag in front of him on the floor, and then took a donut from the box, which was on the seat next to him. He then noticed that the man sitting two seats over, on the other side of the donuts, thrust his hand into the box and took a donut. The man couldn't believe it. What chutzpah! But it didn't stop there. The man continued helping himself, one donut at a time. And so this continued, with both men eating donuts, until finally there was only one donut left. The other man took it, broke it into two pieces, took one piece for himself and left the other half.

The man could not believe his eyes. This was outrageous. How can someone steal someone else's food so flagrantly?

He finally got on the plane, and when he got settled into his seat, he opened his bag to get something. He was shocked to see the full box of donuts that he had purchased, still unopened.

It had seemed as though the man next to him was taking, but in reality he was giving.

> *"Sometimes it seems that Hashem is taking things away from us. One day we will realize that in truth Hashem only gives, and gives, and gives."*

Sometimes it seems that Hashem is taking things away from us: our peace of mind, and the assets that are most important to us. But one day we will realize that in truth Hashem only gives, and gives, and gives.

The *sefer Ki Atah Imadi* cites a comment by Rashi indicating that Yosef HaTzaddik endured the test of Potifar's wife throughout the twelve years he spent in the Egyptian dungeon. However, as we know, the test of Potifar's wife lasted only one year, after which Yosef was thrown into prison. How could it be that the test lasted throughout the time Yosef was in the dungeon? Evidently, the author explains, the test continued because Yosef was made to suffer bitterly as a result of his piety. He could have thought to himself, *I was so good, and this is what Hashem does to me? I deserve to be rewarded!* For twelve years, Yosef was tested by this challenge of faith. He did not once regret his good deed, despite the dire straits to which he was subjected as a result.

Often, the challenges that one confronts after overcoming one of life's tests are more difficult than the test itself. When a person chooses to become religiously observant, making the significant and difficult adjustments necessary, and then experiences hardships, he is tested. But he must remember that the reward for trusting Hashem could be even greater than the rewards for the mitzvos he has now begun to observe. As a result of Yosef's faith throughout the twelve years in prison, he became worthy of serving as ruler of Egypt for eighty years. Hashem knew exactly what He was doing. All those years, He was making Yosef worthy of the blessings that were in store for him. There are hidden jewels beneath every form of suffering we endure. And when we accept the suffering with love, these jewels become even more valuable.

> A woman told me that she had been waiting a long time for her daughter to marry, but nothing was working. One day, she borrowed a relative's car, and while she was out it was stolen. She felt terrible. It would not have been as distressing to her had it been her own car, but to cause her relative to lose her car after doing such a big favor — this she simply could not bear. She said that she was in agony over the incident, but worked on internalizing that Hashem is the One in control. The very next day, she received a call with an offer of a *shidduch* for her daughter, and they married.

We don't understand Hashem's ways, but everything He does is for our benefit. We must never regret a good deed that we've done. We must remain strong, and one day we will be shown how even when it seemed as though Hashem was taking, in truth, He was only giving.

106 According to the Effort Is the Reward

It is told that the Chozeh of Lublin once made an announcement after Yom Kippur: "If anyone wants, I can tell them exactly what they prayed for this year." The congregants were taken aback by the Rabbi's proposal, and they were afraid to come forth.

Finally, there was one man who approached the Rabbi and said, "O.K., Rabbi, tell me what I prayed for."

"You had a very difficult time learning Torah this past year," the Rabbi said. "You came home late from work every night, had to rush through dinner, and then ran to learn, managing to learn for only one hour. You prayed for an easier schedule so you could learn for longer periods of time and with greater peace of mind."

"Wow," the man marveled, "that's exactly what I prayed for. Tell me, what was Hashem's response?"

"He said 'no,'" the Chozeh answered, much to the man's astonishment.

"What?!" the man exclaimed. "All I want is to be able to serve Hashem better by having an easier time learning Torah. This is His response?"

The Rabbi explained, "The way that you managed to learn Torah for one hour a day amid great difficulty, with such a pressured schedule, is so precious to Hashem, and worth far more than learning for longer hours with ease and peace of mind."

It says (*Avos DeRabbi Nasan perek* 6), טוב אחד בצער יותר ממאה שלא בצער — "One good deed performed with difficulty is worth more than one hundred mitzvos performed easily." Many times we set out to do a mitzvah or raise our religious standards, only to encounter numerous obstacles as we work toward that goal. The natural tendency of many people when this happens is to say, "O.K., Hashem, I'm trying to be good, but if You don't want me to, then I won't." They view the obstacles and challenges as Hashem's way of telling them to stop. In truth, however, it's just the opposite. Hashem loves their mitzvos so much that He wants to give them a hundred times more credit for them.

The *Chafetz Chaim* is cited as saying (*Chayav U'Pealav,* p. תתקע"ה) that when Hashem wants to elevate a person to a higher spiritual level, He will present him with a struggle for him to overcome so he could achieve greatness. Thus, for example, the Midrash relates that when Avraham was bringing his son, Yitzchak, to the site of the *Akeidah* to fulfill Hashem's command, the *Satan* set out to block his path. On one occasion the *Satan* appeared as a tall mountain, and on another occasion as a river, and Avraham proceeded into the river until the water reached his neck, at which point he cried out to Hashem to let him continue on his way to do the mitzvah. Avraham's act of self-sacrifice was so precious to Hashem that He wanted to make it even greater by giving Avraham the opportunity to overcome obstacles along the way.

"When Hashem wants to elevate a person to a higher spiritual level, He will present him with a struggle for him to overcome so he could achieve greatness."

People often look enviously at their peers and think to themselves, *It's just not fair. It's so easy for them to be religious. Why can't it be so easy for me?* A person in this situation must realize that Hashem loves him and wants to reward him a hundred times more for his efforts. The *pasuk* says (*Tehillim* 62:13), ולך אד־ני חסד כי אתה תשלם לאיש כמעשהו — "You are kind, O

Hashem, for You pay a person in accordance with his actions." The simple meaning of this *pasuk* is that Hashem shows kindness by rewarding people for the good deeds they perform. However, many commentators ask: Why is this considered a *chesed*? Isn't this exactly the way things should be: a person who works gets paid for his work? Some commentators explain that Hashem is kind because He pays us not just for the job we do, but כמעשהו, based on how it was done. If it was difficult, we get paid much more, even though it was inherently a simple job.

Imagine a factory with two buildings: one with air-conditioning, and one without. The workers in both buildings do precisely the same jobs, but the workers in the air-conditioned building are paid $50 an hour while the workmen in the other building are paid $5000 an hour. The people in the building without air-conditioning are very happy to endure the sweltering conditions, because they are earning $40,000 a day, while their friends in the other building are bringing home just $400 a day.

The next time we encounter obstacles as we try to elevate our religious standards, we should not feel upset. Instead, we should thank Hashem for giving us this wonderful opportunity to achieve even more exalted levels of greatness.

107 No More Stress

A psychologist was delivering a lecture on the subject of stress management and lifted a glass of water.

"How heavy is this glass?" he asked his audience. Several attendees guessed that it weighed 8 ounces., others figured 10 ounces.

"The truth is," the lecturer said, "that the weight itself really doesn't matter. The more important factor is how long I hold it. If I hold it for a minute, I'll be fine. If I hold it for one hour, my arm will ache. If I hold it for an entire day, my arm will feel numb and paralyzed. The weight remains the same, but the longer I hold it, the heavier it feels.

"This is true of life's stresses, as well. If you think about them for a few brief moments, you'll be fine. Even if you dwell on them for a while, it won't be such a problem. But if you think about them all day, you will feel paralyzed and incapable of doing anything. Nothing good will come out of it. So we all need to let go of our stresses, and not hang on to them the entire day."

This is a very meaningful suggestion, but it leaves open the critical question: how do we do it? How do we let go of our stresses?

Diverting our attention to something else is just a temporary fix; it does not actually address the problem.

> A man went to the doctor and complained that he felt overwhelmed with anxiety. He had many worries in life, and he felt so depressed because of them. He begged the doctor to help him.
>
> "I have the perfect remedy," the doctor proudly said. "Go to the town jester and watch him perform. He will laugh you out of your depression, and then we'll work from there."
>
> "Doctor," the man protested, "I am the town jester. I can't help myself."

What then is the solution?

> *"Hashem is fully in control of our lives, and He wants only the very best for us."*

We have to constantly remind ourselves of two fundamental principles of Jewish faith: 1) Hashem is fully in control of our lives, and no one else has any power over us. 2) Hashem wants only the very best for us. Whether or not we understand how, He is always helping us and looking out for our best interests. If these two beliefs were deeply ingrained within our consciousness, we would never become nervous, no matter what happens to us.

We would immediately recognize that it was all brought about by Hashem, Who has only our best interests in mind.

> Rabbi Ephraim Wachsman drew an analogy to a wealthy businessman who ran a large corporation, and decided it was time to bring his son into the business. He notified his employees that his son would be starting to work for the company, and he instructed them to give his son a hard time. He wanted the workers to send his son every problem that came up, and to point out every mistake he made. The father knew that this was the best way for his son to learn the ropes and get the business training he would need in order to succeed. The son started work full of confidence, having earned his degree and feeling he was fully prepared to succeed in the business. But after just a few days, he was distraught. Wherever he turned, there were problems. Things were going the wrong way, no one was cooperating, and everyone was giving him a hard time. *What's going on?* he thought to himself. *I thought I was prepared for this! Why is this happening?*

He feels exasperated and depressed only because he does not realize that all this was being caused directly by his father. His father is aware of all the problems being sent his way, which people are causing him trouble, and why all this is happening, and all this is done under his complete control. And, his father is doing this only because he loves his son so much and so desperately wants to see him succeed.

Hashem controls every aspect of our lives, and His love for us is endless. He loves us far more than we can ever possibly love ourselves, and only wants to see us succeed. The entire reason why we were created is to receive Hashem's goodness and draw close to Him. He wants us to have the best possible chance to earn all the goodness He has in store for us, and this is the reason behind everything He does, whether or not we understand why or how. If we would think about this, we would always feel secure and at ease at every single step we take in our lives, knowing that everything that happens has been carefully planned by the One Who loves us more than we can imagine.

The next time we are stressed, we need to stop and think that Hashem is in full control of our lives, and everything He does is for our benefit. These soothing thoughts not only have the effect of alleviating stress, but also provide us with great merit. Recognizing that Hashem is in control over everything that happens, and accepting it all lovingly, elevates us spiritually, and, as the Ramban writes, causes us to become "attached" to Hashem.

All we need to do is constantly remind ourselves of these fundamental beliefs until they are fully ingrained in our minds and hearts.

108 Seeing Through the Lens of Emunah

The Mishnah teaches us that we have an obligation to love Hashem under all circumstances, no matter how He deals with us. We must train ourselves to always say, "Everything Hashem does is for the best," and to accept everything He does with love, remaining loyal to Him regardless of what happens. Every time a person is presented with a challenge and says, "Hashem knows what He's doing," he fulfills the Biblical command of, וידעת עם לבבך כי כאשר ייסר איש את בנו ה' אלקיך מיסרך (*Devarim* 8:5), realizing that Hashem treats us as a loving parent treats his or her child.

People who were not taught *emunah* have many questions: "Why did Hashem do this?" "How could Hashem do that?"

"How could something like that happen?" We don't always have the answers, but if we train ourselves to look at the world through the lenses of Torah and *Chazal*, we will never struggle with these questions. Two people could witness the same event and walk away with completely different perspectives. Upon observing a serious car accident, one person might say, "How could Hashem do this to such a righteous person?" But another observer will say, "Wow, what a terrible accident. It is such a miracle that he came out with just a few broken bones, and in a few weeks will be back to normal. Look at Hashem's kindness!" Two people could see a poor man, and one would say, "How could Hashem make such a fine, pious individual struggle so much?" But the other says, "Look how Hashem takes care of him. He always manages to get by and has what he needs." We always have to recognize — in our eyes and hearts — that what Hashem does is just, realizing that things aren't necessarily the way they seem. Even if what we see does not make sense to us, we must affirm our belief that Hashem does everything for the best.

> *"Two people could witness the same event and walk away with completely different perspectives."*

It is told that Rav Yechezkel Abramsky looked up at the early evening sky and said to the Brisker Rav, "How could Rabbeinu Tam say that halachic night begins 72 minutes after sunset? Look how dark it is!"

The Brisker Rav replied, "We don't look at the sky for answers; we look at the *Shulchan Aruch*. Our eyes could be misled by what they see in the sky, but the *Shulchan Aruch* always tells us the truth."

In a similar vein, our Rabbis teach (*Berachos* 60b), כל מאי דעבד רחמנא לטב עבד — everything Hashem does is for the best, even if it does not seem to us that way. When we have the right perspective, following what the Torah tells us, it is much easier to accept everything that happens, and we know we are always correct. The Torah guides us toward the truth. People who do not view things from the Torah's perspective could make grievous errors, whereas those who look at the world through the lens of Torah are always correct. Darwin arrived at his theory that human beings descended from monkeys because he observed people and monkeys, and noticed many striking similarities. Rabbi Pesach Eliyahu Falk noted that if Darwin had learned the Gemara's comments on the topic, he would not have made this mistake. The Gemara relates (*Sanhedrin* 109a) that when Hashem punished the builders of the Tower of Babel who sought to rebel against Him, He divided them into three groups, one of which were turned into monkeys. Darwin was indeed correct: there is a close relationship between the human being and the monkey, only in the opposite direction. Human beings didn't descend from monkeys; the monkeys descended from the human beings! In fact, upon seeing a monkey one recites the *berachah* משנה הבריות, praising Hashem Who changed people into something else.

We have to see things from the right perspective, as the *pasuk* says (*Hoshea* 14:6), כי ישרים דרכי ה' צדיקים ילכו בם ופושעים יכשלו בם. Hashem is always right, and He only wants to help us. The more this belief is ingrained within our consciousness, the happier we will be.

109 Is It a Sign From Hashem?

If a person tries to do something good but obstacles come in the way, he should not interpret this to mean that Hashem wants him to stop. We do not know how to interpret "signs." Our job is to try our hardest to do what is correct, and make every effort to surmount any obstacles that we confront along the way. For all we know, Hashem may have placed the obstacles in our way for the precise opposite reason: so we can earn more reward by having to invest extra effort to overcome the hurdles. Only after one has tried his hardest, there is nothing left to do, and he sees his efforts did not succeed, should he then conclude that Hashem, in His infinite wisdom, felt that this undertaking should not work out, and he should accept Hashem's will joyfully.

> *"Our job is to try our hardest to do what is correct, and make every effort to surmount any obstacles that we confront along the way."*

For example, if a person wakes up early to pray with a *minyan*, but when he goes outside he sees his car is blocked, he should not say, "I guess Hashem does not want me to go to shul this morning, so I won't go." Instead, he should explore other ways of getting to shul. For all he knows, Hashem may have decided to present this challenge so he can overcome it and his prayers will then be especially powerful, and that day he needs a powerful *tefillah*. If, however, one made every effort to get to shul, but through circumstances beyond his control he missed the *minyan*, then he should accept the fact that Hashem, for whatever reason, did not want him to pray with a *minyan* that day.

This lesson applies to many different areas of life. We do not know how to read "signs," and we should not even try. We should always just make our best effort to do what is right.

One area in which this lesson is especially relevant and important is *shidduchim*. Sometimes the road is bumpy and laden with large obstacles. When things do not work out immediately, one should not rush to decide that Hashem does not want the *shidduch* to come to be. Instead, he or she should try to do what seems to be in his best interests, and only if all efforts fail can it be conclusively determined that Hashem did not want this *shidduch* to work.

In the Torah we find two stories of *shidduchim:* one which was effected very quickly and smoothly, and another which was plagued by hardship before working out for the best. And both were quite clearly Hashem's will. In *Parashas Chayei Sarah*, we read that Avraham sent Eliezer to find a match for Yitzchak. Avraham did not give any detailed instructions, saying only that Eliezer should go to Avraham's homeland and find a girl. We might have expected this to be a difficult process, with so little information to work with, but in a matter of several hours the right girl was found and the *shidduch* was finalized. Later in *Parashas Vayeitzei*, we read that Yaakov Avinu's parents sent him to Padan Aram with very detailed instructions, telling him to marry one of Lavan's daughters. It looked like it would be a very simple and straightforward process, but in the end seven years passed until Yaakov was able to marry, and even then he was given Leah, and not the daughter he preferred to wed. At that point, we might have expected him to say to himself, *Look, what can I do? It must be that Hashem does not want me to marry Rachel.* But this is not how he approached the situation. He persisted, doing what he thought was the right thing, and ultimately married Rachel. As it turned out, these obstacles that had to be overcome are what enabled Yaakov and Rachel to have children together. Our Sages teach that Rachel was physically incapable of conceiving, but Hashem gave her the ability to bear children in reward for her giving the signals to Leah before her wedding to Yaakov, to spare her embarrassment. It was specifically because of the difficulties they confronted that the *shidduch* worked out as well as it did.

We should not be trying to give explanations for the obstacles that present themselves as we try to do the right thing. We must persist and try to do what we think is Hashem's will. If even with maximum effort it does not work out, we should then say, "Hashem knows what's best, and for whatever reason He did not want this to happen. I fully accept His decision, and now I'm moving on."

110 Stay the Course

Some people endure very difficult tests — either physical tests or spiritual tests — for long periods during their lives. They are in pain, and they do not understand why Hashem is not helping them. They often think to themselves, *I've been praying for such a long time, and yet nothing is changing; I went to a Rabbi and he told me what to do, but even though I'm following his instructions, I'm still not getting the help that I need; I've gone to so many tzaddikim for blessings, but nothing is working, and life is just not going well; I keep on trying to improve and do more mitzvos, but I don't see Hashem giving me anything in return; What are the mitzvos doing for me? Where is Hashem when I need Him?*

We don't understand why people go through troubles and must endure hardship for extended periods. But we do know that Hashem is with them in their pain, as the *pasuk* says (*Yeshayah* 63:9), בכל צרתם לו צר — "In all their distress, He is distressed." And we also know that Hashem is only doing this for their ultimate benefit. People in these situations certainly have an excuse to just give up and say, "I've had it, I'm not doing any more mitzvos," but they can also say to themselves, *To the contrary, I can give Hashem something that most of the world is never able to give — I can serve Hashem with all the pain and anxiety that I am experiencing*. Every ounce of effort invested in serving Hashem becomes exponentially greater as a result of the difficult challenges entailed.

> "I can give Hashem something that most of the world is never able to give: I can serve Hashem with all the pain and anxiety that I am experiencing."

We sometimes hear people say, "I'm being so good, I'm trying so hard, when am I finally going to get a break?" We must continue what we're doing, maintaining our loyalty to Hashem and His Torah even when it is difficult. All we have is Hashem. One day we will be shown how valuable all the hard work and effort really was.

Rabbi Ephraim Wachsman demonstrated this point by way of the story of Yosef HaTzaddik. The Midrash tells us that when Yosef's brothers sold him as a slave, he went to each brother and cried at his feet, begging for mercy, but they all ignored his cries. At that point Yosef could have thought, *This is how great Torah scholars act toward their own brother?! I've had it, I'm not interested in religion anymore.* But this was not his attitude. He persevered in his faith, and even in ערות הארץ, the most immoral society in the world — ancient Egypt — he remained loyal to Hashem, praying and studying every day. He might have then thought, *Hashem must be seeing how good I am despite my situation, how hard I am trying to remain loyal. Now He's really going to help me.* But then he was subjected to the very difficult test of Potifar's wife, who day after day tried to seduce him (ותשא אשת אדוניו את עיניה אל יוסף) (*Bereishis* 39:7). At that point Yosef could have said to himself, *Isn't it hard enough already? Is this really what I need now?* But yet, the *pasuk* (ibid. 39:8) says, וימאן — he firmly and resolutely refused Potifar's wife's advances, remaining true to his faith and values. He could have then thought to himself, *Now Hashem will really take care of me, after I passed such a difficult test.* Instead, he was thrown into an Egyptian dungeon, forgotten about by the entire world. Yet even in jail, Yosef remained faithful to Hashem and retained his belief. After ten years of imprisonment, he turned to the royal butler and asked for help, and Hashem punished him for placing his trust in a human being, forcing him to spend another two years in the dungeon. An onlooker to such a situation might say, "Enough is enough, how much more can he handle?!"

But finally, after twelve years in the jail, Yosef was suddenly rushed to the king, and instantly became the kingdom's viceroy, the second most powerful man in the ancient world (and retained this position for 80 years). And for all the tests he successfully passed he is forever known as "Yosef HaTzaddik." Hashem knew that every test was making Yosef greater, bringing him to higher levels of spiritual achievement.

We do not know when or how the salvation will come, but every day that a person remains loyal despite the hardship he endures makes him a greater *tzaddik*. And the more one must sacrifice, the greater his opportunity to grow. People facing hardship must try their hardest to stay the course, and one day they will look back and see that this was how they earned their ultimate glory.

111 The Mitzvah of Hishtadlus

Chovos HaLevavos (*Shaar HaBitachon*) writes that although we know everything we have is from Hashem — including our health, our money, our positions, and so on — we are nevertheless obligated to do our *hishtadlus*, meaning, to invest effort. One must try his hardest to obtain what he wants through normal, natural methods, and then believe that his efforts bring him only that which Hashem had in any event intended to give him. When done the right way and with the right intentions, *hishtadlus* is a mitzvah. And thus, for example, the *Taz* (*Yoreh Deah* 336) writes that one fulfills a mitzvah by caring for his health, such as by consulting with doctors and undergoing treatment. The Rabbis apply this concept to *parnassah*, as well. A person actually fulfills a mitzvah by investing effort to earn a livelihood, as long as he has the right intentions.

By "right intentions" we mean that a person realizes that through his effort he finds out what Hashem had in store for him, and regardless of the outcome, he believes that everything he has is precisely what Hashem wants him to have, and he is thus happy, knowing that Hashem always wants only what is best for him.

Several years ago, Rav Menachem Mendel Lemberger, a respected *dayan* in Yerushalayim, passed away after a very difficult illness. A person once accompanied another Rabbi as he visited Rav Lemberger in the hospital, and told the remarkable story of what he observed. He heard the doctor explain to the Rav that his leg would have to be amputated, as otherwise his life would be in real danger. The Rav pleaded with the doctor to try to explore other options.

"I'm very sorry," the doctor said. "We've consulted with leading specialists, and this is the only way to save your life."

Rav Lemberger was devastated. He was desperately hoping to get out of the hospital and fully recover so he could continue his great work. When he saw the Rabbi who had come to visit, he asked him to intervene. "Maybe you can convince the doctors that there are other options," he pleaded, tearfully.

After a brief but intense discussion, the visiting Rabbi told Rav Lemberger that there was no alternative. The only way to save his life was to amputate the leg.

At that moment, Rav Lemberger called over his family, who had been waiting outside the room. He said, "We begged for mercy. We cried. We prayed. We did all we could, all the *hishtadlus* that was possible in a situation like this. But now it is clear that this is Hashem's will. From this moment on, we are not allowed to second-guess the decision, or to cry even one more tear. Not one of us should feel bad. It is clear that this is what Hashem wants, and we will accept His will with love. I know Hashem loves me, and I want to thank Him for giving me the strength to overcome this challenge and have *emunah*."

> *"We begged for mercy. We cried. We prayed. We did all we could … It is clear that this is what Hashem wants, and we will accept His will with love."*

This is *hishtadlus* with the proper intentions. We are obligated to try our very hardest to achieve the results we think are most favorable for us, but once we see that Hashem has decided otherwise, we must fully accept His decision with love and faith, knowing that this is the very best thing.

112

If Everything Is for the Best, Why Pray for Change?

The question is often asked: How do we reconcile the concept of prayer with the belief that Hashem always cares for us and does what is best for us? If we do not have something we want, then obviously this is Hashem's will, and thus, by definition, it must be the best thing for us. So why should we bother to pray? And why would prayer change the situation? If it's best for us not to have what we want, why would Hashem give it to us in response to our prayers?

One answer is that the greatest kindness Hashem can perform for us is to allow us to draw close to Him. When we pray and submit our requests to Hashem, we get close to Him, and establish a meaningful relationship, which is the greatest privilege of all. And so Hashem, in His kindness, waits to give us what we want until we ask Him for it, so that we will be compelled to establish a close relationship with Him.

> *"It might be detrimental for a person to have what he wants, but then become beneficial for him as a result of his prayer."*

This answer assumes that at times it would be more beneficial for us to have something, but Hashem withholds it from us so that we can have the privilege of bonding with him. However, we might also suggest that at least in some circumstances, it might be detrimental for a person to have what he wants, but then become beneficial for him as a result of his prayer. To understand how, we turn our attention to a parable told by the Chafetz Chaim in a different context.

> A man passed away after 120 years, and his soul ascended to the heavens to stand trial. He was told by the heavenly court that he would have to experience some suffering for the sins he committed during his lifetime, and thereafter he would be allowed entry into *Gan Eden*. But then they found on his record that he had once insulted his fellow.
>
> "Suffering will not help you for that," the court told him. "You never asked your fellow for forgiveness, and so you cannot earn atonement for that sin. It's not in our hands." There was no choice but for the soul to return to earth to correct this mistake. He would have to go back down to the world and treat people properly. The last thing a soul wants is to return to earth, but there was no choice.
>
> "Whatever it takes," he said to the court.
>
> They informed him that he would be sent down as a wealthy, handsome, and brilliant man.
>
> "What?!" the man exclaimed. "How can I do my job if I am wealthy, handsome, and brilliant? How will I be able to avoid becoming arrogant and condescending? How can I ensure to treat people properly under these conditions, living this kind of life?"
>
> The court explained that he needed to endure this test in order to earn his share in *Gan Eden*. He pleaded with them to change the decision, noting that he would likely commit even more sins if he returned in this form. Finally, they agreed to send him back as a poor beggar. He was overjoyed, and thanked them profusely.
>
> "I will be so humble," he said enthusiastically, "and that way I will be able to fulfill my mission!"
>
> And so he returned to earth and suffered bitterly from poverty and hardship. Throughout his life, he wondered to himself, *Why is Hashem doing this to me?*

The truth, however, is that Hashem is being so kind to him, placing him in the precise position he needs to be in to achieve what he needs to achieve. The best thing for him was to be poor.

Now if that person would go to a Rabbi to ask for help, and explain how no matter what he does he cannot earn a living, the Rabbi would urge him to pray very hard and beg Hashem for money. And his prayers might very well work. The Mabit (*Beis Elokim* Chapter 2) writes that the purpose of *tefillah* is for us to recognize how needy and deficient we are, and how we must depend on Hashem for absolutely everything. If this man would sincerely pray to Hashem, and truly recognize how dependent he is on Hashem for his needs, then earning money would not threaten his mission at all. After going through the experience of heartfelt and sincere *tefillah* and submission to Hashem, he is now in a position where he can become wealthy without becoming arrogant. If he would acquire wealth without praying for it first, it would be a disaster and undermine the entire purpose of why he was on earth. But being the beneficiary of wealth as a result of *tefillah* is a positive outcome.

We must trust that Hashem knows precisely what He's doing, and that He's full of love and mercy. At the same time, though, He commanded us to pray for all our needs, and there is no contradiction whatsoever.

113 Shehakol Nehiyeh Bidvaro

David HaMelech says (*Tehillim* 28:1), אליך ה' אקרא — "Hashem, I call out to You alone." He understood that Hashem is the only true Source of salvation, as he says (ibid. 86:7), ביום צרתי אקראך

כי תענני — "On the day of my distress, I call to You, because You will answer me."

This must be one of our goals in life. When something is bothering us, our instinctive reaction must be to turn directly to Hashem and ask Him for help. We should ask Him to lead us in the right direction, to open our eyes to the right solution, and send us the right messenger. If there is a medical issue, Heaven forbid, we should say, "I know that You, Hashem, are the only real doctor, and that the cure will come only from You." This is the way to bring the assistance we need. It is not easy, and sometimes we will have to first experience the failure of other alternatives until we arrive at the realization that there really aren't any other alternatives.

> Rabbi Fishel Schachter told of a man named Avraham from Meah Shearim. Everything went well for him, and he was very close to Hashem, until his daughter fell ill. The illness brought him even closer to Hashem, but the situation looked bleak. The doctors told him that medically there was nothing else they could do. There was, however, a certain specialist in the United States who had developed a method of treatment that proved to be successful. The problem was that it was impossible to reach this doctor, and there was a very long waiting list to see him.
>
> One day, a person who was involved in connecting patients with doctors called Avraham and told him that this doctor was visiting Eretz Yisrael, and would be in his office in Tel Aviv.
>
> "Come right away," he said. "If he sees you and hears about your daughter's situation, maybe he'll have mercy and give you an appointment. This is your only chance to get through the red tape and get to see him. Be here in a half-hour."
>
> "A half-hour?!" Avraham asked. "How do you expect me to get from Jerusalem to Tel Aviv in a half-hour?"
>
> "I don't know, just do it. It's your only chance."
>
> The man quickly told his wife what was happening,

grabbed all the money they had in the house — 300 shekels — and ran outside. He flagged down a cab and told the driver he needed to be at the Tel Aviv address in a half-hour, urgently. The driver turned around and said it was impossible. Avraham showed him the 300 shekels. The driver looked at the money, looked at the passenger, and said, "O.K., it's possible."

They took off, and the driver took every shortcut imaginable, and even drove through fields. The car came to a screeching halt in front of the office building, and Avraham looked at his watch. They had gotten there in 29 minutes flat — a miracle! He charged up the steps, knocked on the door, and he saw the man with whom he had spoken.

"I am sorry," the man said. "The doctor left exactly one minute ago. You just missed him."

Avraham's heart sank. There was nothing left to do. He suddenly began feeling very lightheaded, and he looked like he was about to faint. The people around him quickly brought him a cup of water, and he began reciting the *berachah*. After saying the first three words, ברוך אתה ה', he realized something. *My Father in heaven*, he said to himself, *"I don't have to make an appointment with You, I don't have to meet You only at a certain time and place. I don't have to rush by taxicab to see You. Whenever I want, at any time during the day or night, I am standing right in front of You and You listen to what I am saying.* ברוך אתה ה' *— You are right here, I can speak to You at any time. Forget the doctors and cabdrivers. This is between me and You."*

"Whenever I want, at any time during the day or night, I am standing right in front of You and You listen to what I am saying."

As he completed the *berachah* and recited the words, שהכל נהיה בדברו, he said to himself, *You created everything — me, my daughter, everything. You help me, Hashem.* After he drank the water, the people asked him if he was O.K., and he said, "I was never this O.K. in my entire life."

Several weeks later, he brought his daughter back to the doctor. After examining the girl, the doctor said, "It's one in a million. The medication appears to be working, and your daughter should have a complete recovery."

Later, Avraham's wife asked him what it was that helped their daughter. He told her that it was that *berachah* he recited over the cup of water in Tel Aviv.

"But why did you have to rush to Tel Aviv in a taxi and pay 300 shekels to say a *berachah*?" she asked. "You could have made the same שהכל right here in Meah Shearim!"

"Without that taxi ride," Avraham said, "I could never have made that *berachah*."

Sometimes we experience dark periods in our lives, but those are what gives us the opportunity to rise to levels of *emunah* that would have otherwise been unattainable.

114 How Much Hishtadlus?

The Midrash comments that Yosef HaTzaddik was punished with an extra two years in prison because he asked the *sar ha'mashkim* (butler) to help by mentioning him to Pharaoh. The commentators all raise the question of why it was wrong for Yosef to make his *hishtadlus* — an effort to help himself. *Chazal* infer from the Torah itself that it is not only permissible, but obligatory to make our own efforts to better our situation. The *pasuk* (*Devarim* 15:10) says, יברכך ה' אלקיך בכל מעשיך ובכל משלח ידך, indicating that Hashem's blessing depends upon מעשיך — a person's own work and initiative. Why, then, was Yosef punished for making a reasonable effort to get himself out of prison? It is true that the more one trusts in Hashem, the less *hishtadlus* he requires, but Yosef made a very small effort, making a simple request of the butler. What did he do wrong?

The Chafetz Chaim answered that Yosef was punished not for his initial request of כי אם זכרתני אתך (*Bereishis* 40:14), but rather for then repeating his request — והזכרתני אל פרעה. A *tzaddik* of Yosef's stature should have realized that it was sufficient to make one simple request, rather than repeating it again.

Rav Eliyahu Dessler suggested a different answer, noting Rashi's formulation of Yosef's mistake: שתלה בו לזכרו. Yosef was certainly entitled to ask the *sar ha'mashkim* for help, but for a brief moment he depended on the *sar ha'mashkim*, pinning his hopes on him instead of Hashem. We are certainly allowed and required to invest effort, but we must believe that ultimately everything depends solely on Hashem, and the people helping us are merely His messengers. If the person we turn to cannot help us, we need to trust that Hashem can just as easily send someone else. And therefore we must never pin our hopes on any human being, as the *pasuk* says, אל תבטחו בנדיבים (*Tehillim* 146:3).

The work *Ki Atah Imadi* offers a different explanation. Yosef informed the *sar ha'mashkim* that he would be released from prison after three days, yet he made his request for help right then, at the time he conveyed this information. Yosef should have waited before making his request, recognizing that Hashem could release him from prison even before those three days had elapsed.

Although these interpretations differ from one another, they all basically convey the same general principle: *hishtadlus* is necessary, but has to be done the proper way, with a keen awareness of the fact that ultimately it is Hashem, and not our efforts, that bring the results. The *Mesillas Yesharim* thus writes:

> *"After a person put in his normal effort, he must trust in Hashem that He will provide him with what he was destined to receive."*

חייב אדם להשתדל איזה השתדלות לצורך פרנסתו אבל כיון שהשתדל הרי הוא יצא ידי חובה. . .מכאן ואילך אין לו אלא לבטוח בקונו

"A person is obligated to make some effort toward his livelihood, but once he made an effort, he fulfilled his obligation. . .After a person put in his normal effort, he must trust in Hashem that He will provide him with what he was destined to receive."

Reb Zundel of Salant formulated this concept as follows: we must make a *hishtadlus* because Hashem will not make an overt miracle for us; but once we've done enough that it would not look like a miracle for us to receive what we need, we have fulfilled our obligation.

Since *hishtadlus* is just simply opening the pipelines of Hashem's blessings, the *Chovos HaLevavos* writes that one should choose whichever occupation suits his personal skills and has the most appeal.

It must be emphasized that the Torah by no means encourages laziness. Quite to the contrary, while a person is working he is required to work as hard as he can. The Rambam writes that when somebody is hired for a job, he must work בכל כוחו — "with all his strength" — as we learn from Yaakov Avinu, who said about his work for his father-in-law, Lavan, כי בכל כחי עבדתי — "I worked with all my strength." We are to put in a normal hard day's work, but after that, we must return to Torah learning, mitzvos, *chesed*, tending to our families, and so on. And, once we've made our *hishtadlus*, there is no mitzvah at all to worry about the outcome. In fact, worrying is detrimental. Hashem is in charge of our livelihood, and thus in any event it is not our efforts that will yield the desired results. As such, once we've fulfilled our obligation of *hishtadlus*, we must relax and trust that Hashem will give us what we need.

> It is told that Rabbi Moshe Shapiro once sent a student to go try to raise money for the yeshivah. The student worked very hard, but did not succeed. He didn't raise any money at all. Several days passed and a wealthy man came to the yeshivah and unexpectedly made a very large donation. The Rabbi went over to the student and thanked him for his efforts.
>
> "But I didn't even ask this man for a donation," the boy said. "I didn't achieve anything. Why are you thanking me?"
>
> "We had to make our *hishtadlus*," the Rabbi explained, "and you did. And now Hashem has sent down His blessing this way."

Our goal is to serve Hashem with peace of mind, and to trust that He will take care of us. Once we feel we've put in a reasonable effort to create a "pipeline" through which Hashem can send us His blessing, we should be satisfied and then spend time involved in *avodas Hashem*. And if we do not feel satisfied and are worried that perhaps we should be doing more, then perhaps we need to work that little extra until we reach higher levels of *emunah*. There is no mitzvah at that point to do more work, but there is a mitzvah to enjoy peace of mind. We must remember that *hishtadlus* is not a goal; it's the means to the goal of serving Hashem. And we must therefore put in the effort while trusting that Hashem will always take care of us.

115 Hardships — Ours or Someone Else's?

It is told that the students of the Baal Shem Tov once asked their Rabbi, "You've always taught us that every negative character trait can be used in a positive, constructive way. Jealousy can be used to bring us closer to Hashem if we envy those who are more spiritually accomplished than us. We can use pride in the service of Hashem, as the *pasuk* says (*Divrei HaYamim I* 17:6), ויגבה לבו בדרכי ה'. Even desire can be used for the right reasons. But what about *kefirah* [heresy]? How can this be used for a positive purpose?"

The Baal Shem Tov answered that *kefirah* — the denial of Hashem — must be used in situations where one's fellow is suffering and going through a difficult time. The person enduring hardship must try to have complete faith in Hashem, but the other people in his life should approach the situation with a tinge of *kefirah*. They should not tell him, "Don't worry, just have faith in Hashem; He loves you and he'll make sure everything turns out fine." While this is certainly true, this should not be our response to a person facing hardship. Instead, we need to share in his pain and try to help him in any way we can. If our friend lost his job and is worried how he will provide for his family, we should not tell him, "Don't worry, Hashem will take care of it." Instead, we should think of how we can help provide him with the money he needs until he finds a new job, and which connections we have that might help him find new employment. Afterward, once the person sees that we are genuinely concerned and trying to help, then we can offer words of encouragement and try strengthening his *emunah* by reminding him that Hashem can solve every problem and that He loves and cares for all of us. But first we must offer assistance and sensitivity.

"Instead, we need to share in his pain and try to help him in any way we can."

The Steipler Gaon once said that after having untold numbers of people approach him over the course of many years for help with their problems, he realized that no matter what a person's problem is, it fills the entire heart and causes overwhelming pain. He added that the person who is suffering should try to strengthen his *emunah*, but everyone else needs to focus their attention on offering assistance in any way they can.

When we learn about *emunah* and *bitachon*, it's for ourselves, reinforcing in our minds the awareness of how everything that happens is caused directly by Hashem Who always wants only the very best for us. A person's remark cannot break a *shidduch*; a doctor's mistake cannot hurt a patient; a competitor cannot take away someone's *parnassah*. The *pasuk* (*Eichah* 3:37) says, מי זה אמר ותהי ה' לא צוה — who could possibly cause something to happen if Hashem did not first decree that it should happen? He is behind everything that takes place, He loves us, and wants us to trust Him even when we do not understand why things happen. But we must train ourselves ahead of time, before hardship sets in. It is very difficult to teach people to have *emunah* while they're experiencing hardship. In a period of pain and anxiety, people are not receptive to this message. But if we keep reminding ourselves of how everything is caused by Hashem Who wants only the best for us, we are preparing ourselves to be able to remain calm and relaxed in any situation.

Imagine that Hashem comes to a person one morning and says to him, "I know you have a very important business meeting today, with a lot at stake. But I am in charge of your *parnassah*, I love you very much and I will always take care of you, and today, for reasons that you cannot know, I am causing you to have a flat tire on the way to work. Trust me, this is the very best thing that could happen to you." When that person has a flat on his way to work, he will not get agitated at all, because he was prepared ahead of time, and realizes that this was caused by Hashem and it must therefore be the best thing to happen. We have to try to feel that way in every situation in life, realizing that everything is from Hashem and not getting depressed or anxious. Hashem is in full control of our lives, and the more we live with this recognition, the happier we will be.

116 I Have No One Else

The *pasuk* says (*Divrei HaYamim I* 16:10), התהללו בשם קדשו, which means that we should "take pride" in the Name of Hashem. Rashi explains: כל מי שמאמין באלוקים הוא יעזרנו — "Anyone who truly believes in Hashem — He will help him." The *pasuk* then continues, ישמח לב מבקשי ה' — "those who pray to Hashem properly will rejoice in their hearts" because of the salvation they experience.

The *Chazon Ish* wrote in one of his letters that those who pray hard for salvation accomplish more than those who actively pursue it. Prayer is the greatest *hishtadlus* (investment of effort) that one can make. However, it must be approached with the proper mindset. And the proper mindset is expressed by David HaMelech (*Tehillim* 25:16) where he prays, פנה אלי וחנני כי יחיד ועני אני — "Turn to me and have mercy on me for I am all alone, and I am impoverished." *Ashrei Ha'ish* explains that normally, the greater a person's stature, the greater his chances of receiving help when he needs it. If a person is well connected, and certainly if he is a high-ranking official or person of means, people will naturally want to help him, figuring that one day they will need his help. And thus the more prominent a person's stature, the more confident he feels in his ability to obtain the assistance he needs. David HaMelech understood that when it comes to Hashem, the exact opposite is true. The more we realize our lowly stature, that we have no way of achieving the salvation we need independently, the greater our chances of receiving His assistance. David therefore asks for help (ibid.), כי יחיד ועני אני — "for I am all alone, i.e. I have no connections, and I am impoverished." Although he was the king, he truly believed that everything he had was ultimately worthless, as his only means of salvation was Hashem. And when a person truly believes this, that he has nothing and no one to help him besides Hashem, then he can "take pride in His holy Name," because he has faith and Hashem will come to assist him. It is not simple to feel this way, but prayer with this mindset has the power to pierce the heavens.

> *"The more we realize our lowly stature, the greater our chances of receiving His assistance."*

> A man told me that his company restructured and created five different divisions, assigning several salespeople to each division. Nineteen of the twenty salespeople were assigned to the first four divisions — four or five per division — and this man, alone, was assigned to the fifth division. The company had never before sold this kind of merchandise, and this man never had any experience in this area. He found himself in charge of worldwide sales regarding a product that neither he nor his company had ever dealt with before, and he had no one to help him, no contacts, and nowhere to turn.

Recognizing that there was no ordinary *hishtadlus* that he could make, the man turned to Hashem. He said, "Hashem, I am all alone and helpless — כי יחיד ועני אני. No one can help me except You. Please help me."

Out of the blue, a day-and-a-half later, the salesman got a call from someone he had worked with ten years earlier. The man said he called just to say hello and see what he was up to.

"Well," the salesman said, "I've just been put in charge of a division of sales I know absolutely nothing about."

He told his old friend about the product, and his friend said, "Wow! I've been selling that product for the last two years. I have sales representatives all over the country who have close relationships with every major retailer. I've been looking for a new line to sell. Maybe we can get together to work on this."

The next week, 28 sale representatives flew in from around the country for a meeting in this salesman's office, and a partnership was formed. Hashem brought the salvation just like that.

When we believe that only Hashem can help, then, as Rashi writes, הוא יעזרנו — He will assist us, and then we will be able to "take pride in His Name."

117 Nothing Can Disturb Me

The *Chovos HaLevavos* writes (introduction to *Shaar HaBitachon*) that having *bitachon* brings one great tranquility and peace of mind. A person with *bitachon* is not bothered by problems and mishaps that would get ordinary people upset. If his merchandise isn't selling, if he cannot collect debts that are owed to him, or even if he suffers from a physical ailment, he does not become depressed. He knows Hashem is concerned for his well-being even more than he is, and that Hashem does only that which is the best thing for him in all areas of his life. When a person knows that Hashem is in full control of everything that happens, and wants only to benefit us, there is never any reason to be disturbed when things do not go as planned. And thus the *Chovos HaLevavos* writes (Chapter 1) that the essence of *bitachon* is *menuchas hanefesh* — peace of mind.

> The *Chazon Ish* was a master of *bitachon*, and his *menuchas hanefesh* was legendary. Just being in his presence had a calming effect. Somebody said that he was once walking with the *Chazon Ish* in Bnei Brak when a truck came driving recklessly down the road. Another pedestrian, in his attempt to steer clear of the truck, rammed into them, nearly knocking the great sage to the ground. The *Chazon Ish* simply continued walking, and did not even turn around to see what had happened. He was such a master of *menuchas hanefesh* that he did not feel the need to react to the incident or even to stop for a moment.

Having *menuchas hanefesh* is a sign of a great person. The *Chafetz Chaim* commented that a person has to have *middos* in his pocket. This means that when a person feels a legitimate need to express anger, he should take some anger out of his pocket, so to speak, and use it as needed. But it must all be with complete control. One should never be controlled by external forces or circumstances, as they cause one to lose his *menuchas hanefesh*.

> *"One should never be controlled by external forces or circumstances."*

> There was a Rabbi in Eretz Yisrael who would always get ready for Shabbos early on Friday afternoon and would then go to the shul to spend a few hours learning before Shabbos. One Friday, as he was on his way to the shul, a woman poured out a huge bucket of dirty water from the balcony, and it landed

on the Rabbi. He simply turned around, went home, changed, and then headed back to the shul. Someone who witnessed the event later reported that the Rabbi did not even look up. If he would have looked up, this would have evidenced his aggravation, that he was thinking to himself, *How dare you do that!* But this Rabbi knew that this was from Hashem, and so he did not react at all.

Bitachon is so vital because it stems from the realization that Hashem puts us in every situation in which we find ourselves, and wants us to serve Him to the best of our ability in that situation.

Two religious Jews were once imprisoned by the government on false charges. The conditions in the jail were dreadful. They slept on hard benches, all they were given to eat was some dry bread and water, and there was a putrid stench of sewage, which denied them the ability to pray or study Torah. One of them sat there depressed, while the other was perfectly calm and at ease. The one who felt depressed turned to his friend and asked how he could enjoy peace of mind under such horrendous conditions.

"How could you sit there so peacefully?" he asked. "We cannot even serve Hashem in this prison. How can you be happy?"

The fellow answered, "You know we didn't do anything wrong, we didn't commit the crime we're accused of. It is clear that Hashem put us here, and He knows that we cannot pray or learn under these conditions. And so by accepting Hashem's will with love, I am serving Him the best way I possibly can."

This is how we must approach all situations in life. We must realize that Hashem put us in every situation for a purpose; that this must be the best thing for us, and He wants us to serve Him under those circumstances. If a person cannot find his car keys when he is in a rush to leave, he could either shout, "Where are my keys?! I can't believe I can't find my keys!" Or, he can say, "Hashem knows what He is doing (He is not allowing me to remember where I put them), and now He wants me to be looking for my keys. I will be calm and not allow this problem to disturb my *menuchas hanefesh*." The more we internalize these concepts, the more peace of mind we will enjoy.

118 The Opportunity of a Lifetime

Imagine if somebody arranged a meeting with one of the most powerful and influential people in the world, giving us the opportunity to sit with that person and discuss anything we want for thirty minutes. How much money would such a meeting be worth to us?

To give us an idea of how much value people ascribe to such meetings, Rabbi Eisenman noted that on May 14, 2013, a bidding auction was held, and one of the prizes was having a cup of coffee with the CEO of Apple, Tim Cook, who was ranked by Forbes magazine as the 19th most powerful man in the world. An anonymous bidder paid $610,000 for this privilege. Imagine: somebody paid over $600,000 to have a brief chat with another human being. This bidder likely hoped to improve his financial standing through this meeting. But imagine someone had a life-threatening medical condition that only the best physician in the world is able to treat. How much would the patient be willing to pay to have a meeting with that doctor? Imagine a country was bracing for war, and there was someone with a secret that could guarantee them a swift, resounding victory. How much would the leaders be willing to pay to enlist that person's help? Let us bear in mind that the United States has spent over $1.5 trillion on warfare since 2001.

אשרנו מה טוב חלקנו — we are so fortunate that we can meet with the most powerful Being in the universe, the One Who is *Borei refuos*, creating cures that aren't yet in existence; Who is *Baal milchamos* — the Master of wars; and Who is *Matzmiach yeshuos* — capable of rescuing any person from any situation. We can speak to Hashem at any time any day. And not only do we not have to pay any money for the meeting, Hashem so desires that we speak to Him that He even rewards us when we call out to Him. Whenever a Jew has a problem and cries out to Hashem, he is credited with a *mitzvas asei* — fulfilling an affirmative Torah command, the value of which is priceless. The person earns this reward for all eternity. And thus every single "meeting" with Hashem is guaranteed success, regardless of whether we see the outcome we requested.

"Hashem so desires that we speak to Him that He even rewards us when we call out to Him."

The *Midrash Rabbah* (*Parashas Devarim*) comments that sometimes Hashem wants to hear numerous *tefillos* from us before granting our request, because sincere, heartfelt prayer is so valuable and beneficial. But we must realize that the closer we get to completing all the prayers wanted from us, the more the *yetzer hara* tries to dissuade us from praying. Our evil inclination puts in our minds thoughts like, *Why should I bother praying again? I've been asking and asking, and nothing happened!* The harder it gets to continue praying, the closer we are to being answered. And every *tefillah* we recite brings us immense benefit, if not today, then tomorrow, and if not tomorrow, then maybe in a year from now.

> A grandson of the Steipler Gaon once informed his grandfather that he was on his way to the *Kosel*. The renowned Sage asked, "Please mention my name in your prayer."
>
> The grandson was astonished. "What? I have to mention you to Hashem? You are so much closer to Hashem than I am!"
>
> "Please listen carefully," the great Gaon said. "אין שום תפילה חוזרת ריקם — no prayer ever goes unanswered."

It's a fact of creation. Every single word of prayer that

leaves the mouth of a Jew accomplishes something — maybe not now or tomorrow, and maybe only in ten days or in a hundred years. But results are always effected.

We must take advantage of this priceless opportunity that is available to us at all times. We must never underestimate the power of *tefillah*. And we must pray, pray some more, and then pray again. Success is guaranteed.

119 More Than You Deserve

Hashem created a beautiful world for us to enjoy and in which to live in happiness. And yet, when we look around, we see so many people who feel unfulfilled and depressed. Why are so many people miserable, when there are so many wonderful things in the world for us to enjoy?

Rav Eliyahu Dessler explained that people are miserable because they've been trained to believe that they are entitled to whatever it is they desire. We are constantly being told, "You deserve the best in life"; "You deserve more"; and "Don't settle for anything less." None of this is true. We aren't entitled to anything, and we deserve nothing. A Jew is to live his life feeling grateful for all he has, appreciating everything Hashem has given him, and recognizing that anything we have is far more than we deserve. We are to walk around all the time feeling happy, and saying, הפעם אודה את ה' — "I will now thank Hashem" (*Bereishis* 29:35) — just as Leah Imeinu did. We must thank Hashem for giving us so much, beyond what we could deserve. When we walk around with the opposite attitude,

"A Jew is to live his life feeling grateful for all he has, recognizing that anything we have is far more than we deserve."

thinking about what we deserve and what Hashem owes us, then we will always feel that our lives are lacking, that we are cheated and do not receive our fair share in life.

Happiness does not depend on any external source; it comes from within ourselves. A person can be happy under any circumstances. It comes from a proper ideology and outlook. The great Reb Zushe of Anapoli was so poor that once he could not afford a single morsel of food. He turned to Hashem and said, "Hashem, You are so kind — You gave me an appetite. There are people in this world who cannot feel when they are hungry, but I do — thank you!" Everything we have in life, including the sensation of hunger, is a gift.

Someone told me that he visited a museum in Israel where visitors experience a day in the life of a blind person. He told me that ever since that visit, he is so happy and grateful for being able to see. Every time he opens his eyes and sees something, he feels grateful to Hashem for His kindness. If we could feel that way throughout life, we would feel so much happier and our lives would be so much better. Whenever we reach the *Modim* section in the *Amidah*, we should stop for a moment, think about a blessing in our lives, and then express our gratitude to Hashem. This will train us to feel content and grateful for what we have.

If a person's livelihood falls on hard times, and he is forced to sell his home and move his family into a smaller residence, there are two possible ways he could approach the situation. He could say, "Hashem, why are You doing this to me? Aren't I a good Jew? Do I deserve this?" Or, he could turn to Hashem and say, "Hashem, You are so kind to me. You gave me this wonderful, large home which my family enjoyed for many years, and now, when I need the money, I have something to sell so I can continue living comfortably!" If he views the situation from this perspective, he will feel happy and content, rather than bitter and depressed.

I recently attended a *sheloshim* where a man for the second time in his life had to give a eulogy for a deceased wife. He stood up and said, "I know you are all probably feeling bad for me that I've had such a hard life, but I haven't. I don't ask Hashem, 'Why did this happen?' I ask Hashem, 'What did I do to deserve to be married to the two greatest women in the world, who gave me such happiness and joy for so many years?'" The man spoke with such inspiring faith. He realized that each day he was married was a great *chesed* from Hashem, and he appreciated it the way a Jew is supposed to appreciate life.

Every person can be happy. It depends on his mindset. And when we are happy, this will improve the quality of our lives and we'll be far more able to accomplish what we're really here to do — to serve Hashem with joy: עבדו את ה' בשמחה (*Tehillim* 100:2).

120 Hashem's Treasure

In *Parashas Yisro,* Hashem says with regard to *Bnei Yisrael* (*Shemos* 19:5), והייתם לי סגולה מכל העמים — that we are His beloved treasure. Hashem loves us like a "treasure." Later, the Torah says (*Devarim* 7:6), בך בחר ה' אלקיך להיות לו לעם סגולה. Rav Tzadok HaKohen notes that here, too, *Bnei Yisrael* are referred to as Hashem's "treasure," only here the Torah employs the singular term בך, indicating that Hashem's love for us is not only a collective love for the entire nation as a whole, but a personal love for each and every individual. Every Jew is a "treasure" to Hashem.

What exactly does it mean to be Hashem's "treasure"?

The Malbim, in his commentary to the verse (*Tehillim* 135:4), ישראל לסגולתו, explains that when a person has something immensely valuable in his possession, he cannot take his mind off it. It is on his mind at all times. Similarly, Hashem has us in mind, as it were, at every moment. He is constantly thinking about us and never takes His attention off us.

> *"Hashem has us in mind, at every moment. He is constantly thinking about us and never takes His attention off us."*

Hashem has us in mind, at every moment. He is constantly thinking about us and never takes His attention off us.

Rav Tzadok adds that Hashem's love for us is unconditional, and not dependent on anything. Even if a Jew sins, Hashem still loves him. The Gemara (*Yoma* 54b) relates that when the enemies entered the *Beis HaMikdash* and set it ablaze, they went into the *Kodesh HaKodashim* and saw the two *keruvim* on top of the Ark embracing. This is the ultimate symbol of the love that exists between Hashem and the Jewish people, and this was the nature of our relationship at the time of the Temple's destruction. Even when Hashem has to punish us because of our sins, His love for us endures.

Hashem calls us His children (*Devarim* 14:1) — בנים אתם לה' אלוקיכם — "You are children to Hashem, your G-d" — and in our Shacharis davening we call Him our Father — אבינו אב הרחמן — "our merciful Father." The Midrash (*Tehillim Rabbah* 103) comments that as a father has an abundance of mercy for his children, Hashem has an abundance of mercy for us: כרחם אב על בנים — "As a father is merciful toward his children" (*Tehillim* 103:13). And as a mother comforts and cares for her children, Hashem similarly comforts us, as the prophet says (*Yeshayah* 66:13), כאיש אשר אמו תנחמנו כן אנכי אנחמכם. Hashem is compared to both a father and a mother, but this is only because this love is something we can understand and to which we can relate. The *Chovos HaLevavos* states (*Shaar HaBitachon*) that Hashem loves us and cares for us far more than any human being could ever love us. To understand what this means, we need to just think about the person who loves us the most, and then realize that this person is able to love us as much as he does only because Hashem granted him this ability, and that Hashem's love for us is infinitely greater than that love.

How far does a parent's love for his child extend?

> In 1988, a massive earthquake nearly flattened Armenia, killing more than 25,000 people in less than four minutes. In the midst of the chaos and devastation, a father ran to the school where his son was a student, and saw that the building had collapsed. After the initial shock

and trauma, the father remembered that he had once promised his son that he would always be there for him, no matter what happened. With tears in his eyes, he surveyed the rubble and tried to recall where in the building he brought his child each morning, and he realized that the classroom was in the rear right corner. He rushed over to that corner and began digging through the rubble. The other parents tried to dissuade him, explaining to him that there was nothing he could do. But he just turned to them and said, "Are you going to help me, or just stand there?" He continued digging, stone by stone. Soon the fire chief arrived and tried pulling him away from the scene.

"There are shifting beams everywhere," the chief warned. "It's too dangerous."

"I'm not going anywhere," the father insisted. "Are you going to help me?" The police chief came and tried to pull the man away, but he wouldn't move. He remained there, digging on his own, for 8 hours, then 12, 24, and 36 hours. After 38 hours, he pulled back a large boulder and heard his son's voice. He yelled his son's name, and heard, "Dad! It's me! I knew you were coming. I told all the other kids not to worry — my father promised that he would always be there for me."

It turned out that when the building collapsed, it made a wedge like a triangle, and 14 people were saved, including the son.

כרחם אב על בנים — Hashem loves us like a father, but even this demonstration of love does not come even close to Hashem's love for us. We are Hashem's pride and joy. We must always remember that whatever is happening in our lives is being done by Someone Who loves us more than we can possibly imagine, and He is only doing the very best thing for us.

121

From the Bottom of Your Heart

A person can recite thousands of prayers over the course of his life, but if he is able to pray just one the right way, then, the *Shevet HaLevi* (beginning of Vol. 7) writes, this would be the happiest possible moment — אין לך שעה מאושרת יותר. If a person pours out his worries and problems to Hashem with tears, this brings peace to his soul and forges a connection to Hashem that would otherwise be impossible to experience. The *Shevet HaLevi* writes, אשרי האדם שיש לו שעות מאושרות כאלה — fortunate is the one who has such precious moments in his life.

> *"If a person pours out his worries and problems to Hashem with tears, this brings peace to his soul and forges a connection to Hashem that would otherwise be impossible to experience."*

How do we do it? How do we experience this kind of joy and connection to Hashem through prayer?

When Rabbi Eliezer was on his deathbed, his students gathered around him and asked him to share some words of wisdom before he left this world. He said (*Berachos* 28b), כשאתם מתפללים דעו לפני מי אתם מתפללים — "When you pray, know before Whom you pray." If a person needs assistance, there are two ways in which he could pray. He could ask, "Hashem, please, when I approach people for the loan I need, have them give it to me," or, "Please, have the people I turn to give me sound advice." Alternatively, he could stop for a moment and contemplate to Whom he is praying, that he is speaking to the One Who gave everyone every dollar they have, and Who gave every person the intelligence to offer advice. He can give each individual anything he or she needs in abundance. And if we approach prayer with this mindset, then our prayers will be so much more powerful. The *pasuk* says (*Eichah* 2:19), קומי רני בלילה...שפכי כמים לבך נכח פני ה' — "Arise and pray in the night ... pour forth your heart like water, toward the presence of Hashem." We are to pray נוכח פני ה' — with a keen awareness of the fact that we are speaking to Hashem, Who can give us anything. A prayer recited with this mindset can be a life-changing event, and this experience is available to anyone and everyone.

Rabbi Binyomin Pruzansky tells the story of a man who experienced this firsthand. Moshe and his wife, Chani, were married for five years without children. Their hopes of building a family began to wane. Moshe decided he would visit Rabbi Shimshon Pincus, who lived in the Southern Israeli town of Ofakim and was renowned for his keen understanding of Torah, *tefillah,* and the ways of Heaven. Moshe arrived at Rav Pincus' home one night, and the Rabbi greeted him warmly. They sat down to talk, and Moshe, overcome by emotion, described the pain and frustration he and his wife have endured, unable to fulfill their dreams of having a family. Moshe saw the Rabbi's empathy, but he wanted results, not empathy.

Finally, Rav Pincus said, "I understand. Come back here later tonight, at 2 a.m., and I'll be able to help you. I know this is asking a lot, but please trust me."

Moshe did not understand, but there was nothing he wasn't prepared to do to have a child. And so he left and returned at 2 a.m. The Rabbi opened the door and once again greeted him with a warm smile.

"We're not staying here," the Rabbi said. "Come, let's go to the car." Moshe had no idea where the Rabbi could possibly be taking him at 2 a.m., but he wasn't going to question him. He went into the car and sat there quietly. They drove for a while, leaving the town, and were driving on a remote desert road. Moshe thought to himself that there probably wasn't another soul within miles of where they were. Finally, the Rabbi stopped the car and told Moshe to step out. It was pitch black outside; the only light was from the moon. Moshe could barely even make out the Rabbi's face.

"Moshe," Rav Pincus said, "you are all alone here

in the desert. The only One anywhere near you is Hashem. Cry out to Him and beg and plead with Him to answer your prayers. Speak openly, tell Him everything on your mind. This is how you will be answered. I'll be back in a half-hour to pick you up." The Rabbi got back into his car and drove away. Moshe was speechless.

He began to pray, and he opened his heart to Hashem like he never had before, begging for a child. It seemed like no time had passed at all when he heard the Rabbi's car approaching. The Rabbi got out of the car, approached Moshe, looked at him closely, and said, "Moshe, I can see you prayed, but where are your tears? You have to pray with all your heart. You are here alone with Hashem, your Father. He's your only hope, and you have to feel this when you pray to Him. That is why I brought you here." Rav Pincus got back into his car and drove away.

Moshe took a deep breath and began to imagine that he was standing all alone with just Hashem. He thought of all the anguish he and his wife had endured, and suddenly tears started pouring down his face. He felt the years of pain and frustration flowing from his eyes. And as he prayed and cried, he felt his soul starting to soar. He felt a sensation he had never felt before, a completely unobstructed attachment with Hashem. He told Hashem about all his pain and how badly he wanted a child.

When the Rabbi returned and saw Moshe, he placed his hand on his shoulder and said, "This is what I meant, Moshe. Now you'll see that Hashem will answer your prayers." Ten months later, Moshe and Chani were holding a beautiful baby boy.

Nothing can compare to sincere, heartfelt prayer, when one prays with a genuine realization that he is speaking directly to Hashem.

122

Fear of Heaven Is Your Job

Although we know that everything we have is given to us by Hashem, and every situation we confront was placed before us by Hashem, there is one area which Hashem left up to us, and that is the decision between right and wrong. Our Sages teach us (*Berachos* 33b), הכל בידי שמים חוץ מיראת שמים — "Everything is in Hashem's hands except for fear of Hashem." The Rambam elaborates on this concept (fifth chapter of *Hilchos Teshuvah*), where he writes that one should never think that his religious level is predetermined, that it has already been decided whether he will be a *tzaddik* or a sinner. Each and every individual, the Rambam writes, has the power to become as great as Moshe Rabbeinu.

However, the *Chovos HaLevavos* (*Shaar HaBitachon*, Chapter 4) notes that even within the realm of mitzvah observance, there is one aspect regarding which we can and must plead for Hashem's assistance. He explains that there are three prerequisites for performing a mitzvah: 1) the decision to do it, such as deciding one wishes to go to shul in the morning; 2) making the necessary preparations, such as setting the alarm clock the night before; 3) the actual execution — making it to shul in time for the *minyan*.

The *Chovos HaLevavos* writes that when it comes to the first stage — the decision to do the mitzvah — there is no room whatsoever for *bitachon*. One cannot say, "If Hashem wants me to go to shul He'll put in my heart the desire to do so." Hashem has already told us what He wants from us, and now the decision whether or not to do it is entirely up to us. This message is conveyed in a powerful pair of verses (*Yirmiyah* 9:22-23):

כה אמר ה' אל יתהלל חכם בחכמתו ואל יתהלל הגבור בגבורתו אל יתהלל עשיר בעשרו. כי אם בזאת יתהלל המתהלל השכל וידע אותי כי אני ה'

"So says Hashem: The wise man shall not take pride in his wisdom; a strong man shall not take pride in his strength; a wealthy man shall not take pride in his wealth. Only in this shall one take pride — understanding and knowing Me, for I am Hashem..."

Having wisdom, strength, or wealth are all gifts from Hashem. The only thing to be proud of is our spiritual accomplishments, the extent to which we believe in Hashem and follow His commands. And thus deciding to perform a mitzvah is entirely up to us.

This is true of the second aspect, as well: preparing for the mitzvah. This is our responsibility, not one that we can leave to Hashem. If a person is asked how he is doing in his religious observance, he should not respond, "*Hashem ya'azor*" ("Hashem will help"). He, and only he, is the one who needs to help himself. If one is asked how business is going, then it is certainly appropriate to answer, "*Hashem ya'azor*," because financial success depends only on Hashem.

Hashem comes into play in our mitzvah observance only when it comes to the third stage: the execution. Will the alarm ring on time, or will there be some malfunction? Will the person feel healthy and strong so he can get out of bed? Will external conditions enable him to get to shul on time? These factors are out of his control, and depend on Hashem. We therefore need to pray to Hashem to help us earn the additional merit of successfully performing a mitzvah by ensuring that we are able to execute our decision.

> *"Hashem determines the circumstances, and He determines whether we can actually get the job done."*

The *Ben Yehoyada* adds that we must beseech Hashem to make the difference between right and wrong clear to us. The *yetzer hara* is often able to fool us into thinking that what's right is wrong and vice versa. And thus, for example, Moshe Rabbeinu prayed that Hashem should save his disciple, Yehoshua, from the evil scheme devised by his fellow spies. Moshe prayed that Yehoshua would be able to clearly see that the spies were doing the wrong thing, so that he could then choose with his free will to oppose them.

Finally, the *Chazon Ish* noted that one must pray to have an environment around him that exerts a positive influence upon him, and, especially, that his children will be surrounded by the right friends who influence them in the proper direction.

Hashem determines the circumstances, and He determines whether we can actually get the job done, but we bear the responsibility to always make the right decisions and do all we can to act upon them.

123 Giving Life

Giving someone *chizuk* (encouragement) is like giving him life itself. When a person is emotionally broken or depressed, when he cannot sleep at night or does not want to get out of bed in the morning, his life is not a life. And thus lifting his spirits with words of encouragement can truly restore his life. Saying the right words, in the right way and in the right time, can change a person's entire outlook on his situation. And oftentimes just listening to a person speak about his problems and frustrations is a great act of kindness, the importance of which cannot be overstated.

The Torah says (*Vayikra* 25:36), וחי אחיך עמך — "Your brother shall live with you," which Rabbi Akiva (*Bava Metzia* 62a) explains to mean that "your life takes precedence over your fellow's life." The case under discussion is a person trudging with his fellow in the desert, and they are both literally dying of thirst. Rabbi Akiva says that if one of them has only enough water to sustain himself, he is allowed to drink it, and does not have to share it with his fellow, because one's own life takes precedence over the lives of others. Many commentators raised the question of how to reconcile this ruling with the oft-quoted command (*Vayikra* 19:18) ואהבת לרעך כמוך — "Love your fellow as yourself." How can we be required to love other people as much as ourselves, and yet be allowed to save ourselves before saving others? The *Chasam Sofer* (*Toras Moshe*, *Parashas Kedoshim*) answers by distinguishing between physical matters and spiritual matters. When it comes to physical matters, we may care for our own needs before those of others. If someone needs a couch and his friend needs a couch, but he can afford only one couch, he can buy one for himself. But when it comes to spiritual matters, the *Chasam Sofer* asserts, no one takes precedence over anyone else. He holds that we all share the same *neshamah* (soul), and thus we have an equal responsibility toward other people and to ourselves. If a person spends hours helping someone draw close to Hashem, explaining to him Who Hashem is, how everything He does is good, and He is always helping us even when He does not appear to, the person is not sacrificing anything. He is doing precisely what he is here to do. As the *pasuk* says (*Yeshayah* 41:6), איש את רעהו יעזורו ולאחיו יאמר חזק; we are here to help and encourage each other as much as we can.

> There was a man living in Radin who was still not married at an advanced age. He said that once he stayed in the synagogue after the evening services on Yom Kippur night, figuring he had no family to go home to anyway. He thought he was alone in the synagogue, until someone unexpectedly came and sat down next to him. It was the Chafetz Chaim. The great sage began talking to him about the problems he had himself experienced in his life. His father died when he was just ten years old, and he suffered extreme poverty. He went away to yeshivah and was on his own without family for many years. When it was time to get married, he was part of an elite group of young men who were offered enormous dowries by wealthy men eager to have them marry their daughters. However, the Chafetz

Chaim's stepfather, who was very poor, urged him to marry his daughter, who was older than the Chafetz Chaim. The Chafetz Chaim agreed for the sake of his mother's marriage. At the time he did not understand why all his friends were able to marry wealthy girls and live comfortably, while he would be forced to struggle. Eventually, however, he saw that his friends who married girls from wealthy families were led away from Torah, while his wife was kind and supportive, encouraging him to devote himself to Torah learning so he could become the great sage he became. Hashem led him along the path he needed to take.

"Throughout all my ordeals," the Chafetz Chaim said, "I stayed strong by knowing that Hashem was holding my hand and taking me precisely where I needed to go."

> *"Throughout all my ordeals I stayed strong by knowing that Hashem was holding my hand and taking me precisely where I needed to go."*

The Chafetz Chaim sat with this man throughout the entire night of Yom Kippur giving him *chizuk*. This was the holiest night of the year, and the Chafetz Chaim spent it giving encouragement to a downtrodden person, saying not a word of Torah or anything about repentance and the judgment of Yom Kippur. The Chafetz Chaim obviously knew the value of Torah study, but he also knew the value of giving encouragement to one's fellow, telling people about Hashem's benevolence and about how He is always holding our hand and doing what is best for us.

We need to give people *chizuk*, but we need to ensure to do it the right way: with love and sensitivity, feeling the other person's pain as if it were our own, and listening attentively to anything he feels the need to say. If one is afraid of saying the wrong thing, he can give his friend a recording or a book on relevant topics, or ask a Rabbi to help. The more we work to encourage others, the more life we will be giving them.

124 "Charm Spray"

We live in a very competitive world. At times there are one hundred people vying for the same position, and one hundred companies trying to sell the same product. And so we become apprehensive. We see so many people who seem to be better than us against whom we need to compete, and other products that are better than ours whose companies are fighting for the market. A medical student sits in class with dozens of other aspiring doctors, and he thinks to himself, *They're all much smarter than I am. I don't have a chance!*

We need to repeatedly remind ourselves that we know the One Who made other people smart, and He can just as easily make us smart. There are no boundaries in life. Everything is available to everyone. All we have to do is speak to the only One Who truly matters.

> *"There are no boundaries in life. Everything is available to everyone."*

Even if the product one is trying to sell is clearly inferior to others, it could still generate sales. Sometimes companies who have had limited success will suddenly find that a product starts selling like crazy, everyone wants it, and the company cannot even keep up with the demand, causing the price to skyrocket. A man I know sold children's costume wigs and made a nice living. In 2007, there was a craze for Hanna Montana, and so this fellow took the same wig he had been selling for many years and put a Hanna Montana label on it. Millions of his wigs sold. In 1996, there was an Elmo doll selling for $28.99 apiece until there was a sudden demand, and the price rose by hundreds of dollars. There were even reports of that doll selling for $1500 apiece. The same thing happened again in 2006.

Why does this happen? How could a product suddenly become popular?

In a *shmuess* Rabbi Moshe Malka said that Hashem has a special "spray," so to speak, which we might call "charm spray." When He decides a product should sell, He "sprays" it, and suddenly everyone wants it. Hashem can give products a certain "charm" that makes them popular, and He can also give people a certain charm. A person could be less qualified than others for a certain job but yet be hired because Hashem gives him *chein* — charm — in the employer's eyes. *Chazal* teach us (*Bereishis Rabbah* 39:13) that Esther was 75 years old at the time Achashverosh chose her over all the other maidens in his kingdom, from Hodu until Kush, to be his queen. And the Gemara (*Megillah* 13a) says that she had a greenish complexion and refused to wear cosmetics or perfumes. She was chosen, the Gemara (ibid.) explains, because חוט של חסד משוך עליה — "Hashem granted her a certain charm," and this was all she needed. Similarly, when Yosef HaTzaddik was thrown into jail, Hashem gave him *chein* in the eyes of the prison warden — ויתן חנו בעיני שר בית הסהר (*Bereishis* 39:21) — "And he was appointed the one in charge of the prison."

How does a person earn this special "charm"? We have to recognize that Hashem is the only One Who counts, and not become sidetracked by our impressions. It appears as though the people with whom we deal are the ones who control our fate, and we therefore enslave ourselves to them, trying to please them and earn their favor. But the truth is that our fate depends only on G-d. The *Chovos HaLevavos* (end of *Shaar HaBitachon*) writes that the more directly a certain cause appears to affect us, the less powerful that cause actually is, and the more indirect the cause appears, the more powerful it actually is. For example, when a police officer issues a ticket, his decision and actions are the direct cause of the ticket. But the truth is that he does not have the power to make you pay for that ticket. He is under the authority of the sergeant, who is himself under the authority of the lieutenant, who is under the authority of the police chief, who is under the authority of the mayor. The higher up one is in this hierarchy, the less directly he was involved in the ticket, but the greater his authority to determine whether you are responsible for that ticket. Similarly, the people we deal with in our lives are not the ones with the authority and control. Let us not be fooled. Everyone is under the authority of G-d and answers to Him. And the more we recognize this, the more blessings we will enjoy.

125 The Solution for Anxiety

A young man named David Rosmarin was a college sophomore in 1999, when he began feeling anxious. His anxiety over his academic performance and social life were fairly typical of anxieties experienced by college students, but eventually he was having difficulty falling asleep, at which point he considered consulting with the campus psychologist. After his weekly Torah class, he approached the Rabbi and asked if he thought it was a good idea to seek professional help for his anxiety. Without answering the question, the Rabbi proceeded straight to the bookcase, removed a book, and brought it to the photocopying machine. When he finished photocopying, he handed David a sixty-one-page document: the *Shaar HaBitachon* ("Gate of Trust") segment of the *sefer Chovos HaLevavos*.

> *"To my surprise, within eight weeks not only was I able to fall asleep without difficulty, but my anxiety almost completely vanished."*

"I don't know if you should speak to a mental health professional about your problem," he said, "but I do know that reading these pages will help you. Study this text for ten to fifteen minutes each night before you go to sleep, and contemplate the concepts you read."

David followed the Rabbi's "prescription," and later gave the following account of the results: "To my surprise, within eight weeks not only was I able to fall asleep without difficulty, but my anxiety almost completely vanished. Even more remarkable was that the improvement in my psychological state had occurred despite the fact that the anxiety-producing factors had only accelerated. I was faced with a grueling exam schedule, worse social woes than ever before, and I remained completely uncertain about my future. What had changed was my attitude toward my difficulties and toward life in general. I had increased my level of trust in Hashem, and I realized that the events in my life were ultimately controlled by Hashem, and therefore I had little to worry about."

David eventually became a psychologist, and in his practice, uses "*Shaar HaBitachon*" to help people struggling with anxiety.

Developing trust in Hashem is the greatest medication. There are no side effects, and no expenses. *Menuchah U'kedushah* comments that someone who has not studied *Shaar HaBitachon* has "never seen the light in his days." *Emunah* and *bitachon* is what Judaism is all about.

In the introduction to the "*Shaar HaBitachon*" section, Rabbeinu Bachya describes the benefits enjoyed by somebody with *bitachon*, the beautiful life he is able to live by placing his trust in Hashem. The first benefit mentioned is enjoying peace of mind from anxiety: the ability to live without stress. Imagine a stress-free life! We know that stress causes a person significant emotional and physical harm, and we have been given a way to overcome it. By mastering *Shaar HaBitachon*, we can attain inner peace and serenity. We will come to recognize that Hashem always has complete control over everything that happens, that He loves us more than anything and that He therefore does only that which is best for us. Once we've come to this realization, we will never face a challenge that is too difficult to overcome, because we know we have the greatest source of help available to us at all times, Someone Who can solve any problem in but an instant.

> A man told me that once his physicians predicted that he would not live for more than another few months. He placed his trust in Hashem, recognizing that only He, and not any doctor, has the final word. With tremendous

inner strength and pure faith, he overcame the challenge. He said that the doctors prescribed antidepressants for him to use throughout the entire ordeal but he never once needed them, he did just fine with *emunah*.

The more we learn about Hashem, the calmer and more upbeat we will be even before help arrives. We need to always remember Who our Father is. The son of a billionaire never worries about his livelihood even if he does not have a penny to his name, because he knows that his father could provide him with anything he needs. The more we recognize how Hashem can do anything, that He is our Father Who can and wants to help us, and can solve any problem in the blink of an eye, the calmer we will feel. If our prayers aren't answered immediately, we will know that our loving Father knows what is best for us right now, and maybe soon the situation will change.

There is no substitute in the world for *bitachon*. May we all continue to grow in our *bitachon* and feel the inner peace that it brings into our lives.

126 Your Ticket to Olam Haba

We read (*Bereishis* 1:31) that after creation, וירא ה' את כל אשר עשה והנה טוב מאד— "Hashem saw all that He did and behold it was very good." The Midrash (*Bereishis Rabbah* 9:5) comments that the word "good" in this *pasuk* refers to the beautiful world that Hashem created for us to enjoy, whereas the phrase "very good" refers — surprisingly enough — to *yissurim* (afflictions). The Midrash raises the obvious question of how afflictions can be described as "very good," and it answers that indeed, afflictions are "very good" because they enable us to earn our share in the Next World. As Shlomo HaMelech teaches us (*Mishlei* 6:23), דרך חיים תוכחות מוסר; the path to eternal life is through מוסר, enduring afflictions without complaint.

> *The path to eternal life is through enduring afflictions without complaint.*

Every minor inconvenience we endure in life qualifies as *yissurim* and helps us achieve our share in *Olam Haba*. Of course, greater afflictions are more valuable in this regard, but even minor forms of "suffering" are beneficial, and when a person endures any kind of inconvenience without complaint, it becomes of inestimable value.

One of the greatest Torah Sages in the early 19th century was Rabbi Akiva Eiger, who was a towering scholar who authored numerous halachic works. Ordinarily a student needs hours to get through one passage of Rabbi Akiva Eiger's writings, as they are especially intricate and involved. Once his son-in-law, the Chasam Sofer, mentioned Rabbi Akiva Eiger's name while speaking to his students, and as soon as he uttered the name, he tore his shirt in anguish.

"You cannot imagine," the Chasam Sofer said to his students, "the kind of suffering and anguish my father-in-law went through during his lifetime. From the age of 16, he suffered terribly each and every day of his life." The Chasam Sofer proceeded to tell his students that before his death, Rabbi Akiva Eiger requested that nothing be written on his tombstone other than סבל יסורים כל ימיו — 'He endured suffering his entire life.' He did not want to be called *Gadol* or *Gaon;* he wanted to be known not for his enormous contributions to Torah scholarship, but rather for enduring afflictions without complaint. When his students questioned this decision, he said, "I had so much suffering during my life, but I never questioned Hashem. This is my ticket to *Olam Haba*. With this I can go to the Next World with confidence, knowing that I accepted all of Hashem's decrees with love."

❖ ❖ ❖

The great *maggid* of Jerusalem, Rav Shabsai Yudelevich, told of a man who lived a life of suffering, never able to make a proper living, and enduring many problems in his family. Once he decided to go visit the great Kabbalist Rav Shalom Sharabi to ask why Hashem was subjecting him to so much suffering. He journeyed to the sage's home, and when he arrived, Rav Shalom's wife invited him to sit down and wait for the Rabbi. While waiting, he fell asleep and had a dream that he had left this world and was standing before the heavenly court. There was a giant scale there in the court, and a voice summoned all his sins to come forward. Suddenly, thousands upon thousands of dark angels came and stood on one side of the scale. The voice then summoned all the mitzvos, whereupon many thousands of beautiful white angels appeared and stood on the opposite side of the scale, nearly balancing it. The man watched, anticipating that the scale would tip in his favor, but the white angels stopped coming, and the scale was still tipping toward the side of sin. The voice then summoned all of the man's afflictions to come, and thousands upon thousands of angels came. Once again, he thought the scales would tip in his favor, but then the angels stopped coming. It seemed that he would receive a negative sentence.

The man at that point began to frantically cry out in his sleep, "More suffering! More suffering!"

The Rebbetzin heard the cries and rushed over to the man.

"Is everything O.K.?" she asked, very concerned.

The man woke up, and said, "Everything is fine. I don't need to meet the Rabbi. I already have my answer."

Yissurim are immensely valuable. We are told to pray to be spared suffering only because we are afraid we will be unable to withstand them. But when somebody does confront any sort of *yissurim*, he should know that the suffering is not only טוב, but טוב מאד.

127 Dealing With Tragedy

Av has always been a tragic month for the Jewish people. Nonetheless, we must always remember that its name, Av, means "father," and we call this month "Menachem Av" — "the Father Who consoles." The source of the hardships that have befallen us is the same loving Father Who deeply cares for us. Although we don't understand Hashem's ways, we must have the proper perspective.

There is a story that took place a number of years ago that is recorded in many books, and which I recently heard from Rabbi Pesach Eliyahu Falk. There was a yeshivah student who came from a remote place where he did not receive a Jewish education, and yet somehow became a *baal teshuvah*. He was an outstanding student in his yeshivah and would help many of the other boys with their studies. Suddenly and tragically, this young man died. The entire yeshivah was devastated. They could not help but wonder, how could it be that this boy, of all people, could be taken at such a young age? The students were distraught and could not find any solace.

The Rosh Yeshivah decided to invite the esteemed Rav Sholom Schwadron to the yeshivah to deliver some words of encouragement. Rav Schwadron related an incident that took place in the 1920's, when the yeshivos in Yerushalayim were enduring grave financial difficulties. The Rabbis planned to send Rabbi Balk, a gifted and dynamic speaker, to the United States to raise money. They knew that he would be able to accurately portray the beauty of Yerushalayim and its

Chachamim, and motivate American Jews to provide succor to the city's struggling inhabitants. In Chicago, he delivered a powerful, inspiring speech, and after Shabbos many community members rushed to bring him donations. One of them, a man named Yerachmiel Wexler, was especially moved by the Rabbi's address. He told the Rabbi that after hearing about the Torah community in Eretz Yisrael, he was contemplating moving there and opening a business so he could support the Jews of Yerushalayim.

Yerachmiel traveled to Eretz Yisrael together with his son, Yechezkel, to explore the possibility of moving there. Their first stop in the Holy Land was the famed Chevron Yeshivah, where they met many American boys who were learning in the yeshivah, including the son of Rabbi Yaakov Yosef Herman (whose life is described in the book, *All for the Boss*). With some coaxing from Rabbi Balk, Yerachmiel was very impressed by what he saw, and decided that his son, Yechezkel, should remain and learn in the yeshivah. Even though Yechezkel did not have a strong yeshivah background, he believed this would be his opportunity to grow in Torah. And so Yerachmiel enrolled his son in the yeshivah, and returned to America.

Yechezkel Wexler studied in the Chevron Yeshivah during the winter of 1928-9, and six months after his arrival, during the month of Av, the local Arabs perpetrated a deadly massacre of Jews in Chevron. Many students of the yeshivah were killed. Unfortunately, Yechezkel Wexler was among the victims. News of his tragic death reached Chicago, and the parents, with broken hearts, sat *shivah* for their beloved son.

Sometime later, Rabbi Balk was again asked to sail to the United States to raise funds. He agreed, but he insisted that he would not visit Chicago. He did not want to face Yerachmiel Wexler after having indirectly caused his son to go to Eretz Yisrael, where he met a tragic fate.

As we know, we can never outsmart Hashem. During Rabbi Balk's visit to New York, he happened to meet Mr. Wexler, who extended to him a warm, enthusiastic greeting and embraced him.

"Rabbi," he said, "I've been so much looking forward to seeing you, and I was wondering why you weren't coming to Chicago."

The Rabbi was stunned. He explained that he specifically wanted to avoid Chicago because he felt he could not face Mr. Wexler after the loss of his son.

"What?!" Yerachmiel Wexler said. "Lose my son?! To the contrary, you gave me my son! Twenty years ago, when he was born, his soul was destined to remain in this world for twenty years. I firmly believe that this was his time to go, and he would have left this world regardless of whether he had been in Chevron. If you had not come to Chicago, he probably would have gone to the Next World without knowing much Torah. But thanks to you, he spent six months studying in the Chevron Yeshivah, immersing himself in Hashem's Torah. I am confident that he has a share in the Next World — you gave us a son who merited *Olam Haba*!"

This is the response of a *botei'ach b'Hashem*. No one causes anything to happen. Hashem runs the world, and He knows what is best. Instead of shouting and feeling bitter, Mr. Wexler was filled with gratitude and appreciation.

Rav Schwadron concluded by saying to the boys, "No one gets 'ripped' out of this world. Hashem knows what He is doing. This student who had become a *baal teshuvah* is destined for eternal bliss."

We must always remember that Hashem is מנחם אב, a compassionate Father. Even when we do not understand how He runs the world's affairs, we must have faith.

128 The Big Picture

*C*hazal (*Berachos* 61b) tell us that when the Romans were torturing Rabbi Akiva to death, he recited *Shema* and his soul departed as he said the word, *Echad*. At that point, there was an uproar in the heavens, as the angels turned to Hashem and asked, זו תורה וזו שכרה — "This is the reward for Torah?" They wondered how a great scholar of Rabbi Akiva's stature could be subjected to torture and executed in such brutal fashion. Hashem warned in response that if the angels did not keep silent, He would return the world to the state of תהו ובהו — nothingness — that prevailed before creation (found in *Eleh Ezkerah*).

Rabbi Shlomo Kluger raised the question of how to understand Hashem's response. Why did He not simply say something to the effect of, "You don't understand My ways"? Why did G-d threaten to annihilate the universe?

> The Rabbi answered by drawing an analogy to a king who summoned a tailor to make for him a magnificent garment. The king provided the tailor with the gold and silver from which to make the threads to prepare this exquisite article of clothing. The tailor devoted himself loyally to the task and produced a perfect garment, precisely as the king wanted. Some of the king's other servants were jealous of this tailor, and so they spread the false accusation that he had pocketed a portion of the gold and silver and used other materials in its place. The king heard the accusations and ordered the tailor to come before him. The tailor firmly avowed his innocence, but the king wanted him to prove it.
>
> "The only way I can prove my innocence," the tailor said, "is to take apart the garment and show you each individual thread. This is the only thing I can do.

Otherwise, I cannot prove that it is made entirely of the gold and silver you gave me."

This was Hashem's answer to the angels. He was saying, "If you want to understand how this could happen to Rabbi Akiva, I would have to unravel the entire world since the time of creation, and show you how every single event that ever transpired fits into My plan." All events from the time of creation are all connected and part of the magnificent "garment." Hashem has the past, present and future in front of Him at all times. We try to understand, but we only see a few bits and pieces of the much larger puzzle. Events that occurred millennia ago are closely connected to the events of today, in ways that we cannot possibly begin to understand.

"To understand how this could happen, I would have to unravel the entire world and show how every event fits into My plan."

At a Torah Umesorah convention, Rabbi Avraham Mordechai Segal told a story of a man who was staying at the home of a Rabbi in France. He happened to open a curtain and noticed a little door behind it. The Rabbi was startled and immediately asked the man to close the curtain. The man asked if there was a problem, and so the Rabbi offered to tell him the story behind this little door. When he and his wife first moved to that town, there was no *mikveh*, and the wife had to travel for hours to reach the nearest *mikveh*. They tried raising money to build one nearby, but the fundraising efforts were unsuccessful. Finally, they decided to turn one of the rooms in the home into a *mikveh*. The problem was they couldn't afford to do it. And so they lived on just bread and water, saving every penny they could, for about 5-6 years, until they had enough for the project. Just a few weeks after the project was completed, their two-year-old son managed to get into the *mikveh*, and, tragically, he drowned.

"We were devastated," the Rabbi said. "We sacrificed so much for this mitzvah, and this kind of a tragedy happened. We spoke to many great Rabbis, but we still found no consolation."

One night, however, the little boy came to the Rabbi in a dream. The boy told him that his anguish over the tragedy was causing pain to his soul. "You don't understand," the boy explained. "I lived already over 900 years ago. I was one of the Tosafists [a commentary printed on the side of the *amud* in the Gemara], and I was killed during an attack on Jews in France. I did not undergo purification in a *mikveh* or receive a proper Jewish burial, and therefore my soul was not able to reach the highest levels of *Gan Eden*. For all these years, my soul waited for the purest *mikveh* to be built, one which is prepared purely for the sake of Heaven. Yours was the one. Now that I went into that *mikveh* and received a proper burial, I am allowed entry into the most wonderful place in the heavens. To show you this is real — you are going to have a baby girl within the year in the merit of Mommy's strict observance of the mitzvah of *challah*."

The Rabbi's wife woke up the next morning and said that she had a dream about *challah*. And, sure enough, that year they were blessed with a baby girl.

We have no idea what G-d's calculations are. Our job is to trust that He knows precisely what He is doing.

129 When You Give, You Get

The Gemara comments (*Shabbos* 151b) that a person who treats other people compassionately will be treated with special compassion by Hashem. The *Mesillas Yesharim* (Ch. 19) states that it is obvious that Hashem gives us in accordance with what we give to others; the more kindness we perform, the more kindness we will receive. The *Maalos HaMiddos* explains that helping people arouses Divine mercy because Hashem looks upon a kind person and says, "This person who has his own needs to care for still goes out of his way to help others. Certainly, I, Who have everything, should help him." Furthermore, the *Zohar* (*Parashas Vayechi*) comments, כל העוזר את ישראל כאילו עוזר את השכינה — "Whoever helps a Jew is considered as though he helps the *Shechinah*." Our Sages teach that when a Jew is in pain, the *Shechinah* says (*Sanhedrin* 46a), קלני מראשי קלני מזרועי — Hashem cries out in pain, as it were. Every Jew is Hashem's precious child, and when a person helps a child, he helps the child's parents, as well. And thus the *Zohar* (*Parashas Emor*) writes that when a person performs *chesed*, he brings Hashem's kindness upon himself, and when someone deals compassionately with his fellow, Hashem deals compassionately with him and helps him in his time of need.

> *"When a person performs chesed, he brings Hashem's kindness upon himself."*

The Midrash (*Tehillim Rabbah* 65) teaches us that when we perform kindness, this makes our prayers especially powerful. The Chida (*Pesach Einayim*) indicates with regard to the *pasuk* (*Tehillim* 5:8), ואני ברב חסדך אבוא ביתך...ענני באמת ישעך — when we come to Hashem's "house" to pray bringing the *chesed* that we have performed, then He answers us. The *Shevet Mussar* (Chapter 30) writes that a person who performs kindness is granted a חוט של חסד — a "thread of grace," a certain charm, such that he will find favor in everyone's eyes. When we act with *chesed*, then Hashem treats us with *chesed*, *middah k'neged middah.*

I read a story that — while I cannot verify whether it is true — conveys this message in an especially powerful way. A man whom we will call Joey Cohen worked in an auto shop, and one cold, winter day, after a long, hard day of work, he was driving home when he saw an older woman standing alongside her Mercedes Benz, which she had parked at the side of the road. He noticed that the woman was shivering and had an anxious look on her face. Joey pulled his Pontiac behind her Mercedes and approached her. Driving a run-down car and wearing his soiled work clothes, he looked threatening, and she became frightened.

Joey gave her a warm, genuine smile and said, "I see you have a flat tire. Get inside the car to warm up. I'll change the tire for you." As he jacked the car, he accidentally rubbed his hands against the concrete and scratched his palms badly. After several minutes — and a few more scratches — the tire was replaced. The woman was very grateful and asked him how much he charged, but he refused to accept payment.

"There have been plenty of times when I needed other people's help and they helped me without asking for money," he said. "If you really want to pay me, then the next time you see somebody who needs help, please think of me and help him." The woman warmly thanked him, got into her car, and drove away.

A short while later she stopped at a small restaurant to grab a bite to eat. She was served by an especially kind and warm waitress who was obviously expecting a child. Despite having to be on her feet, walking back and forth taking and filling orders, she was smiling, cheerful and gracious the entire time. The woman marveled at this waitress, who seemed to have so little and yet was able to serve total strangers with such warmth and so pleasantly. She remembered Joey Cohen, and when it came time to pay for her small meal, she gave the waitress a hundred-dollar bill. When the waitress returned to give the customer her change, she found that she had left. On the table she saw a note. It read: "Thank you for being so nice. I could see you need some help. Here's something for you from someone who was recently helped by a kind stranger." The waitress then saw four additional hundred-dollar bills under the note. Her eyes began to tear. She and her husband were indeed struggling, and she felt so grateful.

When the waitress arrived at home that night, she noticed that her husband had already fallen asleep, and she figured he must have put in an exhausting day's work. Although she did not want to wake him, she knew how worried he was about finances and wanted to let him know about the gift she had just received. She leaned down to whisper in his ear, and she saw the scratches on his hand, which she assumed were the result of his work in the auto shop. She then whispered, "Don't worry, Joey, everything will be O.K."

When we do *chesed*, we receive *chesed*.

130 Taking Everything Into Account

As Hashem guides us through life every second of every day, He makes decisions for us that take into account the distant future that we are unable to see. Hashem, of course, sees clearly the past, present, and future, at all times, and He takes all this into account in determining how to deal with us. Our Rabbis teach that if we knew the reason for everything that happens to us, not only would we never complain, but we would beg Hashem to do what He did. Even when in the present we cannot possibly see any good in what is happening, if we trust that Hashem is doing it for our benefit, we will save ourselves so much anxiety and heartache.

Rav Shimshon Pincus (*Sichos, Chanukah, amud* 47) told of a young man who, along with his sister, was hiding from the Nazis in a bunker during World War II. They were the last two survivors from the family, and the young man felt it was his responsibility to protect his sister. Once he left the bunker to search for food, and when he returned, he found that his sister was gone. He was told that the Germans had found her and taken her to Gestapo headquarters. The boy immediately ran to the headquarters, barged right in, and shouted, "Give me back my sister!"

The Nazis in the room started laughing at him, as the general, who heard the commotion, arrived to find out what happened.

"This Jew wants us to give back his sister," the Gestapo members said, mockingly.

The general looked at the boy harshly and said, "When hair grows out of your palm, I will return your sister. Until then, I will kill all of you Jews!"

The boy immediately lifted his hand and showed his palm — which was covered with hair. The Nazi troops were startled.

"He must be the son of the devil!" the general exclaimed. "Take your sister and get out of here at once, before we kill both of you." They fled and eventually survived the war.

It turns out that many years earlier, the boy suffered a severe burn on his hand, and had to undergo a skin graft. The skin was taken from a part of the body that had hair, and thus he ended up with hair on his palm. At the time, this must have been traumatic for him. But it later became clear that this was Hashem's plan for saving his life.

❖ ❖ ❖

There is another story of a Jewish boy who was conscripted into the Polish Army during World War I. His parents were devastated, understanding that both his physical and spiritual future were in danger. They went to the Chafetz Chaim to ask for a blessing that their son would be saved from the draft. After a few moments of silence, the great sage said, "What would be so bad if he learned how to shoot a gun?"

The parents were stunned. It sounded like the Rabbi

was cursing their son that he should be conscripted and taught how to fight.

They decided to bribe the doctor who made the medical evaluations of the conscripts, to have him write a negative report about the boy's condition. Right after the examination, just as the doctor completed the false report describing the boy as unfit for the military, a general entered and caught them. The general announced that the boy should be placed into his own division, where he would be in charge of assembling machine guns under live fire. And so the boy went into the army, and learned how to assemble guns and use them.

He ended up surviving the war, and several decades later, during World War II, he found himself in the Warsaw Ghetto. He managed to escape from the ghetto with a group of friends, and they ran deep into the woods, where they met a band of partisans. The Jews offered to join the partisans to fight against the Germans, but the partisans were also anti-Semites, and threatened to kill the Jews.

Just then, the man who had served in the Polish Army spoke up. "I can really help you," he said. "You see that broken machine gun on the ground — I can fix it and hit any target."

"O.K.," they said, "let's see."

He proceeded to fix the gun and then shot an apple from a distant tree, dividing it into quarters. The partisans were very impressed, and this is how that man and his friends were saved. For the rest of his life, he remembered the words spoken by the Chafetz Chaim: "What would be so bad if he learned how to shoot a gun?" This remark, which sounded like a dreadful curse, actually expressed the way Hashem would save this young man's life.

I once read of a young girl who fell into a pool and was underwater for several minutes. Miraculously, she survived without any trace of brain damage. After some investigation, the doctor determined that she was able to survive because she suffered from sleep apnea, a condition which enlarged her tonsils and trained her body to survive on low levels of oxygen. Imagine — these parents went through the anguish of countless sleepless nights, but this turned out to be a manifestation of Hashem's kindness, as this condition is what saved the girl's life.

Someone told me of a boy who experienced terrible seizures as he was growing up, and the condition was so bad that he had to undergo a special operation involving the removal of a certain part of the brain. The procedure was successful, and he was completely cured. A few years later, the boy was hit by a car, and he landed on his head. Amazingly, he survived. The doctor said that he survived only because there was place in the brain for all the blood to drain. If not for the seizures he had suffered, he would not have survived the accident.

> *"We do not understand Hashem's ways, but this is because of our very limited vision."*

We do not understand Hashem's ways, but this is because of our very limited vision. Hashem always has the complete picture in front of Him, and He always does the very best thing for us.

131 He Answers Before We Call

A woman has recently been experiencing considerable difficulty running the organization she had started several years earlier. She founded the organization purely *l'shem Shamayim*, out of a sincere desire to help others, but numerous obstacles arose and she was seriously considering shutting it down. She was awake almost the entire night worrying about the situation and trying to decide how to proceed, and the next morning she

> prayed with genuine emotion to Hashem, begging Him to guide her in the right direction. That day she noticed an Emuna Daily email that she had received several days earlier but had yet to open. She opened it in the hope that it would provide her with some clarity and guidance concerning her current predicament. As she listened to the recording, she almost fell off her chair. The recording spoke of many people who had started charitable organizations with sincere motives but confronted obstacles along the way and considered giving up. However they persevered and eventually saw the problems resolved. It was as though Hashem was speaking to her to renew her strength. This was precisely what she needed to hear.

But one might ask, how could we be so sure that this was Hashem communicating with her? After all, the email was there in her Inbox even before she prayed. How could this email message be the answer to her prayer if it was there even before?

> A similar question could be asked concerning another story I heard of a Rabbi in Eretz Yisrael who every Thursday night would leave money for his wife for Shabbos purchases. Once, however, he had absolutely no money to give her. He was too embarrassed to tell her and he did not want to cause his wife and children to worry, but he did not know what to do. He went into his room and prayed, saying, "Hashem, I know You run the world and provide food and sustenance to all. I know You can provide my family with our needs at any moment." He prayed for twenty minutes, and when he came out of the room, he saw the kitchen table laden with freshly prepared food for Shabbos.
>
> He asked his wife where the food had come from, and she explained that their neighbors' daughter who lives in a different city delivered a baby boy two weeks early, and the neighbors were going to her home for Shabbos to attend the *shalom zachor*.
>
> "They had already prepared food for Shabbos," she said, "and so they figured they would offer us the

food." The Rabbi's prayers were answered immediately. But once again, we might ask, wasn't the baby born before he prayed? Even before he turned to Hashem, the neighbors had prepared their food and then had to change their Shabbos plans. How could this be the answer to the Rabbi's prayers?

The *pasuk* (*Yeshayah* 65:24) states, והיה טרם יקראו ואני אענה; Hashem promises to answer our prayers even before we call out to Him. Hashem knows what we need even before we do, and prepares the solutions to our problems even before we become aware of them. However, because He loves us so much, He does not provide the solutions until we ask. Building a relationship with Hashem is even more important than obtaining what we want, and Hashem therefore waits for us to cry out to Him and ask Him for help so we can draw closer to Him and build our relationship. The Alshich draws an analogy to a king who has a large cadre of servants. For those servants whom he does not particularly like, he gives them what they need without waiting for them to ask. But for those servants whom he especially likes, he waits for them to come and ask so he can spend time with them. And thus David HaMelech says (*Tehillim* 116:1), אהבתי כי ישמע ה' את קולי תחנוני — "I love when Hashem hears the sound of my supplications." Of course, everybody is overjoyed when Hashem accepts their prayers. But David is saying that he loves that Hashem gives him what he needs only after he asks for it, for this shows how important he is in Hashem's eyes.

> *"Hashem knows what we need even before we do, and prepares the solutions to our problems even before we become aware of them."*

All the assistance we need has been prepared well in advance, but we need to ask for it in order to access it. Maybe if the woman hadn't prayed she would have neglected to open that email, and if the Rabbi hadn't prayed the neighbors would have brought the food to a different friend or just placed it in the freezer. Prayers bring us the help that Hashem had already prepared for us in advance. Hashem loves listening to us pray, and when we pray with the recognition that the solution has already been arranged, our *tefillos* will be even more effective.

132

Cast Your Burdens on Hashem

The *pasuk* (*Tehillim* 25:23) says, השלך על ה' יהבך והוא יכלכלך — "Cast your burden upon Hashem, and He will sustain you."

The Maggid of Dubno explained this verse by way of an analogy to a poor man traveling with a very heavy bag on his back. As he walks along the road, suffering from the weight of the load he is carrying, a wealthy man with a spacious carriage drives by, and takes note of the poor traveler. He stops his carriage and generously offers the poor man a ride. The poor man steps into the carriage, and it continues on its way. After a few moments, the wealthy man notices that his guest is still holding onto his heavy bag.

"My friend," he says, "why don't you set your bag down on the floor? Why are you still holding it?"

"You're nice enough to offer me a ride," the poor man says. "I don't want to make you carry my bag for me, too."

"You fool," the wealthy man says. "My horses are pulling the weight of your bag regardless of whether or not you hold it. It won't make any difference if you put it down!"

The Maggid explained that so many people act like that poor man. They carry heavy burdens in life unnecessarily. We must realize that Hashem is carrying us anyway, so let Him carry our burden as well. The *Midrash Tehillim*, commenting on this *pasuk*, notes that Hashem is not like human beings. When a person asks his fellow for a favor, the fellow will likely be happy to do it. When he is asked a second and third time, he will likely agree to the favor, but with less enthusiasm. By the fourth time, though, he will likely say, "Enough already!" and refuse. This is not the case with regard to Hashem. Whenever we "throw our burden" on Hashem, הוא יכלכלך — "He responds favorably." Not only is He not worn out by our repeated requests for help, but to the contrary (ibid. 145:18), קרוב ה' לכל קוראיו — "Hashem draws closer to us the more we call out to Him." He loves when we ask Him for favors, and the more we ask, the more He loves us.

Sometimes we find ourselves in a situation and we wonder how it will ever work out; it seems impossible. We are so fortunate that we just need to turn to Hashem for help. As the Torah says (*Devarim* 4:7), ומי גוי גדול אשר לו אלקים קרובים אליו כה' אלקינו בכל קראנו אליו — whenever we call to Him, He is eagerly waiting to help us.

Sometimes we feel overwhelmed, having too much to do and not having any idea how it will all get done. A person told me he was given extra responsibilities at work, and the situation was just impossible. There were simply not enough hours in the day to complete all he needed to do. Suddenly, a two-hour period that he had reserved for a separate project freed up. It was unmistakably the *yad Hashem* (hand of Hashem). He didn't lose any money, and now has time to get everything done. No burden is too heavy for Hashem. We have the greatest source of help available to us at all times.

People sometimes think, "I don't want to bother Hashem with this one; it's too trivial a problem." There's no such thing as too trivial a problem. He can't wait for us to come and ask Him for help. We can bring Him any "load" we have. And the more we have for Him to "carry," the more He is willing to take on.

"There's no such thing as too trivial a problem. We can bring Him any "load" we have."

If we feel worried and anxious, then this shows that we are still holding on to our bags, and refusing to put them down and let Hashem carry them for us.

If a person gives his fellow a bag of precious diamonds and asks him to watch it for him, the man might understandably refuse, not willing to take on such a responsibility. But if the person gives him the bag to watch and runs away, he will accept the responsibility, feeling he has no choice. When you totally let go, the other party feels more of an obligation. The same is true, so to speak, with regard to Hashem. The more we "throw" on Him, the more "responsibility" He is willing to take on, as it were. השלך על ה' יהבך והוא יכלכלך; we need to put down our bags, and Hashem will happily carry them for us.

133 A Hug From Dvir

Life is full of tests, challenges, and hurdles that we need to overcome. We all have the ability to persevere and rise above the challenges of life. But it becomes especially difficult when we feel alone and abandoned, when we've been crying for help day and night without seeing our prayers being answered. When this happens, people begin to ask, "Is Hashem with me? Does He know what I'm going through? Is there really a purpose to all of this?" When we doubt Hashem's involvement, it makes the challenges so much more difficult to handle. If we only knew how much Hashem feels every ounce of pain we experience, how close He is to us particularly during difficult times, and how much meaning and purpose there is in every moment of our lives, we would find it so much easier to handle the challenges of life, and our problems would be so much easier to bear.

> *"If we only knew how much Hashem feels every ounce of pain we experience."*

David HaMelech says (*Tehillim* 23:4), גם כי אלך בגיא צלמות לא אירע רע כי אתה עמדי. No matter what he experienced in life, no matter how difficult the situation, he was always able to manage כי אתה עמדי — because he knew with absolute certainty that Hashem was with him. We don't always understand why things have to happen as they do, but if we could feel Hashem's involvement, this would be our greatest source of consolation.

In 2008, Dvir Emanuelof, an Israeli soldier, was killed during the war in Gaza. His mother, Dalia, had lost her husband two years earlier in an automobile accident. This added tragedy was almost too much to bear. Dalia missed Dvir dearly, and six months after his demise, she turned to Hashem one night before going to sleep and said, "Please, this is so hard. Please give me a sign, a hug from Dvir, so I can know that his death had some meaning."

That week, her daughter wanted to attend a crafts festival in Yerushalayim. Feeling down and depressed, Dalia really did not want to go along, but in order not to disappoint her daughter, she acquiesced. While they were there, a 2-year-old boy came over to Dalia and tapped her on the shoulder. A preschool teacher, Dalia loved young children.

"Hello," she said to the boy. "What is your name?"

"Eshel," the boy said.

"That's a very nice name," Dalia replied. "Do you want to be my friend?"

The boy nodded and sat down next to her.

Eshel's parents were seated two rows behind them, and the father called to the boy. "Eshel," he said, "why don't you come back here and sit with me and Dvir."

Dalia was startled to hear her fallen son's name mentioned. She went to speak to Eshel's parents, and saw a baby in a carriage.

"If you don't mind my asking," she said, "how old is your baby?"

"He was born six months ago," the mother said, "right after the war in Gaza."

"Why did you choose the name 'Dvir'?"

Baby Dvir's mother explained that shortly before she was due to give birth, the doctors suspected that the infant might have a serious defect, and there was little they could do. "When I came home that night, I heard there was a casualty in the war. I was so saddened by the news, and I said, 'Hashem, please give me a healthy baby, and I will name him "Dvir" in memory of the fallen soldier.'"

Dalia stood there speechless. After a long period of silence, she said, "I am Dvir's mother, Dalia Emanuelof."

At first, baby Dvir's parents didn't believe her. But then they realized it was true. In a sudden burst of emotion, Dvir's mother handed Dalia the baby and said, "Here, Dvir wants to give you a hug."

Dalia held the boy in her arms and looked at his angelic face. Her emotion at that moment was overwhelming. She had asked for a hug from Dvir, and it was given to her.

Whether or not we realize it, Hashem is always with us, guiding us and placing us in the situations we need to be in to be successful. The more we feel His presence, the happier we will be.

134

Why Doesn't This Ever Happen to Me?

We repeatedly hear stories of people who experienced difficult problems that were solved as a result of their *emunah* and prayers. We have heard of people facing financial distress who relied on Hashem and their troubles ended. We have heard of ill patients whose doctors despaired, but the sufferers were miraculously cured. We have heard stories of childless couples who had a child after years of waiting and unsuccessful treatments.

These are all powerful stories that can strengthen our *emunah*. Each story that one hears reinforces his faith and reminds him that he, too, can be saved from whatever troubles he faces, no matter how seemingly hopeless the situation. These stories make us think, *If a person can finally find a zivug after so many years, then I, too, can find my zivug; If Hashem gave that couple a child after twelve years, then I, too, can still be blessed with a child.* The more stories we hear, the more hope we have, recognizing that ישועת ה' כהרף עין — "Hashem's salvation can arrive in the blink of an eye."

We are so fortunate to know that we have Hashem Who can do anything, Who is not limited by any odds or statistics, and Who has a solution for every problem. This recognition gives us hope that allows us to get through even the most difficult situation, for we always know that tomorrow the situation could change.

At the same time, however, there is also a danger in hearing so many stories with beautiful, happy endings. One might feel resentful and begin wondering, *Why doesn't this ever happen to me? I relied on Hashem for help, and I was let down. I thought I prayed so hard, but I didn't see any results.* Such thoughts can cause people to lose *emunah* and lose hope. We must remember that Hashem is the Source of all kindness, and everything He does is kind, regardless of whether or not we recognize how. He listens to every word of prayer we recite, and He knows every feeling we experience in our hearts and every thought that passes through our minds. Even when we do not see the results we were hoping for, this, too, is a manifestation of Hashem's kindness.

> *"I don't know why this is happening, but I know Hashem loves me, and I will continue to believe and draw closer to Him."*

When a person responds with *emunah* even though he did not receive what he wanted, this is one of the greatest acts of service to Hashem that one can perform. The *sefarim* describe the towering spiritual heights that one reaches when he says, "I don't know why this is happening, but I know Hashem loves me, and I will continue to believe and draw closer to Him." Such people attain greatness, and the entire world rests on their shoulders. And every time they reinforce their *emunah*, they are elevated to even greater heights. If a person was praying for a long time but still did not get the help he requested and he is ready to despair, his next prayer to Hashem is so much greater than any other *tefillos* he has recited. And if even then he does not see the desired results, his next prayer is an even greater spiritual accomplishment.

This is what it means to live with *emunah* — recognizing Hashem's greatness, learning about His kindness, looking to Him for hope, knowing that He can help, but at the same time trusting that He knows what He is doing even when we do not receive what we want, and continuing to serve Him with joy and serenity.

This volume is part of
THE ARTSCROLL SERIES®
an ongoing project of
translations, commentaries and expositions on
Scripture, Mishnah, Talmud, Midrash, Halachah,
liturgy, history, the classic Rabbinic writings,
biographies and thought.

For a brochure of current publications
visit your local Hebrew bookseller
or contact the publisher:

Mesorah Publications, ltd

4401 Second Avenue
Brooklyn, New York 11232
(718) 921-9000
www.artscroll.com